THE IMPACT OF PIAGETIAN THEORY

THE IMPACT OF PIAGETIAN THEORY

On Education, Philosophy, Psychiatry, and Psychology

Edited by
Frank B. Murray, Ph.D.
University of Delaware

Contributors

Millie Almy, University of California, Berkeley
Ioanna Berthoud-Papandropoulou, University of Geneva
David Elkind, University of Rochester
Hans Furth, Catholic University and Boys' Town
Ernst von Glasersfeld, University of Georgia
Kenneth Lovell, Leeds University
Theodore Mischel, SUNY–Binghamton
Jean Piaget, University of Geneva
Irving E. Sigel, Educational Testing Service
Gilbert Voyat, City University of New York
Sheldon H. Wagner, Harvard University
Peter H. Wolff, Children's Hospital Medical Center, Boston

A Publication of the Jean Piaget Society

UNIVERSITY PARK PRESS
Baltimore

UNIVERSITY PARK PRESS
International Publishers in Science and Medicine
233 East Redwood Street
Baltimore, Maryland 21202

Copyright © 1979 by University Park Press

Typeset by Everybodys Press.
Manufactured in the United States of America by the
Maple Press Company.

Library of Congress Cataloging in Publication Data
Main entry under title:
The Impact of Piagetian theory.

(A publication of the Jean Piaget Society)
"Based upon the authors' presentations at the plenary sessions of the
fifth annual symposium of the Jean Piaget Society."
Bibliography: p.
Includes indexes.
1. Piaget, Jean, 1896-   —Congresses. 2. Cognition in children—
Congresses. 3. Knowledge, Theory of—Congresses. 4. Child mental
health—Congresses. 5. Educational psychology—Congresses.
I. Murray, Frank B. II. Almy, Millie Corinne, 1915-   III. Series:
Jean Piaget Society. A publication of the Jean Piaget Society. [DNLM:
1. Child psychology—Congresses. 2. Philosophy—Congresses.
3. Psychiatry—Congresses. 4. Education—Congresses. WS105.3 I34]
BF723.C5I46   155.4'13'0924   78-13551   ISBN 0-8391-1293-9

Contents

Contributors

Millie Almy
School of Education
University of California
    at Berkeley
Berkeley, CA 94728

I. Berthoud-Papandropoulou
Faculté De Psychologie Et Des
    Sciences De L'Éducation
Universite De Genève
CH–1211 Genève 4
Switzerland

David Elkind
Department of Psychology
University of Rochester
Rochester, NY 14627

Hans Furth
Boys' Town Center for the Study
    of Youth Development
Catholic University of America
Washington, DC 20064

Ernst von Glasersfeld
Department of Psychology
University of Georgia
Athens, GA 30602

Kenneth Lovell
School of Education
University of Leeds
Leeds LS2 9JT Yorkshire
England

Theodore Mischel
Department of Philosophy
State University of New York
Binghamton, NY 13901

Frank B. Murray
Dept. of Educational Foundations
College of Education
University of Delaware
Newark, DE 19711

Jean Piaget
Faculté De Psychologie Et Des
    Sciences De L'Éducation
Universite De Genève
CH–1211 Genève 4
Switzerland

Irving E. Sigel
Educational Testing Service, Inc.
Princeton, NJ 08540

Gilbert Voyat
Department of Psychology
City University of New York
3332 Broadway
New York, NY 10031

Sheldon Wagner
Department of Psychology
Harvard University
Cambridge, MA 02138

Peter H. Wolff, M.D.
Department of Psychiatry
Harvard Medical School
Children's Hospital
    Medical Center
Boston, MA 02115

Preface

A principle of the discipline of genetic epistemology is that the mechanisms of development *qua* development are universal. Thus the study of the ontogenesis of the individual's knowledge illuminates the historical development of academic disciplines and vice versa. The principles of the child's intellectual development are isomorphic with those of intellectual history, as Kuhn (1970) for one observed in his account of the structure of scientific revolutions.

No better metaphors than Piaget's assimilation and accommodation principles exist to describe and analyze the impact of his thinking upon education, philosophy, psychology, and psychiatry. Whether the impact in each case has taken the form of a mindless assimilation without accommodation, or of a mindless accommodation without assimilation, rather than an intelligent balance of the two is the subject of this book. In psychology there appear instances of nearly pure assimilation when the early language researchers evaluated egocentric thought as egotistical thought or when learning theorists accepted the twin functional invariants, assimilation–accommodation, as synonymous with the twin conditioning principles, generalization and discrimination. The educational curricular reforms that mandated performance on the concrete operational tasks, particularly conservation, as instructional objectives seems on the other hand to be an instance of "pure accommodation" of one discipline to another. David Elkind pursues this line of observation in the first chapter.

The form of the impact of Piagetian theory on contemporary disciplines has many manifestations. That the subject heading *Piaget* exists in the *Philosophers Index* (an international index to philosophical periodicals) and has existed since 1947 in the *Bibliographie de la philosophie* is as telling a sign of his philosophical impact as the article devoted to his views in *The Encyclopedia of Philosophy* (6:305–307). In 1969, L'Abate's citation count showed Piaget to be the most often cited author in the child development literature; recently Walberg, Rasher, and Mantel's (1977) study of the citations of winners of the Thorndike Award from the American Educational Research Association showed Piaget had the largest number of the research citations (34.5% of the total), followed by Skinner (15.9% of the total).

Piaget's recent impact upon developmental psychology is dramatically illustrated in the amount of the space devoted to his ideas in the 1946, 1954, and 1970 editions of Carmichael's *Manual of Child Psychology*. In the first and second editions, Piaget is referenced 23 and 27 times respectively, less than half of the totals of persons with the highest numbers of citations (e.g., Terman, Bayley, Goodenough, Preyer, Jersild, Jones, etc.). In the first two editions he is cited almost exclusively for his language and thought book. In the third edition of the *Manual*, Piaget not only is the most frequently cited person (168 citations in Volume 1), but was honored as the only theoretician invited to contribute a chapter about his own theory.

Piaget's acceptance in the American educational and intellectual establishment is marked by many events, not the least of which was the creation of the Jean Piaget Society, 1971. He has been awarded honorary degrees from the University of Pennsylvania (1967), Clark University (1968), the University of Michigan (1968), the State University of New York (1968), Yale University (1970), Columbia University (1970), Catholic University (1970), the University of Chicago (1974), and Rockefeller University (1975) and prizes from the American Educational Research Association (1967), the American Psychological Association (1972), and the Kittay Foundation (1973).

Two social crises in the United States and the preoccupation of psychology with S-R and S-S animal learning and psychometry made the adoption of Piagetian theory by educators virtually inevitable. The first was the post-1955 Sputnik concern of a nation preoccupied with its diminished role as a scientific and engineering leader and the second, ten years later, was the civil rights crisis in which a nation grappled with the need for compensatory education for its poor and other minority citizens. The need to educate a new generation of scientifically literate and productive citizens led to the initiation of the "structure of the discipline" curriculum projects of New Math (Beeberman), Minimath (Rosenbloom), and Science Curriculum Improvement Study (Bruner), all of which were based upon Piaget's notions of structure and stages of intellectual development. Given that the content of Piaget's theory and research was largely children's reasoning in mathematics, science, and logic, and given the lack of similar content anywhere else in psychology, it was all but inevitable that Piaget would dominate these curricular reforms.

Similarly, given that Piaget's theory of intelligence claims a hierarchically ordered sequence of acquisitions from birth onward that places great stress on sensorimotor roots of all intelligence, it was also inevitable that day-care and other preschool planners would turn to this theory (as summarized in Maccoby and Zellner, 1970; Hooper and DeFrain, 1974; Schwebel and Raph, 1973). The results were principally the Early Childhood Curriculum (Lavatelli), the Cognitively Oriented Curriculum (Weikart), Piaget for Early Education (Kamii and DeVries), Thinking Goes to School (Furth and Wachs), and the Piagetian Preschool Educational Program (Wisconsin). In searching for sets of teachable skills for preparatory and compensatory education projects that would provide maximal positive generalized transfer to school learning tasks, many planners selected basic cognitive and intellectual skills. Here again Piaget's tasks and theory provided an attractive alternative to the pragmatic, atheoretical IQ skills of the prevailing psychometric approach to understanding intelligence and to the mechanistic operant educational innovations of programmed instruction and the contingency-managed classroom. As the British Infant School movement had already been rationalized in terms of Piagetian theory, Silberman's insistent call for its transplant to America in *Crisis in the Classroom* (1970) only reinforced Piagetian reform in American primary education.

It is ironic that the way for Piaget in education was paved by the demise of the progressive education movement with its preparation for life and social adaptation goals (Cremin, 1961). Its emphasis on the social studies perhaps contributed to its unpopularity during the post-Sputnik attacks on American schools. The irony is that Dewey's and Piaget's theories are remarkably similar (see Seltzer, 1977) and the ostensive educational recommendations of child-centeredness, pre-requisite of interest as a condition of learning and development, and active discovery in place of passive listening are shared by both.

Perhaps the most ironic aspect of Piaget's acceptance by the educational reformers of the last twenty years was the vehicle by which he became widely known—Bruner's *The Process of Education* (1961). It contained a famous hypothesis that, while offered as compatible with Piaget in theory, clearly could be seen as contradictory to it. "We begin," wrote Bruner, "with the hypothesis that any subject can be taught effectively in some intellectually honest form to any child at any stage of development" (1961:32), and with the corollary notion of a spiral curriculum that holds as its criterion for a subject "whether, when fully developed, it is worth an adult's knowing" (p. 52). The issue is begged somewhat by the phrase "some intellectually honest form", but one clear feature of Piaget's account of the child's conceptual development is that the qualitative leaps in development make many later ideas inherently unavailable to the younger child. Bruner's hypothesis ignores the epigenic emergent assumption of Piagetian and other organismic developmental accounts. On the other hand there is a plausibility in Bruner's hypothesis that only points up again the difficulty in deriving educational practices from theory. Neither Bruner's hypothesis nor its opposite (that by virtue of epigenesis some subjects cannot be taught with integrity) are actually proscribed by Piagetian theory. As Elkind (1976) sensibly observes, the issue is not whether or not the geo-board activity is an intellectually honest form of geometry but whether or not it is interesting and contributes to the development of geometric concepts.

The chapters of this book are, with one exception, based upon the authors' presentations in the plenary sessions of the Fifth Annual Symposium of the Jean Piaget Society. The theme of the meeting was the impact of Piagetian theory upon the four disciplines around which this book is organized—education, philosophy, psychiatry, and psychology. The chapters by Piaget and his collaborators, Berthoud-Papandropoulou, Voyat, and Wagner, not only provide provocative experimental data and new theoretical directions, but are symbolic representations of the research program that has continued undiminished in imagination and coherence for more than half a century. While others attempted to assess the contributions of the theory to their disciplines, Piaget, almost oblivious to the grandeur of the symposium's theme, conducted himself as if he were merely presenting a colloquium session for his colleagues about the latest turn in his theoretical analyses that had directed and illuminated his most recent set of experiments.

In their chapters, the Genevans analyze the developmental significance of the child's understanding of correspondences, an unresolved issue in their prior work on the significance of transformations in intellectual development. For example, in the famous conservation problem, until now no explanation has been offered for the process by which the child accepts or establishes the initial equivalence between the two objects to be conserved. The theoretical issue centered instead solely upon the operations by which the child maintained the equivalence after one of the objects was transformed. A complete account of conservation and the developmental structures of which it is a symptom requires an integrated theoretical analysis of the correspondences that support the initial equivalence. Such an analysis is presented in the three chapters which follow David Elkind's account of the conditions in American developmental psychology which supported its assimilation of and accommodation to Piaget's theory.

One of the most critical issues in developmental psychology is the explanation for the emergence of novel behavior in the course of a person's development. In their chapter, "The Possible, the Impossible, and the Necessary," Piaget and Voyat expand the older operational schemata model to include procedural and presentative schemata. These new theoretical constructions provide interpretations for the existence of novelties and other developmental issues like the heretofore unexplained *décalage* interaction between structure and content, and the interaction of competence and performance in problem solving. Two interacting systems of schemata are proposed in this expanded model, which augments the traditional operational schemata account of intellectual development.

Piaget's contributions to philosophy settle largely on the clarification of certain enduring epistemological questions. Theodore Mischel's chapter exhaustively treats the manner in which Piagetian constructions illuminate the nature of an explanation, and in particular a psychological explanation. Von Glasersfeld presents a neo-Kantian analysis of the relationship between knowledge and ontological reality in which the genetic epistemological resolution prohibits the possibility of a rational description of the "real world."

In the mental health fields, Piaget's description of the mechanisms of normal cognitive development has illuminated certain classical clinical issues. Peter Wolff, while acknowledging these academic contributions to psychiatric theory, focuses his attention upon the utility of Piagetian metaphors and discoveries in the improvement of the child's mental health, particularly as an antidote to mindless school environments. The child's understanding of various social roles and institutions is examined by Hans Furth from the sensible perspective that the child's knowledge of the social world is amenable to experimentation by the same techniques, and guided by the same theoretical principles, that the Genevans have successfully used in their accounts of the child's knowledge of the physical world. He reports new data about the development of the child's grasp of some basic social conventions.

Millie Almy presents in her chapter a thorough analysis of the impact of Piagetian theory upon the early childhood education field from the perspective of how the salient elements and constraints of the theory have been accepted by educators. An analysis of specific difficulties a pupil might have with various aspects of the curriculum is presented by Kenneth Lovell, based upon his considerations of numerous Genevan empirical findings and their replications and extensions. In the closing chapter, Irving Sigel examines briefly the question of the process by which a theoretical position, such as Piaget's, continues to survive and develop.

Frank B. Murray

REFERENCES

Bruner, J. 1961. The Process of Education. Cambridge: Harvard University Press.

Cremin, L. A. 1961. The Transformation of the School. New York: Vintage.

Elkind, D. 1976. Child Development and Education: a Piagetian Perspective. New York: Oxford University Press.

Hooper, F., and DeFrain, J. 1974. The search for a distinctly Piagetian contribution to education. Theoretical Paper No. 50. Madison, Wis.: Wisconsin Research and Development Center.

Kuhn, T. 1970. The Structure of Scientific Revolutions. 2nd Ed. Chicago: University of Chicago Press.

L'Abate, L. 1969. Frequency of citation in child psychology literature. Child Development 40(1):89–92.

Maccoby, E., and Zellner, M. 1970. Experiments in Primary Education. New York: Harcourt Brace Jovanovich.

Schwebel, M., and Raph, J. 1973. Piaget in the Classroom. New York: Basic Books.

Seltzer, E. 1977. A comparison between John Dewey's theory of inquiry and Jean Piaget's genetic analysis. Journal of Genetic Psychology 130:323.

Silberman, C. E. 1970. Crisis in the Classroom. New York: Random House, Inc.

Walberg, H., Rasher, S., and Mantel, H. 1977. Eminence and citations in educational psychology. Educational Researcher 6:12–14.

THE IMPACT OF PIAGETIAN THEORY

Part I
Developmental Psychology

chapter 1

Piaget and Developmental Psychology

David Elkind

Assessing the impact of Piaget's work upon developmental psychology is a little bit like assessing the impact of the automobile on American society in 2,000 words or less! The task is not only enormous, it is enormously difficult. An adequate answer requires a historical perspective and a distance that is really not possible to achieve for those of us who live in the Piagetian era. What is here presented, therefore, is necessarily incomplete and limited, but may be useful as a kind of interim progress report.

Before proceeding, it might be well to introduce the kind of distinction that Piaget is fond of making, which is a very useful device. We need to distinguish between Piaget's impact in the broad sense and in the narrow sense of that term. In the broad sense we can look at the effect of Piaget's work upon the growth of developmental psychology as a discipline. But we can also look at Piaget's impact in the more narrow sense of the influence his work has had upon developmental research and theory. In this chapter, Piaget's impact in both the broad and the narrow sense is treated.

IMPACT IN THE BROAD SENSE

If we look at history from a Piagetian view, then the influence of Piaget's work on psychology has to be seen as an interaction between the work itself and the American zeitgeist, the intellectual climate at the time when Piaget was rediscovered—the late 1950s and early 1960s. Because Piaget's work is familiar, my remarks are restricted to the American zeitgeist, to the events that were occurring within and outside psychology that helped to make Piaget acceptable where he had not been before. Many different factors contributed to his acceptance and it is really impossible to rank them in order of importance.

The Demise of Learning Theory

It is really hard to appreciate, in the context of contemporary American psychology, the hammerlock that learning theory held upon the discipline during the period from the 1930s to the 1950s. Nor is it possible to comprehend how involved and intense were the studies and theorizing centered about a rat's behavior at a chosen point in a maze. The maze learning paradigm colored the whole of psychological research, including child psychology. An investigator might build a life-sized maze through which children would run with different weights hung upon their backs to determine the effect of effort on maze running. Much of the research on children was, and in some cases still is, modeled upon research first conducted with rats.

Interestingly enough, one of the most potent voices against the sterility of the maze learning research was himself an animal investigator. The publication of B. F. Skinner's *Science and Human Behavior* (1953) was one of the single most important events that paved the way for the eventual recognition and acceptance of Piaget's work by American psychology. What Skinner accomplished (and only someone within the system could have carried it off) was to challenge the discipline's vain attachment to physics as a model of psychological science. Skinner argued that the kind of data we have in psychology, at least at this stage in our discipline, does not warrant elaborate experimentation and mathematical theorizing. Observing and counting, he argued, are more appropriate to our discipline than delicate experimental manipulations. Skinner, more than any other single psychologist, helped to make a naturalistic psychology more acceptable in this country.

Obviously there were other factors beside Skinner's work that led to the demise of traditional learning theory research. The social upheavals of the late fifties and early sixties made society look to psychologists for help in providing better education for blacks, a better understanding of the psychology of persons who could assassinate a president, and a better understanding of youth who were alienated and alienating. To these demands upon the discipline, traditional learning theory had precious little to offer. Psychologists were suddenly confronted with a concept they had not had to face before—relevance. And they found that their encapsulated concern with rats could not be justified when society demanded a viable psychology of human behavior.

The Emergence of Ego Psychology

Another significant development that helped make possible Piaget's acceptance in the 1960s was the advent of ego psychology. Although Freud alluded to ego processes early in his writings, he did not devote major attention to the ego until the end of his career. For Freud, ego functions (cognitive processes, as we would call them today) arose from a failure of the primary processes, such as fantasy, to satisfy basic needs. We bring ourselves to test reality and to elaborate cognitive processes because hallucinations and fantasies, however elaborate they may be, cannot satisfy real physical hungers.

In the 1940s a group of psychoanalysts led by Heinz Hartmann (1951) introduced the notion of the "conflict-free ego sphere"—the idea that some ego processes were present from the start of life and were not derived solely from the failure of primary process thinking. This development in psychoanalytic theory lent new value and prestige to ego functioning. It prompted psychologists such as David Rapaport (1951), George Klein (1967), and Roy Schafer (1967) to explore such phenomena as ego autonomy, cognitive style, and projective processes from a rational as well as a dynamic point of view. And last but not least, it lent weight to the study of cognitive processes in children. David Rapaport was one of the first psychologists to recognize the significance of Piaget's work for ego psychology and it is not surprising that two of his students, Peter Wolff and myself, are contributors to this volume.

The Advent of Computers and Information Processing

A more general development that helped make Piaget acceptable in psychology was the advent of the computer and information-processing technology and concepts. Computers provided a new and fascinating model for mental functioning that went far beyond the simple switchboard or chemical analogies that had been utilized heretofore. When computers were programmed to play records, or to play tic-tac-toe and chess, there was a beginning understanding of how complex, intricate, and magnificent the human brain really is. Terms like *feedback, storage, programs,* and *memory load* were at first used metaphorically and then descriptively with regard to human thinking. Attempts at computer simulation of cognitive processes also helped legitimize the study of human cognitive processes as complex mental abilities not reducible to simple associative linkages.

Philosophy of Science

Although many other factors that contributed to Piaget's acceptance in the 1960s could be mentioned, only one other general development will be discussed. Although it occurred in the area of philosophy and the philosophy of science, it had relevance for psychology. In the early decades of this century the philosophy of Kant held sway. Kant was critical of pure reason as a basis of knowledge. In his view, we learn about the world through experience but only as that experience is interpreted by the more or less innate categories of understanding, space, time, number, and so on. The Kantian distrust of reason was carried forward by the Vienna circle and their emphasis upon philosophy as the conceptualization of science rather than as a discipline devoted to the discovery of its own special truths.

More recently, however, there has been a rebirth of interest in Hegel and in his resurrection of reason as a source of knowledge. Although Hegel agreed with Kant in some respects, he did not agree that reason always results in purely empty, synthetic knowledge. Reasoning, dialectical reasoning, can help us discover more general truths, such as how diverse concepts and institutions interrelate and how history progresses. The rational dialectic, which was so derided by Kant, was made by Hegel into a method for discovering general or dynamic truths that were not empty, but analytic—filled with meaningful, if general, ideas.

In many respects Piaget's theory presents a kind of synthesis of Kant and Hegel. Like Kant, Piaget holds that we can never know the environment in and of itself, the *ding am selbst,* but only as it is reconstructed to the mind's categories of understanding. But, like Hegel, Piaget denies that understanding comes only from fixed categories of knowing. Hegel argued that the categories changed as a function of culture and history. Piaget argues that the categories undergo change in the course of individual development. The changes, moreover, come about as a function of reasoning about the world. For Piaget, induction and deduction, the analytic and the synthetic, are not separate and apart, as Kant would have them, but rather are phases of the knowing process as Hegel maintained. Hence, from a dynamic point of view, Piaget's psychology of knowing is closer to Hegel than it is to Kant, while from a structural point of view, just the reverse is true. A philosophy of science that was not opposed to a valid role for reasoning in the attainment of knowledge was more hospitable to Piaget's theorizing than a purely empirical one.

These factors, then—the demise of learning theory, the emergence of ego psychology and information-processing technology and concepts, together with the rise of a new philosophy of science more accepting of the role of reason in the acquisition of knowledge—all helped pave the way for the acceptance of Piaget's work. But Piaget's writings played their part. However crude Piaget's research appeared to be, however far-fetched his theory seemed, there was no denying one fact. In Piaget's books he portrayed recognizable children, children who spoke, behaved, and thought as did children in our own everyday experience. It was this consensual validation, this intuitive sense that somehow Piaget had captured something essentially true about children, that is what made his voice heard—once American psychologists and educators were ready to listen.

The rest is factual history. The growth of developmental psychology in this country over the past fifteen years has been phenomenal. The Society for Research in Child Development was then an intimate society of a small group of scholars. It is now a major organization. Two new journals, "The Journal for Experimental Child Psychology" and "Developmental Psychology," have been founded. The Minnesota Symposium series has been in operation for some years and other enterprises, such as the Review of Child Development Research, have been undertaken to keep up with the outpouring of research and theory in the field.

It is well to remember that hardly more than a decade ago child psychology was at the bottom of most university psychology departments' priority lists. Today, no major psychology department could call itself that without having a prominent division of developmental psychology. Certainly Piaget does not deserve all the credit (or the blame!) for this situation. But his work was a major force in lending respectability to developmental psychology and in highlighting its role as a core discipline for psychology as a whole.

IMPACT IN THE NARROW SENSE

Piaget's impact upon research and theory in developmental psychology has gone in three directions: accommodation without assimilation; assimilation without accommodation; and assimilation with accommodation, or equilibration.

Accommodation Without Assimilation

My favorite Piaget story, and one that illustrates accommodation without assimilation, occurred during my stay at the Institute of Genetic Epistemology in Geneva. At one of the weekly meetings, after my French had become passable, I said to Piaget that I was going to take the part of the devil and ask him a difficult question. I then proceeded to ask him why he insisted upon using the concepts of assimilation and accommodation when the terms stimulus and response would serve just as well. You can imagine the consternation in the room! The students looked at me as if they expected lightning to strike me where I sat. But Piaget was highly amused and with a twinkle in his eye he replied, "Well, Elkeend, you can use stimulus and response if you like, but if you want to understand anything, then you use assimilation and accommodation."

A simple translation of Piagetian terms into more familiar ones is an example of accommodation without assimilation. A more pernicious kind of accommodation without assimilation occurs when Piagetian terms are misused. A case in point is the concept of conservation. Many investigators have tried to show that even young children have conservation if you make the task easy enough. But the tasks that they have employed do not really measure conservation in the Piagetian sense. For Piaget, conservation can only be assessed when the child is confronted with a task that presents him with a conflict between his judgment based on perception and his judgment based on reason. If this conflict is not present in the task, there is no way of demonstrating the victory of reason over perception that marks the appearance of concrete operations. Hence it is really not possible to say anything about cognitive structures on the basis of these tasks.

The problem arises because of a confusion between performance and competence and the fact that you can change a child's performance without changing his competence. A concrete example of the way in which you can get a change in performance without a corresponding change in underlying competence is to have a 4-year-old child who knows his numbers tell time with a digital clock.

The digital clock takes all the logical complexity out of telling time. On a clock face, one and the same figure, say a one, stands both for one o'clock and for five minutes. In effect, to tell time from a clock face the child has to recognize that one number has two different meanings. That feat is generally only accomplished by the concrete operational child.

The question then becomes one of definition. In what sense can the child be said to be "telling time?" Clearly, at the performance level he can, with the aid of the digital clock, read off the hours and minutes. But can he tell time from a regular clock, and, more importantly, does he grasp the concepts of hour, minute, and second? It is not until two or three years later that the 6- or 7-year-old is able to tell time, to read, and to make conservation judgments. Performances like telling time from a digital clock reflect quite different competencies than those required by standard tasks. Much confusion would be avoided in the field if the distinction between performance and competence were kept in mind and if investigators stated clearly which aspect of behavior they were attempting to demonstrate.

Another example of accommodation without assimilation comes from workers who start from a learning theory persuasion. Some of these investigators are convinced that any child can be trained to perform at any level in the Piagetian scheme of development. A three-choice discrimination problem, for example, is not a formal operational task. One of the most dismaying developments growing out of Piaget's work is the trend toward teaching the concepts Piaget has explored in his research. Such an approach assumes that what Piaget has provided us with is a new school curriculum that should, if not supplant the old one, at least accompany it. Nothing could demonstrate more clearly the phenomenon of accommodation without assimilation than this misperception of the educational implications of Piaget's work.

The cause of this misperception is the failure to distinguish between a school curriculum on the one hand and a developmental curriculum on the other. The school curriculum consists of the skills and knowledge in mathematics, language arts, science, social studies, and fine arts that have been accumulated and passed down in the course of cultural history. In contrast, what Piaget has revealed to us is the developmental curriculum, which encompasses the abilities and conceptions that children acquire as part of their basic adaptive apparatus. The developmental curriculum derives in large part from the evolution of the species, although its realization in any particular child depends upon the environment at every point in development.

The real task for education, which has been made prominent by Piaget's discovery of the child's developmental curriculum, is *the coordination of the two curricula*—not the substitution of one for the other. And this coordination, for the most part, must occur at both the macro and the micro curriculum levels. The developmental curriculum can suggest when children might best be taught subjects like reading and geography. And it also provides guidelines at the micro level of day-to-day teaching—it can provide insights into the logical substructure of particular exercises and instructions.

At both the macro and micro levels of instruction, Piaget has not provided us with a new curriculum to be taught, but rather with powerful tools for the analysis of existing school curricula. It has to be recognized that Piaget's work has not made the teacher's work any easier; if anything it has made it harder and more exacting. Piaget demands that the teacher be an investigator who is constantly observing, testing hypotheses, and modifying materials and strategies to adapt to the child's continually changing developmental propensities. But if that is true, it is also true that teaching from a child-centered Piagetian perspective is also far more interesting, exciting, and rewarding than is teaching from a purely adult perspective.

Assimilation Without Accommodation

Research and theory that reflects an assimilation of Piaget's work without an accommodation to American values and practices is less common than accommodation without assimilation, but there are significant instances. Recent work on moral development provides an illustration. Some of the work on moral development has involved Piagetian procedures, i.e., moral dilemmas, and has yielded an innovative elaboration of the stages of moral development as outlined by Piaget. Unfortunately there has been a reluctance of workers in this field to move toward more valid and reliable measures of moral development. The continued reliance upon Piaget's semi-clinical interview is an instance of assimilation without accommodation. (Since this chapter was written, an objective scale of moral development has appeared.)

To be sure, the semi-clinical method is an important and very delicate tool and one that should form part of every developmental psychologist's armamentarium of technical skills. But it is a method that is appropriate to the initial stages of research in a particular domain. The semi-clinical method allows one to map out the domain, and to get a detailed picture of its topography. Once that is done, more objective and standardized procedures can be introduced without fear that meaningful information will be overlooked. For example, now that the basic facts about the conservation of quantity by children and of objects by infants are known, objective methods of assessing these conservations are both necessary and useful. The publication of standardized concrete operational tasks (Goldschmid and Bentler, 1968; Botson and Deliege, 1974) are examples of how Piagetian tasks can be standardized and validated.

Piaget himself is very much aware of the fact that it is the nature of the subject matter and the state of development of the field that must determine the research methodology. In his work on perception (Piaget, 1969), an area where a great deal of his previous work was done, Piaget did employ the experimental method and did report his findings quantitatively. It is wrong, therefore, to identify the semi-clinical method with developmental theory and research. Rather, it is a method that is usefully applied to any field of psychology during the first, or natural history, stage of inquiry into a problem. But the method cannot be justified once the problem is reasonably well delineated. To do so is to show assimilation of one of Piaget's methods without accommodation to the demands of the scientific community.

There is another kind of assimilation without accommodation that (we are thankful) has not been too common in developmental psychology. This type of unaccommodated assimilation occurs when Piaget's work is taken as a kind of dogma, and the investigator takes the stance of "Protector of the Faith." From the standpoint of these workers one must always start from Piaget's work and not deviate from it in significant ways. Certain large scale replications of Piaget's work and certain applications of

Piaget's work to education have had echoes of Piagetian purism. And yet a slavish adherence to Piaget's work is entirely contrary to his position. It is the reason that Piaget has said "to the extent that there are Piagetians, to that extent I have failed." Unlike Freud, Piaget never wanted a cult, and "The Centre D'Epistemologie Genetique" was expressly founded for the purpose of bringing together scholars from diverse disciplines with, often, conflicting points of view.

There is, however, a sense in which one can be a Piagetian without being dogmatic. It is the sense in which most of us are Piagetians. That is to say, we appreciate and value his momentous contribution to psychology and find it a fruitful starting point for our own research and theorizing. But at the same time we feel free to criticize Piagetian research and theory where it seems to be wanting and to follow our own research and theoretical views wherever they will lead us, even if it is into territory not explored by Piaget. It is perhaps the highest tribute to Piaget that one can be a Piagetian without thereby sacrificing one's freedom to grow as both an individual and as a scientist.

Assimilation With Accommodation

So far the focus has been upon the negative parts of Piaget's impact upon developmental psychology. Without question there is a good deal of work in developmental psychology that shows a healthy respect for Piaget's work together with a vigorous desire to go further and to expand some of the new terrain Piaget has opened by showing us the heretofore "hidden side" of the child's mind.

Consider John Flavell's work. Both Flavell's early work on role-taking (Flavell et al., 1968) and his more recent work on memory, particularly the child's conception of memory (Kreutzer, Leonard, and Flavell, 1975) was much influenced by Piaget. But Flavell, with his knack for ingenious research and careful theorizing, carried the issues of role-taking and of memory in directions left unexplored by Piaget. Flavell has never felt constrained to limit himself to Piagetian terminology or methodology and yet readily acknowledges his debt to Piaget.

Consider, too, Hans Furth and the extension of Piagetian theorizing and methodology to work with the deaf (1966). More recently, and with considerable success, Furth has spoken to the problem of education as well and his *Piaget for Teachers* (1970) is a very useful discussion for practitioners. And in a similar way, Burton White (1969), among many others, has built upon Piaget's infancy studies in his research with young children. In still another domain, Anthony (1956), Feffer (1970), and more recently Chandler (1973) have brought Piagetian concepts to bear upon clinical problems and interpersonal relations.

Perhaps one of the currently most exciting areas of work is that dealing with the interface between language and cognition. Unfortunately the field is changing so fast that one must, as George Miller said recently, join "a theory-of-the-month club" in order to keep up. Even so, Sinclair-deZwart's (1967) work, which suggests how developmental psycholinguistics can be built upon the sensorimotor coordinations of infants, is an exciting first step. More recently, Roger Brown (1973), Lois Bloom (Bloom, Lightbourn, and Hood, 1975), and Harry Beilin (1975) have made important theoretical contributions that demonstrate the close interdependence of cognitive development as described by Piaget and of language development as described by the linguists.

Many more illustrations of how one can assimilate Piaget's work and yet accommodate it to new problems could be given. But these examples may suffice to illustrate the positive impact Piaget has had upon developmental research and theory. To be sure, Piagetian influence does not pervade the whole of developmental psychology and there is still work done, such as that in discrimination learning, that does not reflect his influence. But it is fair to say that the flavor and texture of developmental psychology today is very heavily Piagetian.

CONCLUSION

The impact of Piaget in developmental psychology can be found in both the broad and the narrow sense of that term. In the broad sense, his impact upon the discipline as a whole, Piaget's work made itself felt at a time when the American zeitgeist was finally ready for it. The demise of learning theory, the emergence of ego psychology, the advent of computers and information-processing apparatus to cognition, and a new mood in the philosophy of science (more comfortable with the constructive role of reason in the construction of knowledge) all made it possible for Piaget's work to be recognized and valued. The growth of developmental psychology thereafter was, to a measurable extent, a function of the impetus and distinction that he lent to the field.

In the narrow sense Piaget's influence in research and theory has gone in three directions: accommodation without assimilation, assimilation without accommodation, and assimilation balanced by accommodation. The last approach seems to be the most productive in that it takes Piaget as a starting point without at the same time being bound either to stay within the system or to refrain from criticism of it. It could hardly be otherwise for a man who advocates that education should teach people "to be critical and not to accept the first ideas that come to them."

It is really not possible to assess Piaget's scientific impact with any accuracy at this point in time. But there is one type of impression that can be assessed, and only at this time. That is Piaget's personal impact upon his students, his colleagues, and his friends. That personal impact is something that all of us fortunate enough to have had personal contact with Piaget cherish in a very special way and that, for us, will always be the most important impact of all. As I have written elsewhere, "It is Piaget's courage and steadfastness in the face of prevailing zeitgeist condescending towards his methods, suspicious of his results, and hostile toward his theorizing, that have been an example to all of his students of that independence of mind and commitment to truth that is the motive force behind all genuine scientific progress."

REFERENCES

Anthony, E. J. 1956. The significance of Jean Piaget for child psychology. British Journal of Medical Psychology 29: 20–34.

Beilin, H. 1975. Studies in the Cognitive Basis of Language Development. New York: Academic Press.

Bloom, L., Lightbourn, P., and Hood, L. 1975. Structure and variation in child language. Monographs of the Society for Research in Child Development 40 (No. 160).

Botson, C., and Deliege, M. 1974. Le Développement Intellectuel de l'Enfant. Liege, Belgique: Direction Générale de l'Organisation des Études.

Brown, R. 1973. A First Language: The Early Stages. Cambridge, Massachusetts: Harvard University Press.

Chandler, M. J. 1973. Egocentrism and antisocial behavior. Developmental Psychology 9: 326–332.

Feffer, M. H. 1970. A developmental analysis of interpersonal behavior. Psychological Review 77: 197–214.

Flavell, J. H., Botkin, P. T., Fry, C. L., Wright, J. C., and Jarvis, P. E. 1968. The Development of Role-Taking and Communication Skills in Children. New York: John Wiley & Sons, Inc.

Furth, H. G. 1966. Thinking Without Language: Psychological Implications of Deafness. New York: Free Press.

Furth, H. G. 1970. Piaget for Teachers. Englewood Cliffs, New Jersey: Prentice-Hall, Inc.

Goldschmid, M. L., and Bentler, P. M. 1968. Concept Assessment Kit—Conservation. San Diego, California: Educational and Industrial Testing Services.

Hartmann, H. 1951. Ego psychology and the problem of adaptation. In D. Rapaport (ed.), Organization and Pathology of Thought. New York: Columbia University Press.

Klein, G. 1967. Peremptory ideation: Structure and force in motivated ideas. In R. R. Holt (ed.), Motives and Thought: Psychoanalytic Essays in Honor of David Rapaport, pp. 78–128. New York: International Universities Press.

Kreutzer, M. A., Leonard, C., and Flavell, J. H. 1975. An interview study of children's knowledge about memory. Monographs of the Society for Research in Child Development 40 (1, Serial No. 159).

Piaget, J. 1969. The Mechanisms of Perception. New York: Basic Books.

Rapaport, D. 1951. The autonomy of the ego. Bulletin of the Menninger Clinic 15: 113–123.

Schafer, R. 1967. Ideals, the ego ideal, and the ideal self. In R. R. Holt (ed.), Motives and Thought: Psychoanalytic Essays in Honor of David Rapaport, pp. 129–174. New York: International Universities Press.

Sinclair-DeZwart, H. 1967. Acquisition du Langage et Développement de la Pensée. Paris: Dunod.

Skinner, B. F. 1953. Science and Human Behavior. New York: Macmillan.

White, B. L. 1969. The initial coordination of sensorimotor schema in human infants. In D. Elkind and J. H. Flavell (eds.), Studies in Cognitive Development, pp. 237–256. New York: Oxford.

chapter 2

Correspondences and Transformations

Jean Piaget*

For some 50 years we have studied the development of cognitive
functions in the child guided by two hypotheses. The first of
these hypotheses is that knowledge comes from action and not
simply from perception. There is also sensorimotor knowledge
with its organization of schemes of action before language. The
second hypothesis is that certain of these schemes of action can
be interiorized and transformed into operations, the operations
being, for example, the operations of ordering, of reuniting, of
reversing actions, etc. Our central hypothesis was that knowledge is based essentially on systems of transformation. To know
is to transform objects, or rather it is to transform groups of objects to make them assimilable to our structures. From this point
of view, we have described the familiar four main stages in the
development of the child's intelligence. The first, the sensorimotor period where there is pure action, is followed by the
period of preoperatory representations where actions begin to be
interiorized. The third is the period of concrete operations,
where there are already logical inferences and logical structures,
but always accompanied by real or imagined manipulations of
objects—action still plays a role. Finally, the period of formal
operations follows, in which transformations become mental
transformations and entirely interiorized but are still transformations. The significance placed on transformations conformed to
everything that we then knew about the evolution of logic and
mathematics. These two sciences are essentially sciences based
on operations. Geometry is not simply a description of figures.
According to Felix Klein, the geometries are based on groups of
transformations. It is the same with algebra, which is essentially

---

* Translated by Leonard DiLisio.

a system of operations and transformations. However, recently an entirely new current has developed in the study of the foundations of mathematics. It is the study of correspondences, in general, and particularly correspondences that are called morphisms. These are correspondences that conserve structures, and are equally based on the notion of categories, which is a class of objects with all their possible morphisms.

A correspondence is not a transformation. A correspondence is simply a comparison, such as when the child places 10 red tokens in correspondence with 10 blue tokens, thus making a term-to-term or one-to-one correspondence. The child does not transform the tokens, he simply compares them, and there is no transformation. These comparisons or correspondences were naturally already studied by us many years ago in the particular case of numerical correspondences in the genesis of the number. This is only a very specific case and in reality there are correspondences everywhere, and correspondences of various types.

We have posed two general questions for ourselves. The first is the role of correspondences as instruments of comparison in cognitive development. The second is the relationship between those correspondences that we have studied up to now. It is obvious that we have here two complimentary systems. The transformations succeed each other and engender each other according to a tree structure. Figure 1 (part 1) outlines a tree where the branches are constituted one from another. For example, in the evolution of classifications the child first begins by making juxtaposed collections that evolve into collections with subcollections and finally grow into classes with inclusions and intersections. In the end he will construct multiplicative matrices. In other words, there are successive branches that are engendered, so to speak, vertically or successively from a certain point of departure. Correspondences, on the other hand, are transversal comparisons, which are represented in Figure 1 (part 1) as dotted lines that connect any term to any other term on the same level. A transversal comparison consists in comparing states without modifying them. It is necessary to compare them without transforming them. One can even compare transformations themselves, but again without modifying them, only considering them as states of thought to be compared. We have two sorts of entities that are complementary but that are distinct and not reducible one to the other.

Figure 1.   Photograph of Piaget's chalk drawings of: 1) tree of transformations; 2) partial conservation transformation; 3) conservation of length transformation; 4) various angles of incidence and reflection trajectories; 5) rotating disc; 6) indeformable tracing object; and 7) tracing paths.

It is clear that there are correspondences at all levels of development. On the sensorimotor level the assimilations to schemes of action are already correspondences. After a child has by chance touched a suspended object and has seen that he can make it swing, he will, everytime he sees a hanging object, tap it to make it swing. He has made a correspondence between the new situation and the situations that he already knew. Consequently, on the level of representations, whenever there is such a generalization there are correspondences between the new elements and the elements already known. At the level of operational thought—indeed for all direct operations—there is a necessary correspondence between the two sorts of operations, one of which is the inverse of the other, as the presence of one implies the presence of the other (for example, addition corresponds to an inverse operation—subtraction). The feedback regulations themselves also consist of correspondences between successive corrections, and between a perturbation and the compensatory perturbation that nullifies it. Therefore at all levels and in all operational or preoperational activities, of whatever sort, there are correspondences.

Our general hypothesis is that there are three distinguishable stages in the relationships between correspondences and transformations. At first, correspondences pave the way for the transformations, since there are no transformations that the child discovers without first having made certain correspondences. In effect, it is necessary to know the details of the objects to be able to compare them. It is from comparisons of changes of state that the child little by little comes to discover transformations. The second stage is where the transformations and the correspondences are in interaction, that is to say, render each other mutual services. The one helps the other in their effective formation. At a third stage, new correspondences, such as the correspondence between direct operations and inverse operations, result from the construction of operational structures themselves. This time they are necessary correspondences that can be drawn deductively from the structure, whereas the initial correspondences, those that prepare the transformations, were only empirical correspondences that are based simply on the perception of observables. These initial correspondences are not yet necessary, but are simply empirical declarations. Correspondences are general and everywhere, and although they prepare for the transformations they also result from them—because they have a transversal direction, they can tie any operational structure to any other for the sake of comparison. That is why in modern mathematics, the theory of morphisms and of categories results in generalizations that are greater than the simple operational structures.Ioanna Berthoud-Papandropoulou and Sheldon Wagner in the next chapters present two examples of research on the formation and the evolution of certain correspondences or certain morphisms.

Another very simple example of correspondences that renews in part the problem with which we have been occupied for at least 40 years is the problem of conservation. Conservations were conceived as always being conservations across a transformation. When a little ball of modeling clay is changed into a sausage, it is transformed, but the quantity of matter is conserved. There is a transformation but at the same time conservation. However, for young children, when there is transformation in form everything else changes at the same time, positions as well as quantities, quantities as well as positions.

What are the conditions needed to acquire the notion of conservation? These conditions seem to be two in number. First, it is necessary to understand that the change of form, from ball to sausage, consists of a displacement of part of the ball. Second, and it is here that correspondence comes in, the child must realize that when one displaces a part of the object, that part which is added at one point corresponds to that which was taken away from another point. The young children do not understand that what is added at one end corresponds to what was taken away at the other end. They think only about the point of arrival, and see only that the little ball is elongated; they do not ask from where that which produces the elongation comes. They forget about the point of departure and that something has been taken away, and therefore lack a necessary correspondence in all domains because they are centered on the point of arrival. Consider conservation of lengths (Figure 1, part 3), in which one of two congruent sticks is displaced by being pushed up beyond the end of the other. Children who think the displaced stick has become longer fail to consider the correspondence between what is longer at one end and shorter at the other end.

To verify this hypothesis, we did some new experiments with Bärbel Inhelder on conservation with the following technique. Instead of deforming the little ball into a sausage simply by pulling or pushing by hand, we take off a piece and we ask the children if the same amount of clay is in the ball. All the children tell us, "No, you have taken something away, there is less." Then the piece that was removed was placed on the other end (Figure 1, part 2); thus, a small piece was taken away on the left and placed on the other end at the right. The children were asked, "do we have the same quantity of clay as in the small ball before the transformation was made?" Now a very interesting thing happens—after the age of 5½, on the average, three-fourths of the children say immediately, "It is the same thing, you took it away and then put it back and it's always the same quantity of clay." Thus after age 5½ these children arrive at a stable conservation. If, instead of taking away and adding again, the traditional experiment in which a small ball is pushed into another shape is performed, the children tell us, "But that is still the same quantity, you have only stretched it." The children have understood that there is displacement, and that when one displaces, what is added at one place has been taken away from another place. There is a notable advance of the discovery of conservation due to this technique of taking away and adding again, which introduces a notion of correspondence. There is a necessary correspondence, an isomorphism between what is taken away and what is added, and this brings on this precocious conservation.

Another general example of correspondence is the correspondence between affirmations and negations, or rather between positive and negative factors. It is a very general phenomenon. The child who acts always centers his attention on the goal to be attained (in other words, to the positive elements of the action), whereas he does not think, or thinks much less, about the negative elements of the action (that is, what is suppressed or left behind so that the goal can be reached). This produces a fundamental disequilibrium that is the rule at the preoperational level. The operations, on the other hand, with the correspondence of direct and inverse operations, end up by introducing an exact correspondence between the positive elements and the negative elements. Conservation is already an example of this—taking away is negative, and adding is positive. In the field of physical observables, we find a very amusing example that our collaborator, Andrew Rodriguez, observed about the notions of "full" and "empty." If a child is given a water glass and asked to fill it half way, (half full) he rather quickly produces a glass half full. If a glass almost full is asked for, he will fill it almost full and he understands that it is not completely, but almost, filled. If a glass filled only a little bit is asked for, he will put very little water in the bottom. All this is accomplished rapidly. If, instead of speaking of full and filled (positive terms), empty is spoken of, i.e., the same things are said in negative terms and a glass is asked for half empty, or almost empty, or only a little empty, there is a delay. Children of age six, two or three years past the age at which they comprehend "filled," very often do not realize that a half empty and half full glass have equal amounts. The quantification of "empty" is therefore a much later development than the quantification of "full," despite the fact that logically it is exactly the same expression, only in negative terms.

The same phenomenon is found in logical or numerical fields. A child is shown two collections of tokens, 10 tokens for the child and 10 tokens for the experimenter, who says, "I'm going to give you two tokens" as he does so. The child will then have 12 of them and not 10. If the experimenter hides his reduced set and asks the child, "What is the difference between what you have now and what I have now?", the child says: "The difference is two. You gave me two, I now have 12, and the difference is 2." Of course, the difference is not 2, but 4 (not n, but $2n$). It is necessary to understand that what is added to one set is taken away from the other one, as in the conservation problem. The realization that the necessary correspondence between what the child has gained and what the experimenter has lost is a very late development, coming at an older age.

There is regulative character in all these cases of correspondences. When there is no correspondence between positive and negative factors, contradictions result that bring the disequilibriums common to the preoperational stage. One could ask why there are so many disequilibriums and contradictions in the beginning, since for simple problems it would seem that simple solutions should not bring these disequilibriums. It is essentially the disequilibrium between affirmations and negations resulting from a lack of correspondences that is the source of the cognitive disequilibriums. The restoration of equilibrium consists in seeing a necessary correspondence between positive and negative elements.

Another very general example of correspondences is the discovery of covariations or dependency; that is, the notion of function, $y = f(x)$. Take as an example the function of the angle of incidence and the angle of reflection when a ball hits a wall. For young children, when the ball reaches the wall it follows the wall. At a little later age they will tell you (Figure 1, part 4) that the ball goes right near the wall but it avoids touching it, and it continues in that fashion. Finally the child discovers the exact function, i.e., the equality of angles. The functions are interesting because they contain simultaneous correspondences and transformations. There is a correspondence between the values of y and the values of x because y depends on x. Therefore the angle of reflection depends on the angle of incidence. There is a correspondence between the two values. There is even in this case a bijection, an isomorphism. On the other hand, when x is transformed to x' or x'', or y is transformed to y' or y'', it is a transformation. Therefore in the case of function there is a correspondence between the results of two transformations, and it is this correspondence between transformations that leads to the idea of dependence.

The initial hypothesis was that in the beginning the correspondences prepare or pave the way for the transformations. Then

they render mutual services by interaction, and finally correspondences become determined by transformations in the capacity of necessary correspondences, or morphisms. As an example
of this preparation of transformations by correspondences, consider this experiment (Figure 1, part 5). Two boxes of different
colors circulate on a disc, one above the other, as the child
watches. The child is asked to tell if, when on the left the dark
one is above the light one, how the boxes will be situated on the
other side, when turned (the light one then being above the dark
one). It is a difficult problem for the child if he has not understood the transformation, i.e., in so far as he does not follow the
cyclical order of the positions in the rotations. He begins by
discovering certain correspondences and then he discovers
rather quickly the fact that the dark box, which is on top when on
the left, becomes the bottom one when on the right. He foresees
this simply by a type of symmetry. It is by little successive correspondences that the child discovers suddenly that there is a
general order. He reestablishes the cyclical order, and then the
partial correspondences that he had discovered by empirical
method in the beginning become instruments permitting him to
understand the transformation as such. In that case the correspondences will be deduced from the transformation. It is from
the cyclical order conceived as transformation that the child de-
duces the different correspondences in the different positions.

The problem of indeformable solids is interesting from the
point of view of the philosophy of geometry. When one displaces
a solid it does not change its form, and the empirical geometri-
cian of the 19th century claimed that geometry is mathematics
applied to indeformable solids. Certain modern epistemologists
agree that the notion of an indeformable solid already supposes
the entire geometry and supposes the notion of the group of
transformations of invariance, etc. Consider an experiment about
a wooden indeformable object formed of three rings linked by
rigid sticks which cannot be moved in reference to each other
(Figure 1, part 6). The upper circle is pierced by a small hole
through which a pencil is passed. The object is displaced in a
straight line up or down, right or left or in the form of a Z (Figure
1, part 7), or in more complicated motions with curves. Now the
child is asked, once he has seen the path of the pencil-tracing
from the first ring on the paper, to reproduce the paths of the two
other rings. Theoretically the question is quite simple—because

the solid is indeformable there must be parallel paths; knowledge of one path is sufficient to generate the others. This correspondence takes a long time to be constructed. The youngest child supposes that being displaced from left to right, the three rings of the object have changed their respective positions so there is no correspondence between the position of the elements at the arrival and the position of the elements at the departure. At an older age, the child understands that, if the object left with the three rings in a certain position, it must be found with the rings in the same position at the arrival. He will correctly sketch the object at the point of arrival and departure, but he will sketch the intermediary stages in any way, as if the three elements could change position with respect to each other in transit. It is only at the operational stage that the child succeeds in finding the parallel correspondences passage between the rings when he has been given only the path of one at first.

By examining these several examples, the different relations possible between correspondences and transformations can be distinguished and separated into five types. First, correspondences exist without transformations when it is a question simply of comparing two states (for example, comparing an immobile figure to another immobile figure) and finding the common elements or the different elements. Second, there are pretransformational correspondences that prepare the transformations, as with the rotating disc and the two boxes in different positions. The correspondences discovered empirically are the source of the discovery of the transformation of movement of cyclical order. Third, there are intertransformational correspondences that make a transformation of a certain type correspond to a transformation of another type. For example, when a child has made a seriation of sticks, with sizes from the smallest to the largest, and is asked to make a seriation with, say, cubes, from the smallest to the largest, he should see immediately that there is identity of the two structures and that the transformations are the same in the two cases. This will be an intertransformational correspondence. Fourth, cotransformational correspondences exist when the correspondence is based necessarily on a transformation and its reciprocal. If, for example, the sequence of natural numbers 1, 2, 3, 4 . . . is taken, there is a correspondence that is the well known morphism of the successor. Each element has one and only one successor or, inversely, each element except the first has one and only one immediate predecessor. This correspondence, which is designated by the name of morphism of the successor, is necessarily based on a transformational operation of $n + 1$. Each number is the preceding number plus one. Between the transformational operation $n + 1$ and the morphism of the successor there is, therefore, a narrow solidarity of a co-transformational correspondence. Finally, there is what could be called protransformational correspondences, which announce transformations not yet discovered and permit them to be engendered in so many free transformations. This last category will not be found to a great extent among children, but rather among adolescents. In mathematics, it happens that those studying morphisms and categories have discovered new structures and new groups of transformations by simply relying on the theory of categories.

The systems of transversal and simultaneous comparisons, or correspondences, are all as necessary for cognitive development as are operational transformations. For a long time transformations seemed to us sufficient for explaining cognitive development and sufficient for practical action, because a practical action always consists in modifying reality. They seemed sufficient to us for the objective comprehension of physical phenomena because, in order to understand physical laws or physical relations, it is always necessary to modify things more or less to study the variations. They seemed sufficient to us for the logical or mathematical construction, because all logic and all mathematics are based on operations. But the study of correspondences and of morphisms has shown us that comparisons are also quite necessary. These correspondences are not transformations, but may accompany transformations. Even though as comparisons they transform nothing by themselves, these comparisons are necessary for the discovery of transformations, because in order to discover transformations it is necessary to know the data and in order to know the data it is necessary to begin with the systems of comparison. And they are necessary once the operational structures are constructed, because the latter necessarily comprise morphisms and correspondences. Nevertheless, even though both comparisons, or correspondences, and transformations are necessary, they are not identical. They remain rather profoundly distinct. Transformations are based essentially on reversibility. The evolution of transformations in the sense of a progressive equilibration is the gradual conquest of reversibility. A comparison or a correspondence does not permit the inverse. If a is isomorphic to b, then b is isomorphic to a. There is a reciprocal, but there is no negation in the domain of correspondences themselves. There are no negative correspondences as there are negative operations. In particular, in the domain of the progressive equilibration of correspondences there is a notable and interesting difference between the two types of systems.

The equilibration of transformations is therefore the movement toward reversibility. As for correspondences, because they are comparisons they consist essentially in discovering common forms between two structures, two objects, two states, or the terms to be compared, whatever their number or their nature. But this comparison essentially amounts to searching for resemblances, since it is the common form. Differences as such do not give rise to correspondences. Here we find ourselves in the presence of this interesting problem—the relation between resemblances and differences is not the same as the relation between affirmation and negation in the domain of reversibility. Actually, there exists an absolute resemblance, i.e., the identity $a = a$ means that there is no difference between a and a itself. That is clear and there is no need for demonstration. There is no absolute difference. Now take two objects that seem to be completely different, but are nevertheless two objects and, as objects, they resemble each other. They both belong to the physical world, and that's also a resemblance. They are objects of thought that both belong to the world of concepts. That's still a resemblance. There is no absolute difference. The progressive equilibration of correspondences or of morphisms, of comparisons, consists in subordinating the differences to the closest unifying resemblances, and it is this progress toward the common form that seems to me to be the distinctive character of the progressive equilibration of correspondences.

Given, therefore, that we are dealing with two sorts of systems that are distinct, but both indispensible, both necessary, the conclusion is that there is a solidarity between transformations and comparisons, between operations and correspondences, and that even if their forms of equilibration are different, the forms are complementary forms that have nothing contrary or contradictory in relation to each other. We have, while working on this problem of correspondences and morphisms, glimpsed an aspect of cognitive development that for the most part had escaped us until now.

chapter 3

Children's Constructions of Correspondences in Double Seriation Tasks

Ioanna Berthoud-Papandropoulou*

This experimental study consisted in an investigation of the seriation of lengths, but this time from the specific point of view of looking at correspondences and their link with transformations. In order to carry out such an investigation, we developed a special technique and a specific research situation.

POPULATION

Thirty-four children aged 3 to 10 were interviewed; thirty of them were between the ages of 3 and 7, and four were between 7 and 10. They were students in the elementary grades of the local Genevan schools and were chosen only on the basis of their chronological age.

RESEARCH MATERIALS

In front of the experimenter were the following:

1. Eight sticks, each of a different color and seriatable according to their length. The smallest was 3 cm long, the longest 10 cm, with a regular difference of 1 cm of length between each successive stick and the next

---

* This piece of research was carried out in collaboration with D. Voelin-Liambey, Center for Genetic Epistemology, Geneva. Translated by Harold Chipman.

29

2. The bottom half of a box and a sheet of standard-sized paper to be used as a lid
3. Two wooden objects of different shapes: a block and a half-egg. They were used in the introductory part of the experiment
4. A pair of scissors
5. Pencils

GENERAL TASK

The child is asked to find a means of putting an object into the box without removing the sheet of paper, which acts as a lid, but rather by cutting a hole that enables the object to pass into the box. In order to achieve this, the child is asked to draw the outline for a hole of appropriate size on the sheet of paper. As an introduction to this type of task, the child is asked to draw on the sheet of paper a hole that "fits well" for passing the block and another for passing the half-egg while wasting as little of the paper as possible. The child is then asked to draw a hole that fits neither the block nor the half-egg. This is done in order to bring about in the child the idea that there is a correspondence between the shape and the size of the object and the hole required to pass these objects into the box. It must be noted that an actual cutting of the hole with the scissors was done only by our youngest subjects; the other subjects displayed sufficient awareness that they could imagine the hole once they had drawn it and could even imagine the disappearance of the object through the hole.

EXPERIMENTAL PHASE

The child was told the sticks must pass into the box in the horizontal position (i.e., lying down). Several different experimental situations were used, but the results of three of them that were particularly interesting are described here.

Situation I: Hole(s) For All the Sticks

The child was asked to find a way that "all the sticks may go into the box." The solution to this is obviously a hole corresponding to the size of the largest stick. (But, so the story goes, even Isaac Newton had a large hole drilled in his door to let his cat in and a smaller hole for her kitten.) In the event that the child solves this problem correctly, the next situation (Situation II) is immediately proposed. In the event that the child draws several holes for several sticks, he is asked to reduce the number of holes: "Can you draw fewer holes?"; "Can you draw the least number of holes possible for all the sticks?"

The following notation was used for the children's acting out behavior: the numbers 1 to 8 for the sticks (the smaller numbers corresponding to the smaller sticks) and the letters A to H for the holes (the smallest hole being A, which corresponds to stick 1). Hole H is therefore the correct solution to Situation I. This notation was of course not used in the instructions spoken to the child during the task.

Situation II: Hole For a Certain Number of Sticks Only

Item 1:   A Hole For Three Sticks Only   The child was asked to draw a hole that fits three sticks only, excluding the others. The exact formulation of the task is: "Make a hole that fits three sticks only and so that the other ones cannot pass through this hole." The sticks involved are numbers 1, 2, and 3, and the measuring stick is number 3, the longest of the three.

Item 2:   A Hole For Six Sticks Only   The task is the same as for Item 1, but this time the correct sticks are numbers 1 to 6, and the correct measuring stick is number 6.

Situation III

The child was first asked to seriate all the sticks: "Put them in order so that we can see all the sizes." Then the following question was asked: "How many sticks are bigger than the smallest (number 1)?" Then, without allowing the child to count: "How many sticks are smaller than the largest (number 8)?" Finally, the child was asked to explain his answer.

The order of the tasks was the same for all the subjects. The form of interrogation was clinical, and the child was constantly asked to justify his actions or anticipations.

PRELIMINARY CONSIDERATIONS

Before detailing the results of the experiment, it is important to briefly describe the results of work carried out on seriation prior to our experiment and to stress the importance of the seriation scheme from the point of view of Piaget. Research carried out by Piaget and Szeminska (1941) on the seriation of 10 sticks of different lengths (today called the "classical" seriation task) evidenced three developmental stages:

In the first stage (around age 4 to 5), the child groups two or three sticks, thus forming pairs and triads without coordinating them into a single series

During the second stage (around age 6 to 7) the child constitutes a single series through trial and error. However, he is unable to place in this series additional intercalary elements proposed by the experimenter, and he solves the task only through extensive trial and error procedures or starting the entire series again

In the third stage (around age 7 to 8) the child uses a systematic method that may be called operatory; this consists in finding the smallest element, then the smallest of those remaining, and so on, exhaustively. (He may also start with the largest element and proceed regressively.) This solution is termed operatory as it evidences reversibility: any one element of the series is both larger than the preceding and smaller than the following. The child of the third stage can insert without trial any supplementary element—a further sign of operatory reversibility

These stages were described later (Piaget and Inhelder, 1959) in more detail. In particular, intermediate forms of behavior were distinguished, such as the seriation of the tops of the sticks alone without consideration of the base line, or the construction of a roof shape (up and then down). Additional control tasks were introduced to verify the operatory nature of the children's reasoning. Another proof of the operatory nature of the seriation task is the phenomenon of transitivity. The children who build the series by trial and error do not exhibit transitivity behavior at all times. If the child is shown $a < b$ and then $b < c$, hiding a, the child does not necessarily discover the relationship between a and c when these are not directly compared.

Although experimental investigations of seriation have long been carried out, the present experiment concerns certain specific aspects involving correspondences. Involved is a spatial and physical experimental situation but one where the task proposed is logical. The spatial aspect is due to the length and seriation aspects of the sticks. The physical dimension is linked to the task material, to the concrete possibility or impossibility of having a stick pass through a given hole. The logical aspect governs the following fundamental principles necessary to the solution of the problem: the sticks must be at least partly mentally seriated in order to find the largest, and the child must understand that a hole of length l admits all sticks equal to or shorter than l and only these, excluding those longer than l. Thus are constituted equivalence classes of sticks having as common characteristics the possibility of passing through a hole large enough for the longest. In this type of seriation, it is to be emphasized that the concrete elements are given for only one of the two series, i.e., for the sticks. The aim is precisely to constitute the second series mentally and to design, depending on the task proposed, some of its elements (the holes). It is in the constitution of the second series that we have studied the problem of correspondences. The two terms, *correspondences* and *transformations* are defined at the Center for Genetic Epistemology in the following manner:

Correspondences are "comparisons that do not modify the content upon which they bear." In the present task, correspondences can be established between the sticks themselves, the holes themselves, and the sticks and the holes. These correspondences are used by the child to construct one or several holes for the sticks.
Transformations, on the other hand, are "activities that modify the content upon which they bear or that generate their own content."

In the present task there was no question of modifying any part of the concrete materials used, but there are transformations of the content, in the sense that this material has to be apprehended by the child in terms of certain principles or parameters:

First, the double relationship "bigger than" and "smaller than"
Second, the possibility of grouping elements into equivalence classes so that a specific relationship (such as "all the sticks equal to or smaller than l will pass through hole l") is requested
Third, the transitivity aspect of the relationships. These are thus not effective actions but regroupings and mental transformations on the given content

The interaction between correspondences and transformations will be outlined in the discussion that follows the presentation of the results. It is indeed very difficult and sometimes almost impossible to distinguish the two aspects at the level of the children's overt behavior. The analysis is carried out in terms of levels and not of stages because a child may evidence one, two, or several of these levels in the course of the interrogation, whereas this is not the case for the stages.

RESULTS

Situation I

Five levels of correspondences may be distinguished in the acquisition pattern.

Level 1—Global Correspondences (Ages 3 to 5)   The child draws a very large hole and proposes to put all the sticks in at the same time. He also admits that other objects may fit into the hole too. There is thus no particular relationship between this hole and any given stick, and no stick is used as a measure to make this hole.

> GUY, age 5;5,[1] when in front of the eight sticks, says "They can also go through the big hole" (previously made for a big object). After a series of trials and errors, he draws a hole bigger than stick 8 and says "Each at a time." In order to demonstrate that this hole fits all the sticks, he places stick 1 in the hole.

In a sublevel 1b, the sticks are divided into two or three small groups (small and large, or small, medium, and large) to which correspond holes with analogous properties (big hole for big sticks etc.). The evidence that this correspondence remains global is that the stick chosen as a measuring stick for the hole is not necessarily the largest stick of each group.

> ANA, age 3;6, chooses holes D and F (corresponding to sticks 4 and 6) for all the sticks. Then she places stick 8 on F ("Because it's big") and stick 5 on D ("Because it's small"). The child does not consider the *relative* size of the sticks, but rather the absolute size.

Level 2—Strict Correspondence (Ages 5 to 6)   The child draws one hole for each stick, each stick being considered different from the others; therefore, each stick must have its own hole. Certain amusing expressions of this one-to-one correspondence were noted.

> DAN, age 5;8, says "We must pass this stick (number 2) in the same hole, the same size of hole." For stick 7 he says "We draw its hole

---

[1] Names are code names. Age is given in years;months.

and we pass it through" (despite the fact that hole H is already drawn).

LEO, age 6;0, says "We have to make each same size."

Some children, upon suggestion that they should make fewer holes, say that it is not possible because you would need either fewer sticks or two sticks the same length.

Despite apparent differences, a common trait may be found between levels 1 and 2: there is no specific relating of the sticks among themselves. Either the child considers them as equivalent and having to be passed through a large hole, or he considers them different and that as many holes are needed as there are sticks. However, the existence of level 1b suggests progress between levels 1 and 2. The sticks first considered equivalent begin to undergo a process of differentiation in 1b. This process leads each stick to become different in the child's mind (the anticipation of one-hole-per-stick thinking in level 2).

Level 3—Early Correspondence (One-To-Several) The child understands that to one hole, drawn with the help of a measuring stick, correspond several sticks. But these sticks are not all contiguous, hence the child feels the necessity to make more than one hole for all the sticks. This type of behavior often follows effective drawing of at least two holes: the child notices that several sticks can pass through these holes. However, he has to try these out, and this one-to-several correspondence is not anticipated with any degree of certainty, as is the case later in development.

CED, age 6;6, anticipates a one-to-one correspondence and designs holes F, G, and H. Later, by trial and error, he notices that stick 5 fits hole F, stick 2 fits hole H, and stick 4 fits hole G.

FRAN, age 5;7, draws several holes (B, C, D, and H), then he places sticks 5, 6, and 7 in correspondence with hole H, stick 1 with hole B, and keeps stick 3 for hole C and stick 4 for hole D, in strict correspondence.

We can see that this idea of one hole corresponding to several sticks does not affect the entire series (otherwise one hole would have sufficed). The reasoning behind this is interesting: more than one hole is needed because "large sticks cannot go through small holes." The children thus do not reason inversely, that is, that small sticks fit both small and large holes. The two possible directions, ascending and descending, remain undifferentiated, betraying a misunderstanding of the fundamental asymmetry of the series.

However, the progress of this level is that the individualized and differentiated elements resulting from the one-to-several correspondence begin to be integrated and structured in classes of "elements passing through a same hole." But this integration is not as yet general, owing to the absence of transitivity and recurrential forms of reasoning.

Level 4—Structured Correspondence (One-To-Several) The children's responses all display the comprehension of the principle that "the hole must be drawn according to the largest element of a group." This principle is expressed and sometimes explained by the children and no longer discovered during or applied after any trials, as was the case previously. The children start by drawing several holes, as do the children of the preceding level, but this time they reach the concept of hole H being large enough for all the sticks by reuniting all the sticks, which are apprehended as linked together by a single size relationship.

> DID, age 7;0, first supposes a one-to-one correspondence, then reduces the number in his anticipatory behavior and announces the principle: "All those that are smaller than the others can go into the other holes." Then he further reduces the number of holes and retains only D and H, with the argument that sticks 8, 7, 6, and 5 are larger than sticks 4, 3, 2, and 1. Then he spontaneously seriates all the elements correctly, and ends up with hole H because "All these (sticks 1 to 7) are smaller than 8."

At this point we can infer from the children's behavior that both directions of the series are distinguished with final recognition of their reciprocity that respects the asymmetry.

Level 5—Immediate Structuring This level begins at age 6 but is true for the majority of 7- to 8-year-olds. Without drawing several holes and without trial and error the child immediately seeks out stick 8 as a measuring stick and spontaneously seriates the eight sticks.

> YVES, age 7;7, says: "I take the biggest, I make a hole, and all can go through."

Situation II

In this situation the problem is to make a hole for n sticks only, and this turns out to be more difficult for the children than Situation I. The reason for this could be the following: in Situation I, all the sticks are given and the task is to draw a hole by one-to-several correspondence as we have outlined. On the other hand, in Situation II, the task is to *choose* the sticks in terms of the number asked for; in other words, a subclass has to be formed by opposition to other subclasses, which is not the case in Situation I.

The earliest reactions (ages 4 to 5) consist in one-to-one correspondences. The child deforms the instruction "one hole for three sticks" and proposes three holes for three sticks. But it is interesting to note that these same young children spontaneously choose the three smallest sticks, which is correct in terms of the task. Furthermore, they sometimes reach the point where they admit to keeping only one hole, hole C, which is also perfectly correct. We are thus confronted with the following paradox: the young children find the correct solution in a "one hole for three sticks" situation without even seriating the sticks. The explanation that can be put forward runs as follows. The young children establish a relationship between "small number" and "small sticks." Thus "a hole for three sticks" evokes the idea of searching for the small elements. An indication in favor of this interpretation is that when a greater number of sticks is asked for by the experimenter, the children choose the large sticks.

> SAM, age 5;2, succeeds in finding hole C for three sticks. When the experimenter asks him to make a hole for five sticks only, he then chooses among the largest sticks (i.e., 4, 5, 6, 7, and 8).

This type of behavior presents two complementary characteristics:

First, it neglects the asymmetrical characteristic of the series: if the small holes only admit small sticks, the large holes admit both large and small sticks

Second, it consists in a structuring of the sticks in two disjoined classes (small/large) and not in a relationship of inclusion (small included in large)

Among the older subjects (ages 5 to 6), some of the subjects choose *n* sticks but not from among the smallest. Furthermore, these sticks are not contiguous and the hole does not correspond to any of them.

> DAN, age 5;8, when the task is a hole for three sticks, draws hole H for elements 1, 2, and 7.

These older children all notice post hoc that the instruction has not been fully executed. The children who evidence this type of behavior are in the process of building up the idea of "any element whatever" of the series. At the same time they develop the idea of "any content whatever" of the number three in its cardinal aspect—that is, that three objects may be either big objects or small objects. Later on, the ordinal aspect of the number three is respected and it fixes the extent of the subclass to be chosen: the child is thus successful in the different tasks and sometimes says "The three first" (sticks 1 through 3) for one hole for three sticks or "The six first" (sticks 1 through 6) for one hole for six sticks. We can see in these responses that the ascending direction is conserved, whatever the number of sticks to be chosen. There is thus inclusion of the three first sticks into the six first sticks. The child thus divides the series of eight sticks into two complementary classes (three vs. five, then six vs. two).

Before outlining the results of Situation III, a general remark concerning Situations I and II is called for. It is easier once the hole is drawn to make the appropriate sticks correspond to it one by one than to anticipate which hole is needed for all or for n sticks. This difference is due to the status of anticipations compared to the effective realization of a correspondence. This fact is apparent in a great number of pieces of research. In this experiment, this may be translated by the difference existing between the "all" or "n" on the one hand and the "each" on the other. The "all" or "n" is to be structured in anticipation, the "each" is to be carried out by single and successive actions.

Situation III

Only the following aspect of the task will be discussed: counting the number of sticks greater than 1 and inferring, without counting further, the number of sticks smaller than 8. The most elementary forms of behavior (which may appear as late as ages 6 to 7) evidence the need for further counting when the relationship is reversed. For these children, the fact of having to scan the series in the opposite direction, changing the referent for comparison, probably constitutes a new operation. There seems no necessity for there being, in a given series, as many "smaller" elements as there are "bigger" elements. The final success responses are those where the child anticipates without hesitation the same number in both directions and accompanies this statement by one of two possible arguments:

The number is the same because both times one element only
    has been removed
The number is the same by considering the reciprocal relation-
    ships (this may be considered more sophisticated at least in
    argument)

> vɪv, age 6;8, says "These seven are smaller than 8 because it's the
> contrary, the same as for the other but the other way round."

FINAL REMARKS

The results of the experimentation raise several questions. The
first question is: starting with the isolated relationships "3 larger
than 2" and "2 larger than 1," how does the child attain the
transitive inference that 3 is larger than 1? It seems that for the
young child, the relationship "bigger than" established by correspondence for the first pair (3 > 2) is not exactly identical to the
relationship "bigger than" established for the second pair
(2 > 1). Therefore, if the relationship "bigger than" is not
conserved for different comparisons by the child, then we have
here perhaps an explanation of why operatory structures appear
so late in the course of development: a composition of relationships that are heterogeneous for the child cannot possibly be
expected.

At the most elementary levels, after the global approach to
sticks, the correspondences between sticks lead to the conclusion that all the sticks are different (one-to-one correspondences). Later on, duads and triads begin to be structured
according to the relationship "greater than" or "less than": these
are localized correspondences owing to the contiguity of the
sticks and not transferred to the entire series. Furthermore, the
child very often has to verify them by effective trials. The need
to draw more than one hole for all the sticks (Situation I) can be a
sign of these nongeneralized local correspondences.

At a higher level, the relationship "larger than" becomes
homogeneous in the sense that it governs not only the close but
also the distant sticks in the series. Thus are constituted classes
of sticks having a common characteristic, and this step forward
from the "each" of the preceding level to the "all" of the present
level is accompanied by: (1) anticipations that replace effective
trials; and (2) a feeling that such relationships are *necessary*,
which also replaces the need for empirical verification.

We feel that this more or less sophisticated structuring of the sticks according to the developmental level is dependent upon the transformation aspect. Indeed, there is no simple possibility of reaching operatory necessity starting from simple juxtapositions of correspondences. These relationships and correspondences are important, however, in the sense that they lead to adequate knowledge of states. It is necessary to compare terms in order to determine their linkages in terms of the task proposed, but the criterion for a comparison and the choice of terms used in the comparison (parameters that change with age) depend on the dynamics of the transformation aspect. This idea appears even more clearly when the development of the reciprocity concept and of the inverse operation in general is examined. A correspondence cannot of course be negative, as there would be an absence of correspondence in that case. By contrast, inverse operations do exist, which does not exclude, at a certain level, correspondences between direct and inverse operations, but these correspondences are also positive in nature.

Such considerations should not lead the reader to believe that at lower levels only correspondences exist and at higher levels only transformations. These are complementary aspects—both are present at each level and each is necessary to the other. It may be said that correspondences prepare transformations and these in turn lead to new correspondences. The study of these correspondences has enabled a better understanding of the process of operatory development itself and to detailing the levels of the latter. This is within the focus of the recent investigations of the Center for Genetic Epistemology, where the object of study is not the different areas of knowledge themselves nor the different notions themselves, but the *mechanisms* that engender the creation of novel notions.

REFERENCES

Piaget, J., and Szeminska, A. 1941. La Genèse du Nombre Chez l'Enfant. Neuchatel et Paris: Delachaux et Niestlé. Translation published 1952: The Child's Conception of Number. London: Routledge and Kegan Paul.

Piaget, J., and Inhelder, B. 1959. La Genèse des Structures Logiques Élémentaires. Neuchatel: Delachaux et Niestlé. Translation published 1964: The Early Growth of Logic in the Child. London: Routledge and Kegan Paul.

chapter 4
Experimental Incursion into Correspondence Systems

Sheldon H. Wagner

After having studied the formation of the more important cognitive domains (space, number, causality, etc.), attention in Geneva has recently been directed to what was often called "le fonctionnement"—that is to say, the more dynamic processes involved in intelligence, such as "functions," "reflective abstraction," "contradiction," "generalization," and "realization."[1] But there remained the problem of how these dynamic processes were coordinated and in what way they were implicated in the preparation of the englobing cognitive structures. A new research series (which is still continuing) took up this problem of coordination at a more primitive level. The research on correspondences is one aspect of this analysis. The behavioral items that are presented should provide some concrete feeling for this new language of correspondences and morphisms and how it can be applied to intellectual development.

THE EXPERIMENTS[2]

Imagine that you are a child. A strange man walks in and shows you five boxes that go from small to large in size. The boxes are all different colors and are labeled weights A, B, C, D, and E, with A being the smallest. In addition, it is obvious that A is the lightest, B is a little bit heavier, and C is heavier than B but lighter than D, which in turn is lighter than E.

---

[1] Cf. the recent volumes of the Etudes d'Epistémologie Génétique, Paris: P.U.F.

[2] The two experiments that follow were conducted in Geneva with the collaboration of Eduardo Marti and Jean Piaget. Their insights and analyses are gratefully acknowledged.

Also on the table are five piles of chains. Each chain is made out of six metal rings with one colored paper ring in the middle. The five piles of chains have colored rings corresponding to the five different colors of the boxes. The chains from the first pile have the same color middle ring as weight A and you are shown that all these chains (hereafter called 1, 1', etc.) are *just able* to hold up A.[3] It is the same with chains 2 and weight B (notation: 2-B), and so forth up to 5-E.

Now we play a game in which you are the operator of a large crane. The weights are houses. The chains can hang from the crane.

Problem 1: You have just lifted up C with 3. The man replaces C with B. What will happen? How about 2-C? Now watch 1-C; 1 breaks. How about 1-D? Try a bunch more.

Problem 2: Take any two chains and hook them together so that the two small chains make up a long chain. Say you picked 2 and 3 (notation: (2-3)). Which houses could you lift up? What other long chains would be the same as (2-3)?

This is the essence of the experimental design. There are two parts. First, we search out the child's correspondences between the two series by asking him what will happen with most of the 25 possible ones. We refresh his memory if need be as to the initial pairings (1-A, 2-B, 3-C, etc.). Sometimes he is shown whether he is right in his predictions, and other times he is not. We then pass on to the composition of the chains (two or more chains hooked lengthwise), asking for predictions of different combinations (e.g., (2-3)-C?). Subproblems of this section include asking for all chains equal to, say, chain (4-2), or for a hierarchical ordering of several different chains. Finally the weights are combined (e.g., (A + B)) and the child is asked which chains can hold up the different combinations of weights.

In general we followed a clinical interview format, switching from weight-to-chain predictions to chain-to-weight predictions. Because of the exploratory nature of the experiment, we were not very interested in systematizing the positive and negative feedbacks to the child's judgments.[4]

---

[3] The weights of the houses were 200, 400, 600, 800, and 1,000 g respectively. The resistance of chain 1 was a little over 200 g and so on for the others.

[4] Experimental sessions sometimes lasted over an hour and on rare occasions were spread over two days. Fifty-five children ranging in age from 2 to 16 were interviewed. They were spread fairly evenly over the different age groups. The

There are, of course, two fundamental problems here. The first has to do with the understanding of certain necessary transitive relations between the two series. The second has to do with the construction of a function: will the resistance of a composed chain be a function of only one of the chains (the stronger or the weaker) or of the total length of the chain or even of the relative positions of the composing chains? It should be clear that when we speak of a function $y = f(x)$, there is both a correspondence aspect (the bijection between the values of y and those of x) and a transformational aspect (variations of x engendering the variations of y). One of the most intriguing problems in the development of intelligence is to understand how these two aspects are related to each other. And in fact, a large part of current Piagetian theory addresses itself to precisely this problem ("morphisms of state," "morphisms of transformations," "categories," etc.). In this particular experiment, the understanding of the initial correspondences between the two series should show in what way they are united with these two aspects of function.

It should be noted that this experiment differs in one important respect from the traditional battery of tests. Here we will be concerned with a dynamic progression of understanding on the part of the child. Depending on what his lifting experiments tell him, he will react in different ways. What this means is that within any test setting there will be a "micro-development" that will perhaps be interesting relative to the macrodevelopmental stages. Professor Inhelder, in her recent work on strategies in problem-solving situations, talks about "micro-formations" that occur within any one task. The point is that we can analyze the data here in two fundamental ways. This chapter will treat only the global developmental question because we are concerned with the pattern of correspondences that children make across time. Correspondence-type tasks are, however, rich in the second, more local, question as well.

THE CONSTRUCTION OF SIMPLE CORRESPONDENCES

This is the first general problem space in which the child operates. We attempt to seek out the criteria upon which the children

---

interviews were more detailed and structured than the account in the text suggests—but not so much as to justify a full exposition.

base their different predictions. The material is fully explained and the children are shown several chains holding or breaking when lifting the different houses (weights). One should remember that our overall research goal is exploratory rather than strictly experimental. Such a research outlook is necessary whenever one starts looking into a new domain.

Before beginning the stage-style analysis that is common to Genevan research, it should be noted that the youngest children interviewed (age 3 and under) showed no coherence whatsoever in their responses. During the short periods of time that they were tuned in to the task, they did not understand what we were interested in finding out—and, for that matter, we could not understand what they were interested in. This is mentioned only because it serves to distinguish quite precisely the difference between these Stage 0 children and the Stage I children. First of all, think for a moment about all the implicits involved in the most elementary correspondence (chain-weight) possible. Take as an example the case of chain 3 holding weight C. What happens if we put the weight down and then try to lift it up again? Will it lift? Most of us would say "of course" (ignoring metal fatigue, which children do) but what does this imply? It seems that it implies a certain vision of the physical world: namely, that events are repeatable given replication of circumstances. But certainly not all events are repeatable. If you play darts and aim for the bullseye and then hit it, you do not immediately assume that your next throw will also be a bullseye. The reason is obvious. Most of what we do (and what the child does) in the world does not give the same results upon repetition.[5] Indeed, schools and mothers are constantly repeating this to children. They usually don't tell a child who has failed: "Try it again but *do something differently.*" We generally (perhaps wrongly) leave it up to the child to manipulate experimentally the particular variables involved. For the Stage 0 child the physical event of the chain holding or breaking must be seen as not *independent* of the child's act of lifting. An adult immediately sees the event

---

[5] Perhaps a concrete example will help. There have certainly been many times you were frustrated by a recalcitrant lock that just didn't want to open. Sometimes you will try and try for several minutes until finally it opens. The curious thing is that you usually feel sure that you have done nothing different in the last few seconds than in the first few. Most people's conceptions of locks are not such that they think that they can do anything else but repeat over and over again what they did in the first few seconds. It is as if we wait for the universe to stop being capricious.

of breaking or holding as a function of the chains themselves and in such cases the decision of equality of circumstances (necessary for a repeatability judgment) is quite direct. The Stage 0 child, however, believes that none of the physical events he is shown are in any *necessary* way repeatable. If he is shown that 2 breaks with D (notation: "2 br. D"), and is then asked whether 2′ will lift D (notation: "2′-D?"), he will respond either "yes" or "I don't know" or "we have to try harder" or "I don't think so."

We are not dealing here with a problem of memory. These children have no trouble telling us what happened in the first instance. The judgments and predictions all take place within a few seconds of each other. Memory does play a role when the time frame extends over several minutes, but in these cases we always refresh the child's memory by showing him the pertinent correspondences for the particular inferences we are interested in. Nonrepeatability refers to a very "local time" sense. With this in mind, the case of Stage I responses can be considered.

Stage I (Age 3 to 4)[6]

In Stage I, the children have understood that some of the results they observe are independent of them. When presented cases where the holding relation is involved, they see a repeat of the event as necessarily giving the same result. (If 2-B in time 1, then 2-B in time 2.) They will even give arguments like "it held before." What is fascinating, however, is that the breaking relation is much less "repeatable." Children who think it obvious that if a certain chain holds a certain weight the first time, it does so if you try again, do not think it is at all obvious if it is a question of the chain breaking. PAM (3;5)[7] for example, sees that 2 br. D and we then ask what will happen if we try 2′-D? He responds, "Maybe it won't break." This is just after he has responded on the obviousness of 4-D because "it held before."

One could argue that what the child is really saying is that chain 2 does not equal chain 2′. We made sure, however, that these children accepted easily the fact that if chain 3 *held* weight C, then chain 3′ also held C. Therefore it is not the equality of like-colored chains that is being questioned by the children.

---

[6] The ages that characterize these stages are meant to be approximate, because their value as a delimiting device is questionable.

[7] Names are code names. Age is given in years;months.

The general finding then, is that there is a slight but clear advantage of holding repeatability over breaking repeatability for these younger children. Even in cases where the breaking of a chain is predicted correctly (in the context of repeatability) many of the predictions are "hedged" with qualifications like "probably" or "I think so." Such incertitude is in itself significant, but when compared to the certainty expressed about holding, it is arresting. Other research in Geneva has shown that many relations are seemingly well understood by children at one time but their corresponding negations are not (e.g. "full-empty"; "pass through-not pass through," etc.). We shall return to this point during the discussion of transitive inferences.

So far only isolated instances of correspondences (i.e., the ones dealing with repeatability) have been presented. One might think that the children show no conceptualization whatsoever of the two seriations taken as a whole (weights and chains). This is generally true of Stage 1 except for the extreme elements of the two series, which seem to have a privileged status. Chain 5 is often seen as being able to hold up anything and chain 1 as breaking in all uses. Another characteristic response pattern of these children is to fixate on the initial color coding (weight-chain) and insist that a given chain (say, 4) can only hold up the weight (house) of its same color (in this case D).

In Stage 1, then, we are witness to the first attempts at putting into correspondence ("mises en correspondance"); however, there is an absence of any serial transitivity.

Stage II (Age 3 to 4)

So far the pattern of correspondences across children for one or two predictions has been discussed. If we extend the time frame somewhat (memory will thus start to play a role) we can see a more global pattern to the predictions for several chain-weight correspondences. Two characteristic schemes seem to be operating. The first, which one might call the "friendly neighbor scheme," consists in extending the hold (H) or break (B) relation to adjacent members of a series. For example, one sees several predictions of the following type:

Experimenter	Child
2-A?	"It will lift"
2-B?	"Lifts"
2-C?	"Lifts"
2-D?	"Lifts"
2-E?	"Breaks"

The pattern is thus H-H-H-H-B. Correspondingly we might find B-B-H-H-H where the direction is from heavier to lighter weight. The general scheme seems to be that "an effect observed for one chain on one house (weight) will repeat itself on the next house that is slightly different." The strategy is in a sense a good one. Often in problem-solving situations a good heuristic is to try out an already known rule on situations not very different from the initial one. Because of the nature of the physical system these children are presented with, this neighborhood rule leads to apparently correct seriation of the weights ($E > D > C > B > A$). However, things are not that straightforward. Seriation, according to Piaget, can not occur without transitivity, and transitivity, because it reflects an underlying structure, should give 100% correct results within a given task. The second characteristic scheme of Stage II shows quite clearly how partial the orderings of these children are. Consider the following typical case of EVA (3;6). She is shown that 2-B and decides that 2-C and 2-D also. But she says that 2 br. E. This seems to suggest the correct partial seriation: E is heavier than D and C. Soon after, she is shown 2-A and concludes that 2-B and 2-C but 2 br. D—again, an apparent seriation (although 2 br. D had been rejected earlier). But then she surprisingly predicts that 2-E. Perhaps a clearer example of this second scheme is given by another 3-year-old (PIE) who is shown that 5-E. He then predicts that 5-D, 5-C, 5-B but that 5 br. A (which is obviously wrong).

One reaction to such strange behavior is to say that the children are simply randomly predicting "hold" or "break" because they don't understand anything about the task. This is not the case for several reasons. One, that is sufficient, is that the respective children are internally consistent in their judgments. For example, in the case cited above PIE gave the same answers on three consecutive passes. This inversion of the direction of the relation (H-H-H-B) is quite interesting and is very common. One is tempted to see it as a sort of "distance anxiety scheme"—the further one goes up (or down) the series, the more one is tempted to go back to the initial prediction.

The neighborhood and distance schemes, however, do not give the full picture of Stage II. The deductive apparatus of these children is very active and two very interesting examples of rule transferences, which are so important in the understanding of correspondences, will be given. The first is implicit in the neighborhood scheme and consists in a kind of over-generalization of a perceived effect. When shown, for instance, that 4-C and 4-D, children will often spontaneously say "4 will lift up all the houses." Conversely (and this is slightly more common) after seeing, for instance, 3 br. D, they will say "3 will break everywhere."

What is even more interesting about this stage are the false symmetries that the children construct to account for what they see. For example, they will make conclusions to the effect that "if a weak chain doesn't hold a heavy weight, then a strong chain won't hold a light weight!" NIC (4;5) is a good illustration of this. He sees that 5-C and predicts (by symmetry) that 3-E. He is then shown that 3 br. E and he concludes that 5 br. C!

One should not fail to see the significance of these incorrect symmetries and the general response pattern of Stage II. These children show signs of an active participation in trying to set up a stable system of correspondences. Often this results in an "over-extension" of the rules they are constructing in an effort to *preserve* relations. The notion of "preservation" is the essence of morphisms and correspondences systems.

Stage III (Age 4 to 5)

Stage III heralds one vital event that is of considerable interest. Here the serial correspondences of the hold relation are acquired by trial and error, even to the point of justification. But curiously, this is not the case with the breaking relation. CLA (4;4) sees that 4-D and concludes that 4 will hold C, B, and A "because they are lighter." But right after seeing that 2 br. C she predicts that 2 br. D (correct) but that it will hold with E! This seems reminiscent of the distance anxiety scheme behavior of the previous stage. Another illustration is given by SAM (5;6). She sees that 4-D and predicts 4-C and 4-B "because they're light." We ask her "What about A?" She responds "Even more so" ("Encore plus"). Such language is hardly different from that of an adult in the same situation. But when we show her 2 br. C, she says that 2 br. D but that it will hold with E!

We are forced to conclude that the fact that if a chain holds a certain weight it also holds lighter weights (Holding Necessity Axiom) does not imply the consequence that if a weight breaks a certain chain, all heavier weights have to break chains of the same resistance (Breaking Necessity Axiom.) Now we should be prudent and realize that the Breaking Necessity Axiom requires an assumption not present in the Holding Necessity Axiom—the one of equality of chains (we must replace the broken one). This alone could account for the startling *décalage* (shift) between the understanding of the two axioms. However, the proper controls that allow us to reject this hypothesis were done. We periodically replaced chains that were holding a given house with chains of the same color, and even Stage I children accept the identity of like-colored chains. This suggests that there is a deeper reason for the asymmetry between the holding and breaking transitivity axioms. It seems that the children of this stage do not conceptualize the act of breaking as being the exact negation of "lifting" or "holding." Maybe this is because breaking is such a "unary" phenomenon: when a chain breaks, it breaks completely. There is no middle ground between breaking and not breaking. On the other hand something can hold weakly or hold very strongly. We have seen that chain 5 is often thought by children to be quasi-indestructible. This of course is still not an explanation but it does redirect our attention from the specific correspondences (which cannot explain the asymmetry, since they justify both transitivities) to questions of force, direction, etc., that is, to the physics of the affair. Indeed, the arguments of the children become more and more weight oriented. Instead of saying "The chain is strong (or weak)," they speak more frequently now in terms of "heavy weight" and "light weight" and explicitly make the correspondence heavy weight-strong chain.

One cannot help but think, in this light, of the previously mentioned *décalage* between holding repeatability and breaking repeatability. It seems that here in Stage III, the asymmetry between the holding and breaking relations has been rekindled.

Stage IV (Age 5 to 6)

Stage IV is the end of simple correspondence development. Responses of this stage cannot be distinguished from adult ones, which is moderately surprising since both the transitivities (Holding *and* Breaking Necessity Axioms) pose no problem for these children. POS (5;4), for instance, is shown that 5-E and says "If it (5) goes with that house (E) then it can go with all of them." He then sees that 2 breaks with C and says that it can't go with D "because D is heavier and it'll break there, too." We ask him then if 2-E? He responds that "It'll break even more." The use of the comparative "heavier" as opposed to "heavy" is common in this stage.

The real novelty relative to Stage III is thus the acquisition of the breaking transitivity, which is the result of the child's understanding that breaking is the exact negation of holding. On what is this new understanding based? Research in Geneva on the notion of weight during the causality research series (late 1960s) suggests that the problem of weight is one of direction. Once the weight of an object is represented as all tending downwards, it becomes the exact opposite of lifting. (Preoperational children, for example, believe that depending on where you place a single ball of clay on a scale, the weight of the ball will be different.) This representation can only depend on internal transformations that the child makes and not on the observed surjections (weights to one chain) that are its necessary precursors.

It is precisely this point of transformations that are reconstructed on the basis of observed correspondences (in this case the surjections between weights and individual chains) that is developed in a crisper way in the next section on the composition of correspondences.

THE COMPOSITION OF CORRESPONDENCES

After interviewing the children about the correspondences that can be made between different *single* chains and single weights, we move on to a different problem entirely, which is that of the correspondences between composed chains and one or more combined weights.

There are two fundamentally different ways of combining chains. One can put them on the crane parallel—in which case their resistances are added together to form a stronger chain—or one can attach one to the other lengthwise to form a longer chain—in which case the absorption law of the weakest link will determine the total resistance of the longer chain (which we can make arbitrarily long). Only results obtained using the second paradigm are presented because of the limitations of space. There are, however, interesting effects when the problem is one of additivity of forces.

The combining of the chains introduces a whole plethora of issues and is much richer in possibilities than the simple correspondence case. If we assume that each chain has its own unique correspondence pattern (with the houses) for the child, what will happen when two of these patterns are vying with each other?

This discussion will proceed more easily if we establish some abbreviational notation. Instead of writing: does the long chain made up of chain 2 and chain 3 lift up house C?", I will simply write (2-3)-C? The order in which the chains are written indicates which chain is nearest the house. In the above case chain 3 is linked *above* chain 2. This will prove to be important later. It is also possible to combine the houses. The houses are five-sided and hollow, and because the heaviest is the largest it is possible to combine their weights by slipping a smaller house inside a larger one. In this case the notation will be, for example (B+C).

Stage I (Age 4 to 5)

With two important exceptions, the general pattern of responses for this first stage is one in which there is a centration on one or the other of the chains. There seems to be no firm rule as to which chain is centered upon. In some cases it is the weaker and in others the stronger chain (even for one child) that determines the predictions.

The first exception to the above centration rule can be anticipated from what we know about Stage I of the simple correspondences. Here, too, the extreme elements of both the chain and weight series seem to be privileged. For example, (2-5) is supposed to lift up E "because the 5 is strong" or "house A can't break anything." In these cases length does not play a role; for example, (5-1) is thought to be equal to 5 (in a sense a resorption law).

Interestingly, the two rules (centration and extremes) are both commutative. Once the child has centered upon one chain, it does not change his predictions if we turn the chain upside down ((n-m) into (m-n)). Commutativity is an essential part of the weakest-link law (absorption law).

The second exception to the arbitrary centration rule is much more interesting and consists in the children's assigning special power to two chains of equal resistance. They will say, for instance, that (2-2) is a lot stronger than 2 alone or even than (5-2)! In Stage II we will see a version of this rule that achieves comic proportions.

If we now consider the extension of correspondences, it is important to note that the composition of chains in no way disrupts the holding and breaking transitivities. The Stage I child (in the composition case) is entirely self-consistent. If he says that (2-4) can lift up D, then *a fortiori* it can lift up A, B, and C. Now this is really quite interesting because the composition of weights disrupts almost the entire world-view of older children.

One may wonder how the youngest children (age 2 to 4) behaved in the composition part of the experiment. In general, we could not make sense out of what they said. There is a suggestion, however, of one potentially interesting finding: some of the children who "had" breaking repeatability in the simple correspondence case "lost" it in the composition case. Unfortunately the finding is not a firm one and merits further study. However if this turns out to be true, the "non-disruptability" of the holding and breaking transitivities mentioned earlier becomes all the more significant.

Stage II (Age 5 to 7)

The Stage II responses are some of the more difficult to fashion into a coherent whole. This is due in large part to the dynamic nature of the task we presented to the children. We clearly want to get at least some feel for how their structurings change within the experimental session. The children of this particular cognitive level seem to feel heavily the demands of the real world feedback they receive. Consequently there is strong response variability for each individual child.

Because the essence of Stage I is one of centration (except for the special length rule), many of the children's responses are correct (physically speaking)—if they happen to center on the weaker chain. In some sense Stage II might be viewed as a regression relative to Stage I, because here the children try to take into account the other chains involved and in doing so they are led into rather strange mistakes. We found four response schemes—each peculiar in a different way.

The first scheme might be characterized as "extreme bijectivity." Take two different chains and compare them (e.g., (3-5)). The houses that can be lifted by the resultant long chain are two in number and consist of the houses of the same color as the individual chains (in the above example, C and E) and no others (i.e., *not* A, B or D)! This is extremely odd because the children who explicitly state this rule "believe in" and use transitivity to predict simple correspondences. FAB (5;6), for example, is asked what houses he can lift with (2-4). He responds "D and B." We ask him if (2-4) will also lift up C, since it can lift D. He hesitates and then says no. We then ask if (2-5) will lift up E and he says it will. We show him that it breaks, and then ask him what (3-4) will lift up. He responds "D and C." We ask him again about (2-5) and he says that (2-5) won't break with E and B! Not all children want to preserve their rules so badly. Some will start out using the extreme bijectivity rule and, seeing that it doesn't work, will move on to one of the other schemes characterizing this stage.

From the above bijections the child may start to differentiate his predictions as a function of the relative positions of the chains. In this case he bases his predictions on the lower chain. This creates situations in which, say, (4-5) is thought to break with E and (1-5) is thought to be able to lift up houses A through E. This lower-chain rule is extremely common and many children apply it consistently even when it requires them to say that one composed chain changes its resistance depending on which way it hangs from the crane (i.e. (2-3) is weaker than (3-2)).[8] The noncommutativity of chains is thus in contrast to Stage I. But whereas the reasonings behind the Stage I responses were all "correspondence-type" (e.g. "the 3 goes with C"), the Stage II child is obviously worried about issues of a different ilk. Indeed, in some children the lower chain rule can be so powerful as to induce the child into a rejection of the basic correspondences that he knows so well. This is one of the most fascinating findings of this study. A paradigmatic sequence (this particular one from a 7-year-old) is as follows:

Experimenter	(Result)	Child
"Which is stronger, (4-2) or (2-4)?"		(4-2)
(4-2)-?		D, C, B and A
(2-4)-?		B and A
Watch this: (4-2)-C	(breaks)	
(2-4)-?		Just A

---

[8] In actual fact, (3-2) is less resistant that (2-3) because of the weight of the chains themselves. In pretests almost all adults ignored this. Even if this factor is admitted, it applies only to the relative orderings of composed chains and not to the correspondences with the weights.

This is a simply beautiful example of how much this child is rule bound. He believes that (4-2) is stronger than (2-4), because the 4 is there—right at the bottom—to "absorb" the downward pull of the weight. But look how he assimilates the experiential feedback (and he definitely does assimilate it) that disconfirms his prediction; rather than change his rule (which he sees doesn't work) he changes the correspondence pattern of one of the chains (in this case (2-4)). What is incredible is that he "knows" that by all accounts (i.e., his own), the chain (2-4) should at *least* be strong enough to hold up B, but to admit that would necessitate a rejection of the fundamental rule.[9] It seems—and here is the point—that it "costs less" to change the basic correspondence pattern (i.e. make a new mapping) than to change the function (transformation) that generated the "second-level" mapping (the one that hierarchically orders the composed chains).

The impression should not be given that the Stage II child is completely blind to all feedback when he is in the throes of applying his rules. Stage II is very chaotic precisely because the child is becoming aware of other factors besides the initial simple correspondences. For instance, we found numerous examples of a concern for the length of the chains involved— which in turn engenders an assumption of interaction between the elements of a composed chain. Children will say for instance that (5-4) is stronger than 5 alone "because it is long . . . the 5 helps the 4," or even that (1-1-1) is stronger than 4 alone. In addition, the privileged status of two equal chains that are linked (that was present in Stage I) can come back to haunt even more ferociously. Not only is, say, (3-3) stronger than 3 but it is also stronger than a single chain made up of just steel rings! (You will remember that the center links of chains 1 through 5 are made out of paper.) This rule is tenacious and we will see it again in slightly different circumstances.

There is one more correspondence rule common to this stage that one sees glimpses of throughout the protocols. It consists in centering on the strongest chain of a composed one and establishing the correspondences on the basis of its known

---

[9] This example, incidentally, is what we call in Geneva a "morphism." The relationship between psychological morphisms and the purely algebraic notion is too involved an issue to delineate here.

strength. This is interesting because it is in contradiction with the length rule and it is commutative.

So, in sum, Stage II is a collection of strange and uncertain attempts on the part of the children to try to reconcile what the real world is telling them with what they are telling themselves. At times the rules they evolve are correspondence-based (e.g., extreme bijectivity scheme) and at other times more dynamically based on properties of the objects themselves (e.g., lower chain scheme). Clearly, nothing we have seen so far qualifies as a causal argument. In Piaget's terminology the arguments are still "legalities" consisting simply in supposing certain regularities in the observed variation.

Stage III (Age 7 to 9)

This is a very curious stage because it is characterized by a seemingly complete understanding of the weakest-link law (usually after a few incorrect predictions). One would not expect, after the confusion of Stage II to see the game over so soon. Here is an extract of a protocol from a 6½-year-old:

Experimenter	Child
"(1-2)-?"	—"A. Because 1 is weak"
"(1-2)-B?"	—"No, 1 will break"
"Which is the strongest chain of all of these: (2-4); (5-1); (4-2); (3-3); (1-5)?"	—"(3-3)"
"Which is stronger, (4-2) or (5-1)?"	—"(4-2) because the 2 is stronger than the 1"
(2-2) = 2?	—"Yes"
(4-4) = 4?	—"Yes"

The responses are all correct. Yet it can be shown that these arguments are simply a generalization of a correspondence rule that says that if the weaker of the two chains cannot go "beyond" a certain weight, then the union of that chain with another does not keep it from breaking. Now this rule is true (it gives correct answers) but it is not a rule of physics, i.e. it is not based on any projection of directional forces equally distributed along the chain so that every single point of it is experiencing the same amount of "pull."

The way we can tell that Stage III answers do not reflect true understanding of the different mechanisms involved is by changing the situation slightly. When the weights are combined (e.g. (B+C)) and we ask for the relevant correspondences, we are witness to spectacular regressions on the part of the children who had ostensibly "caught on." The regressions are truly amazing! This is one example:

Experimenter	Child
"(2-3)-C?"	—"No. The 2 will break."
"Is (B+C) heavier than C?"	—"Yes"
"(2-3)-(B+C)?"	—"Yes"
"Why?"	—"Because the 2 can hold B and 3 can hold C."

When these children are shown that (2-3) breaks with (B+C), they will all exclaim "Oh, yes, the 2 breaks with C." We then ask, "What about (3-3)? Will that lift (B+C)?" There are those that will say "yes"! Of course when they see that (3-3) breaks with (B+C) they all see why—at least they say they do. But some we can take even farther along by asking if (3-4) will work ("yes, because the 3 can lift C and the 4 helps it lift B"). One child went all the way to (3-5)-(B+C) after seeing (2-3), (3-3), and (3-4) all break! Each time she verbally expressed understanding that the 3 was too weak for any weight heavier than C, and yet when presented with each succeeding case, the temptation to split the weights into two separate entities was too strong.

What is so fascinating about these regressions is that they seem to reproduce the old rules of the previous stages—at the expense of well-established (i.e., well-understood) transitive laws. If we think back over the results presented so far, the glimmer of a pattern emerges. When the composition part of this task was presented to the younger subjects (age 4 to 5), some of them who had used breaking repeatability arguments in the simple correspondence part of the task "lost" that capacity in the composition part. In addition we have seen children use transitivity arguments in the simple correspondence part and fail to use them in the composition part. Indeed, some explicitly deny them. In a partially similar vein, we have seen quite clearly that the understanding of holding repeatability does not necessarily imply the understanding of breaking repeatability; nor does the understanding of the holding transitivity law imply the understanding of the breaking transitivity law. Why are these children's rules so fickle? To an adult the particular change in the situation (for example the addition of the weights) does not alter in any way the kind of rule he will apply. More significantly the rules we do apply are the *same ones* the child has. If we look at the formalization of our transitivity law and compare it to the child's, the incredible fact is that ours is no better—the same quantifiers are there, the same number of variables are bound, the same sets (or classes) are being called upon. And yet, there is, of course, a difference. It seems that when we introduce a variant in the task it is like asking a child who has laboriously designed a monkey wrench to design a left-handed one. He starts again from scratch, whereas we rotate it. The problem of the left-handed monkey wrench is merely a convoluted way of posing the general, very grave problem in Piagetian theory of content bias—which is the real problem behind *décalage*. Unfortunately, the scope of this chapter merely permits the evocation and not really the exploration of such considerations.

Stage IV (Age 9 to 10)

If we exclude the composition of weights case, Stage III is characterized by essentially correct responses. Stage IV is then, relatively speaking, a regression. This is, however, the general finding of research on physical concepts and is certainly due to the posing of *new* questions generated by the increased activity of the internal operations. The new questions have to do with dynamic processes and the directionality of forces. In our task we hear arguments reminiscent of Stage II with the crucial addition of a type of additivity law that makes linearly explicit the supposed interaction of the chains. For example, (2-3), (1-4), and (2-2-1) are all seen as equal to chain 5. Interestingly, children of this age group who are presented with the task of inducing the law of the parallelogram of forces believe that the value of the two component vectors are added together to form the resultant vector.

These children are also still seduced by the length rule as it applies to the doubling or tripling of the same chain. Just as in Stage I, 4 alone is weaker than (4-4), which is weaker than (4-4-4), etc. The important development of this stage is not, however, in the wrong answers, but in the clearly physical arguments that are used. Significantly, the transitivity laws are applied consistently, even though the specific predictions might be wrong. If, for instance, (2-2) is thought to lift up D, then it necessarily lifts up A, B, and C as well. As a result, the composition-of-weights questions, which had such catastrophic effects in Stage III, are here handled easily.

Stage V (Age 10 to 12)

Stage V marks the end of the developmental sequence. The children of this stage are not discernably different from college students given the same task. One excerpt from a protocol suffices:

Experimenter	Child
"How can you tell when a chain will break?"	—"It suffices that the weaker one breaks and it's kaput!"
"(4-2) = (5-1)?"	—"No, (4-2) is stronger. All you have to do is compare 2 to 1. 4 and 5 can be ignored. You'd have to put them parallel to make them equal."

This stage marks the first reference to putting the chains in parallel. Almost every child mentioned it spontaneously.

The image these children have of what a chain is is very different from anything we have seen so far. It is above all a whole acted upon by two directionally opposite actions that are felt equally at every point along the entire length of the chain.

This does not mean, however, that any Stage V child understands all there is to understand about the resistance of chains. If you will think back to the perhaps frivolous metaphor of the left-handed monkey wrench, we might find another one here. Imagine a hypothetically perfect wire. By perfect is meant a wire that has no part weaker than any other part (the parts can be arbitrarily small). Every part of the wire is thus the strongest *and* weakest link in the whole. Assume also that the wire breaks at *exactly* 100 lbs of force. Now imagine two robots facing each other and holding on to the two ends of the wire. They have perfectly calibrated arms and they each pull slowly (at the same time) with exactly 50 lbs of force. Does the wire break?

Next consider a very, very long chain made up of links that are exactly equal in resistance. There is no single weakest link. The chain will break at exactly 1000 lbs of force. We attach one end of the chain to the moon and we stretch it all the way to the earth (ignore gravity). A robot with an unbreakable arm is on earth and he pulls the chain with exactly 1000 lbs of force. Where does the chain break first?

There is a touch of vengeance in these thought problems (which, by the way, are not trivial). They give an idea of how the Stage III child might feel when he is thrust into the composition task. If you are asking yourself similar questions, perhaps you are trying to design a left-handed monkey wrench.

Overview (Age 5 to 12)

It might be useful here to take up the problem of transformations mentioned at the beginning. Piaget believes that physical phenomena always suppose two types of transformations. There are first those that have as their origin and home base the object itself (these the child discovers or merely observes) and second, those that are the result of an operatory reconstruction of the objective transformations that experience has shown him. Without this reconstruction, the objective transformations remain simply observable variations and covariations, for it is the reconstruction process, Piaget believes, that allows the child to extract meaning from the observed covariations. Of course, the objective transformations must be linked up to the correspondences on the basis of what the child is shown.

This dichotomy is quite clear if we remember the types of hypotheses that are verbalized by the children. Piaget has tried to demonstrate in the research series on causality that "causal explanations" by children are often no more than "legalities." That is to say, the explanations consist simply in supposing certain "regularities" in the observed variations and correspondences. Causal explanations, on the other hand, tend to be "explicative" in that they try to reconstruct the transformations of which the correspondences are the necessary consequences.

Legal hypotheses abound in Stages I through III. For example, when the children say that (4-2) will lift up D and B "because 4 goes with D and 2 goes with B," Piaget would say that they are in effect merely anticipating "legal regularities" without any causal explanation of the mechanisms that play a role in the breaking. These legal arguments are based on the preliminary correspondences (bijections). A major advance is apparent in Stage IV when the children say, for example, that putting two chains together "redoubles the solidity" or that "the stronger chain 'helps' the weaker one." These explanations, although false, are qualitatively different from those of the earlier stages because they are not based on initial postulated correspondences. The correspondences have become *deduced* results. This is a "temporal jump" that has vast consequences, for it changes the nature of what an explanation is for the child. These causal hypotheses that appear on the scene in Stage IV try in a rather ambitious way to trap deducible transformations that engender the correspondences as necessary consequences.

It should be said that we are still not at the level of "true causal explanations." The first level of causal hypotheses are "incorrect" because they are "locally bound." They try to come to grips with each successive case (often *ex post facto*). The novelty of the children in the final stage is that they construct a system of transformations that attempt to englobe all the observed correspondences. This can only be done if the old explanations are modified. But this modification occurs on a plane in which the correspondences are considered as final states and not initial premises.

To sum up this analysis, it is Piaget's view that any function that is verified by experience *prepares* the effective transformations that inhere within it. If $y = f(x)$, the observed bijective correspondences between the values of y and x suggest a dependence (in our particular case, that the breakage of the chain depends solely upon the weakest link) and, sooner or later, the child must seek the reason for this observed dependence. It is at this point that he must construct simultaneously a system of operating transformations and morphisms conceived as necessary consequences. As that one child put it so well, "It is sufficient that the little link breaks and the whole thing goes kaput!"

ST. PETER AND ST. PAUL

There remains a need to discuss a bit more discursively some issues that spin off from the preceding, forcibly sketchy, experimental presentation.

The first thing to ask ourselves after all this talk of correspondence systems is whether in some sense we have merely "clothed St. Paul at the expense of unclothing St. Peter." Is this new language merely dress or do we come to a cleaner, crisper understanding of some of the salient processes involved in the development of the concepts we are studying? Clearly, the behavioral analysis so far traced does not allow a definitive

answer. There do exist formal mathematical (specifically, algebraic) arguments that demonstrate that coexistence between
St. Peter and St. Paul is not only possible but fruitful. There
are as well psychological ones that speak for some potential
promise in further developmental studies.

The immediate concern is whether or not the nascent
conceptual spectacle that we have witnessed so far is relevant
only to processes that have a substantial infralogical "load," that
is, processes linked to empirical abstraction (as opposed to
reflective abstraction). The problem that we investigated was a
trivial one of physics and bound to a somewhat artificial and
highly structured problem space.[10] The essence of the problem
was, however, somewhat special in that it obeyed what can be
called an absorption law (some would say a minimum law).
Absorption obtains whenever one has an element (from a
defined set or class) such that when it is put in binary relation
with another element (also from a defined class) the result gives
the first or absorbing element. (In our case the binary operator
is composition of chains.) The most obvious example is zero in
the real number system under multiplication.

One of the truly great powers of human intelligence is its
ability to recognize absorption-type situations. Consider the case
of proof by induction. Seymour Papert did a clever little experiment years ago in Geneva. On a table there was a cardboard
representation of a lake with a road going around the perimeter
and a model car with two dolls in the front seat. The problem
posed to the children was to see if there was a way to move
the car so that the person who did not have the lake directly
alongside him would after the movement. Of course, lifting the
car up was not allowed. The younger children all believed that if
you drove around the lake enough times, then sooner or later the
switch would be made. The older children, who saw through the
ruse, reasoned to the effect that "if a little movement won't do it,
then a large one won't either." The quintessence of this subtle
argument is really that none of the movements beyond the first

---

[10] I hope it is clear that the weakest link phenomenon could have been
attacked on any number of fronts, many not even paying token attention to the
explicit kind of correspondences we used. This of course in no way detracts from
the research validity of correspondence systems and their role in the development of intelligence.

matter. In other words, whatever effect one sees in the first instance, one can apply to the whole. The analogy with the chain experiment is quite direct.

The general issue of recursive processes (upon which induction in large part depends) is also representable within the absorption framework. Piaget is fond of quoting a 5-year-old who, after being pushed by him to consider more and more variants of a particular task, exclaimed exasperatedly, "If you know it once, then you know it for everytime."

Consider now the cloudier case of class inclusion. If we are trying to determine whether or not some element is a member of a certain class, and we come across a property that is a negation of one of the defining properties of the class in question (e.g. the absence of a backbone when looking for a vertebrate), then no addition of properties congruent with the defining ones can change the decision of "non-membership."

The thrust of the argument is as follows: if a plausible case can be made for the substantially infralogical situation of the chain and weight experiment, then we might also be able to make the same or better case in the above-mentioned domains, which are essentially logico-mathematical in nature.

There is also a second, perhaps better argument for the importance of the correspondence-style analysis that consists in suggesting a compelling new avenue of research. Consider again the monkey wrench metaphor. The general point is that often a new task does not demand new operations to solve it. Intelligence is an opportunist and to function efficiently must possess redundant rules. As we saw throughout the stage analyses, one of the fundamental impediments to confronting experimental variations successfully was the childrens' inability to "retranscribe" the new situations *in terms of* the old. Often we saw that, had this transcription process been effectuated, the children would have had the operational weaponry to solve the problem successfully.

Developmental psychologists should explore the research possibilities in structuring experiments where *situations* are the independent variables. It would be extremely useful to know what specific correspondence patterns are constructed by the child when he compares situations among themselves and also what the minimal conditions are for proper transcription of one situation into another (i.e., what proper transcription is). The thought problems with the hypothetical super chains is one incomplete example of what could be done.

chapter 5

The Possible, the Impossible, and the Necessary

Jean Piaget and Gilbert Voyat[*]

THE POSSIBLE

The central problem of constructivist epistemology is the problem of the construction or creation of something that did not exist before. Immediately, however, there are encountered two incompatible ways of understanding "the possible." The first interpretation is the common sense view; it is also, in some disciplines (for example, biology), the "preformist" view. In this view all possibilities are predetermined by the initial conditions, so that in principle a sufficiently sophisticated computer, by working out all feasible combinations, could generate a complete list in advance. In biology, for instance, primary DNA (deoxyribonucleic acid), the source of inherited characteristics, is made up of components that can be combined in an unlimited number of ways. Thus the evolution of living beings might be conceived of as the simple outcome of different combinations of possibilities; this entails that the creative aspect of evolution be discarded as illusory. According to a frequently drawn analogy, components of DNA are comparable to the letters of the alphabet, which may be used to spell any word or sentence. From this point of view even a great literary work, a Shakespearean tragedy, for instance, is simply one possible combination of letters, words, and sentences among millions that it is possible to produce (though naturally with varying degrees of probability). But, as Cellérier has said in this connection, the tragedy still had

---

[*] Translated from the French by Donald Nicholson Smith.

to be written: good combinations have somehow to be chosen
and organized.

The other way of understanding "the possible," and the one
that we hope to justify by appealing to the facts, even though fact
and interpretation are especially difficult to separate in this area,
is that possibilities are constantly coming into being and that
they have no static characteristics. A possibility "becomes possible" inasmuch as it enters the sphere of the realizable, inasmuch
as it is perceived as having entered this sphere by a subject, and
also inasmuch as it is not just so perceived by him but also "comprehended" with respect to the preconditions of its actualization.
Each possibility is thus the outcome of an event that has produced an "opening" onto it as a "new possibility;" and its actualization will in turn give rise to other "openings" onto other
possibilities, and so on. From this perspective the combinatorial
computation of a set of possibilities itself constitutes an incipient
actualization on the part of the subject who is making the calculation, albeit a limited attempt in that it remains on the level of
mere "conception" and lacks any comprehension of the preconditions of actualization. These preconditions can be fairly complex: the subject knows all the combinations of letters of the
alphabet but he "still has to write the book."

In this chapter we shall opt for the second way of understanding "the possible," basing this choice not just on deduction
but also on facts. Thus the subject of study here is the invention
or comprehension of the possible by the subject, and the assumption is made that the idea of the possible *per se*, conceived of
apart from such activity, is a meaningless notion.

This formulation of the problem is not espoused without
good reason. That fact is that, aside from instances where one
may speak of a "deducible possibility," as determined by an
already formed structure (e.g., seriation), "the set of all possibilities" is usually chimerical because it cannot be circumscribed, since every possibility tends to give rise to others.
More specifically, the notion of a "set of all possibilities" is an
antinomy because the "all" in question is itself no more than a
possibility, and an aggregate that, because it is forever expanding, can never be defined.

Let us turn our attention now to the facts. First of all it
should be noted that the experiments consisted in getting children between 4 or 5 and 11 or 12 to discover the maximum

possible number of variants of an action. Questions such as, "Can this be done some other way?", "Is there still another way?", and so on were asked. Five kinds of situations were set up. The first was a situation in which free combinations were permitted in the context of an activity presenting no difficulties for the subject. The child might be asked, for example, to cut up squares in as many different ways as he can think of, to arrange trees and houses however he sees fit, to place three small cubes on a piece of cardboard in various ways, to show all the possible ways between two points, or to make an unlimited number of shapes from jointed sticks. The second involved solving easy practical problems in all possible ways. Here the child might be called upon to place various objects at an equal distance from fixed points, to build the "largest possible" construction out of differently shaped building blocks, to fix "legs" on to balls of dough so that they stand off the floor, to make the water in a receptacle reach various levels by placing light and heavy objects in it, or to place cubes so as to give specific aspects of them maximum exposure. The third situation consisted of drawing variants of one kind of figure, for example, a triangle. In the fourth, the child, starting with a partial depiction of some object, completed the picture in different ways. In the fifth situation the child was asked to find all the possible uses of a single object, for example, a compass.

The major general conclusion produced by all these experiments is based upon the clear difference between the youngest and the oldest children in the number of possible variations they devised. Thus the younger children only think of a very small number and develop disconcertingly monotonous attachments to the same procedures, but the quantity and variety of alternatives increases in quasi-exponential fashion with increasing age, so that 11- to 12-year-old children even speak spontaneously of infinite possibilities where this is indeed warranted. When the children were asked to decide what possible routes might be taken by a toy car within the confines of the room in which the experiment was being carried out, the smallest children restricted themselves to straight lines except for going around obstacles, and did not vary these unless these obstacles or landmark objects were moved. Those between 6 and 7 invented curving and zigzag routes, through these were limited in number. Children who had attained the level of formal operations, however, made such statements as "You can go further, or not so far, and make as many turns as you want. There's no limit." In another experiment, in which the children were asked to arrange three dice on a piece of cardboard, the youngest would produce a very few regular arrangements, and if asked whether there were ten, a hundred, a thousand, or a million possible solutions they would say "ten." By contrast an 11-year-old girl answered without prompting "If you keep changing the positions, or if you throw the dice, there is any number of ways." When it came to cutting up a paper square in different ways, one 9-year-old had already realized, after producing five variations and using only straight lines and one circle, that he would be able to think of "thousands" of new ideas. A 5-year-old, on the other hand, who also set out by cutting in straight lines, could only conceive of "big," "small," and "middle-sized" shapes as possible alternatives; he then proceeded to cut out meaningful shapes such as houses. The other children in this age range for the most part started off by cutting our representational forms like apples or keys, and they did not consider the discarded pieces of paper as alternative shapes themselves. Even in an experiment where objects were half-concealed by wadding and where the children were asked to imagine the possible forms of the invisible portion (the visible part being rounded, pointed, etc.), the 11- to 12-year-olds replied that "it can be any shape," whereas the younger children could only think of two or three possibilities.

In sum, in situations where the possible solutions are in fact infinite a spectacular progress was found to occur between the lower and upper age limits of our subjects. This consisted not merely in the increased capacity to produce various solutions in the form of different material realizations, but more importantly in the acquisition of the capacity to infer more or less immediately that the possibilities are unlimited. This period of development also sees great progress with regard to problems where there are finite numbers of possible solutions, or where only limited means are available for attaining goals set, as has been shown by Bärbel Inhelder's research on strategies (Inhelder, Sinclair, and Bovet, 1974). In one of the present experiments, in which the subjects were supposed to make triangles with sticks, it was notable that the younger children produced only equilateral or isosceles figures while the older ones all shapes and proportions had become possible (see "The Impossible and the Necessary," below).

Thus the basic problem is to attempt to explain this tendency for possibilities to multiply and the concomitant opening up of new possibilities that the younger child could neither actualize nor even conceive. There are two factors that immediately come to mind in approaching this problem—the development of operational structures, and, more particularly, the specific character of the hypothetico-deductive structures that arise during the 11- to 12-year-old stage. Both turn out, despite their undoubtedly contributory role, to be quite inadequate as explanations of this development.

With regard to operational (logico-arithmetical or spatial) structures in general, these are very few in number in the preadolescent, and, although they certainly suffice to endow the child's thinking with a certain degree of coherence in the shape of an intrinsic demand for compositions, they can scarcely be said to account for the inventiveness betokened by the growing openness of the mind to the sphere of possibilities. It is true that the very construction of these structures attests to a self-organization whose regulations apply to an actualization of possibilities. For instance, when a subject generalizes possible vicarious relationships as a category, the operations involved open up a new possibility in the form of that superior and essential structure, the "integrated whole." It is true, however, that a process of this kind may remain largely unconscious. What are involved here are deductive or structural possibilities. These play an incontestable role in the development of possibilities but they explain neither the multiplicity of the combinations that emerge from the subject's groping progress nor that mystery that Claparède said subsisted, his fine analysis notwithstanding, with respect to the "genesis of the hypothesis."

On the other hand, when we consider not just the general increase in the number of possibilities envisaged by our subjects, but also the quantum leap that, as every single experiment showed, occurs at 11 or 12 (that is, concurrently with the stage of formal operations), it seems obvious that there has to be a link between this ultimate explosion of possibilities and the constitution of the particular operational structure characteristic of this age range. There are, in fact, three arguments in favor of such a connection. The first is that formal operations are hypothetico-deductive, that is, they can be applied to simple hypotheses from which they draw the logical consequences irrespective of the truth or falsity of these initial propositions. Hypotheses of this type belong entirely to the realm of possibilities, and the task of formal thinking here is to construct internally necessary connections between these possibilities as possibilities. The second argument is that formal operations lead to the construction of new structures, such as integrated wholes, including the combinatorial structure, which quite clearly plays a part in the proliferation of possibilities. In the third place, as has been shown elsewhere by Bärbel Inhelder (Inhelder and Piaget, 1958), subjects at this formal level start out, when confronted by a new problem, by drawing up a mental list of possible hypotheses, and only when this is done do they proceed to verification (for example, by separating factors) in order to select and retain the right solution. The conclusion to be derived is that at the formal level the subject proceeds from the outset by plunging reality into a world of possibilities rather than by simply inferring possibilities from reality. Clearly this is another reason for the increase in possibilities during this stage.

Although it is well to recall and bear in mind all these factors, they come nowhere near solving the problem of the proliferation of possibilities—first and foremost because this increase in possibilities begins well before the child's arrival at the level of formal operations. From the age of 4 or 5 onwards our subjects begin to find new possibilities, and these continue to increase in number until the children reach 11 or 12, so that the final leap that occurs at this stage is the outcome and conclusion of what has gone before, and not, of course, its cause. Secondly, although the starting point of formal operations consists in the attainment of deductive reasoning (that is, reasoning involving necessity) on the basis of hypotheses conceived of as mere possibilities, and the child no longer needs (as he has needed since the age of 7) to base his thought on concrete facts and material objects, the fact remains that such hypothetical possibilities are not themselves the product of this new inferential mode of thought. Formal operations merely make use of these hypotheses in a new way, and then enlarge their number: they do not create the category of the possible. From the sensorimotor stages, in fact, the distinction between possible and impossible is implicit in the child's actions themselves and requires no further conceptualization: for example, he grasps a nearby object (possible) but makes no attempt to grasp one that is out of his reach (impossible).

Thus there is the specific problem—the increasing opening up of possibilities for the subject, starting from the sensorimotor stages and continuing up to and including the stage of formal operations. The fact that this account of the progressive elaboration of operational structures cannot solve the problem does not mean, fortunately, that we must go back on earlier theoretical formulations. As a matter of fact, operational structures will play a necessary, although partial, role in the solution about to be offered. It will be necessary to eke out that account by giving consideration to new dimensions and complementary forms of organization.

First of all, three types of schemata must be distinguished. The first type shall be called *presentative schemata*. These derive from the permanent and simultaneous characteristics of comparable objects. Representational schemata or concepts (e.g., "squares," "cats," etc.) are the chief members of this category, but it is called "presentative" because it also contains a large number of sensorimotor schemata. For instance, a baby recognizes that an object is held up by a string even if he does not start swinging it, or an object is recognized as being far away even though the child is making no attempt to take hold of it. A second property of presentative schemata is that they are readily generalized and abstracted from their context. A third property is that they retain their individuality even when they are brought under a broader category, for instance, when the concept "cat" is placed in the rubric "animal."

The second type of schemata is called *procedural schemata*. These consist of sequences of actions that serve as a means for attaining a goal. They are characterized by "precursivity," that is, the determination of initial actions by the tendency towards an ulterior state of affairs. These schemata are difficult to isolate from their contexts because they are defined in every detail by specific and heterogeneous situations. In addition, their lifespan is limited, because, where an end presupposes the means $(1, 2, 3 \ldots\ldots n)$, the first elements of this set lose their raison d'être by the time the later ones come into play. It is true that the *evocation* of these schemata tends to preserve them, but only in terms of presentative reconstruction.

The third type is *operational schemata*. These are procedural in one sense, but they are distinct from procedural schemata in that they depend on the use of regulated and general means (or operations). Furthermore, they combine into structures (classifications, seriations, etc.) that are presentative in character (including the group of sensorimotor displacements). Thus operational schemata reinforce the synthesis of presentative and procedural schemata. (N.B.: It is important not to confuse this synthesis with the relative lack of differentiation between these two kinds of schemata in subjects at the sensorimotor levels).

Now that these distinctions have been drawn, one is in a position to discern two great systems lying within the realm of the cognitive mechanisms. These two systems are complementary but they have different functions: the first (System I) aims at the *understanding* of all physical and logico-mathematical realities, while the second (System II) is geared to bringing about *successes* in every area, from the simplest actions to the solution of the most abstract problems. System I is thus made up of presentative schemata and operational schemata as structured entities. Presentative schemata do not remain isolated but combine into classifications (in the case of concepts), seriations (in the case of asymmetrical transitive relations), and so on. In other words, they are integrated into operational groupings of every sort, including infralogical or spatial ones.

By contrast, System II (successes) brings together all procedural schemata and integrates them with operational schemata as goal-directed transformational operations (problem solving). In the context of the problem concerning the opening up of possibilities, it is vital to understand that the procedural schemata are also coordinated among themselves and that they constitute a system of their own, although by different means from those employed in System I and in a different form. It is often even more difficult for this development to take place, because the procedural schemata have to be partially detached from their contexts. The means involved consist essentially in correspondence and in transfers of methods, which eventually encourage the formation of new procedures by allowing comparisons with those that have worked effectively in other situations. As was found previously, such procedural transferences may be effected well before the subject is aware of it, thus contributing to the formation of System II, although only in a hesitant and laborious way and without any of the self-organization that presides over the establishment of System I, especially in the case of operational structures. Here one begins to see the causes of the early sluggishness of the process of the opening up of possibilities.

The connection between these considerations and the problem of possibilities should indeed be clear to the reader. Unlike "the real," which is constituted by the entirety of presentative schemata and of operational schemata in their structural aspects (by System I), the formation of new "possibilities" is dependent on two preconditions. The first is the establishment of free combinations between the givens or the context of an unsolved problem and the procedures employed or tested out in attempting to solve it. Such combinations may be systematic or haphazard to any degree and do not exclude groping or trial-and-error tactics. There is no relationship here with the combinatorial formal structure, which remains a specific instance of higher level operations. The second precondition is that a selection be made from these combinations in order to correct errors. Such a selection is governed by two considerations: (1) that it take into account the results obtained from the procedures already tried out (exogenous selection), and (2) that it take into account those presentative and operational schemata that have already been organized (System I) and those already tested procedural schemata that are susceptible to transfer (System II as the source of endogenous selection).

In short, the process of opening up of new possibilities falls essentially under the aegis of the procedural system, System II. This is natural enough, because any procedure must be based on a belief in the possibility of a successful outcome, while the regulatory principles used to correct or refine such a procedure are designed to improve the action itself, which thus consists in one actualization among many other possible ones. It may be useful at this point to look at the question of the possibility of error. Among the five kinds of experiments described at the beginning of this chapter there are several where any combination supplies an acceptable solution to the problem set (11- to 12-year-olds, as noted, can recognize this infinite number of possibilities); in others, however, error is possible. The status of error, therefore, must be clarified, for although in System I it may justifiably be dismissed as a mere "accident," in System II it has an important part to play in that it constitutes one "possibility" among others. Clarification is even more essential because this system is very specifically characterized by generalized vicarious relationships (*vacariance*) and by *equilibration in action* (as opposed to equilibrium). These traits have to be emphasized because they typify the general role of possibility within the realm of cognitive functioning.

It would seem clear that System II, and procedures in general, must of necessity be distinguished by their transitional nature, for any procedure is directed towards a goal that, once achieved, deprives that procedure of its utility and hence of its existence as a procedure. What happens is that the result, that is, the thing hitherto aimed at as a goal, now becomes a presentative schema, while the procedure, in those cases where it later gives rise to a mental reconstruction (memory, understanding of the reasons for a successful outcome, etc.), acquires a fresh presentative character as a conceptualized object of thought. In fact it even acquires a *representative* aspect, with sensorimotor reconstruction merely a repetition or an incipient generalization, and not yet a representation. The progress made in the coordination of procedures (by means of transfers, simple regulations, regulations of regulations, etc.) leads in the direction of the formation of operational procedures. Two aspects of the matter have to be considered. On the one hand we have the operation considered as a temporal act (e.g., the union of two classes as a global class), and this, once performed, ceases to exist as such. On the other hand we have the operation considered as a concept (U or +, etc.), and in this sense it acquires a "presentative" character (System I) and is thus an integral part of a structure. In short, System II is never in equilibrium, and this is its benchmark. This is indeed a very fruitful feature as currently viewed, because this aspect of perpetual renewal is precisely what qualifies it for its role as a tool of reequilibration. Any attempt to reach a goal, to solve a problem, etc., is an attempt to remedy a lack in order to eliminate an inconsistency and thus to institute that new equilibrium that is arrived at as soon as the goal is attained or the problem solved. Generally speaking, then, the opening up of new possibilities amounts to the transcendence of a given state of affairs in the direction of a new reality, rich in possible actualizations and thus that much better equilibrated conceptually. A typical aspect of this opening-up process is, therefore, that it accompanies the phases of cognitive reequilibration.

To get back to the question of error, it is obvious that this plays quite a different part in a system like System II, one of whose functions is heuristic, than the one it plays in System I, which is an organizing and structuring agency. So far as inventiveness is concerned, an error set right may be more productive than immediate success, because the comparison of the false premise with its consequences produces new knowledge while comparison between errors fosters ideas. To take an example from the realm of higher mathematics, Poincaré (1905) set out originally to establish the impossibility of a thesis the truth of which later turned out to be one of his great discoveries. Generally, if the proposition p is erroneous, the proposition $not\text{-}p$ is true; and where p turns out to be nonsensical, this discovery itself gives access to truthful metastatements.

The whole group of connected and successive procedures that makes up System II leads to possible errors as well as valid ideas, because hit-or-miss tactics and mistaken transfers are intrinsic to its modus operandi. From the perspective of pure theory, where one must choose between an epistemology of overall preformation and a constructivist epistemology that treats the opening on to new possibilities as the creative activity of new beings or events in the process of "becoming," this logically necessary insertion of errors under the heading of possibilities is highly instructive. It shows in fact that the problem of new possibilities cannot supply the basis for a mathematical combinatory system, for such systems can only deal with schemata having a stable and hence presentative character, while errors are both unpredictable and unquantifiable. Possibilities cannot therefore be said to be either preformed or predetermined; they are merely "pre-oriented" by an exploratory activity that tends in greater or lesser degree to bring about improvement. One of the few logically consistent exponents of the preformationist thesis was Bertrand Russell during his early Platonic period. Russell saw the problem clearly and did not shrink from the assertion that if "ideas" are eternal, then the role must hold for false ideas as well as true ones (in the same sense as that in which white roses exist just as red ones do). He later decided that this position was an absurdity. We concur, although drawing the conclusion for our own purposes, that a constructivist epistemology founded on the notion of self-regulation is the correct view. In this context, the possibility of error may be treated as *one instance* of the difficulty of regulating negations and affirmations.

The placing of errors under the heading of "possibilities" has another theoretical advantage. It points up the fact that while System II ultimately results in an enrichment of System I, and especially of the group of logico-mathematical structures, the origins of this system, the working out of new procedures, and the opening up of new possibilities, are comparable to phenomena observed in biology. Thus the combinations between problems and procedures that engender possibilities are analogous to genetic "recombinations;" the selections that follow are analogous to selections both exogenous (operating from the outside world) and endogenous (operating from the internal and epigenetic spheres); and errors are analogous in form to lethal or merely harmful mutations or variations.

One may now conclude this portion of the discussion by distinguishing four kinds of possibilities. The primary kind of possibilities are *hypothetical* possibilities. This comprises a mixture of productive errors and ideas that may be expected to give rise to successful results. The second kind, or those possibilities that after selection permit effective realizations, or at any rate a correct vision of the extent of such realizations (even where this is deemed "infinite"), are *actualizable* possibilities. Next are *deducible* possibilities, where intrinsic variations may be inferred from an operational structure. Lastly we propose to speak of *available* possibilities (possibilities exigibles) for situations where the subject thinks that he can and should generalize a structure without as yet knowing what procedures to adopt.

THE IMPOSSIBLE AND THE NECESSARY

This section focuses on our ongoing research on the impossible and the necessary. These two ideas are closely akin: a necessary proposition *p* is identically equivalent to the impossibility of its negation *not-p*. From the practical point of view, however, it is easier to question children about impossibilities than about necessities, because the notion of necessity tends to be grasped on a purely verbal level.

Current research on the "possible" has already generated some ideas about "impossibility" that by extension allow us to distinguish different kinds of necessity. In thinking about impossibility a number of useful types may be discerned. The first is subjective impossibility or "pseudo-impossibility," where the subject deems something impossible but he is mistaken. The second is logical impossibility, or the negation of a necessity. The third is lawful physical impossibility, which is arrived at by deductive means. The last is empirical physical impossibility, which is always determined by a situation that may be transcended, so it is not really useful for our purposes.

Subjective impossibility, which in its positive form corresponds to what might be called "pseudo-necessity," is important for two reasons. In the first place it teaches us much about the sources of necessity. Secondly, it is relevant to our theory of possibilities itself, in that it imposes arbitrary limits upon possibilities that are all the more constraining precisely because of their arbitrariness. Two examples from a host of possible ones may be cited. It is necessary in the mind of a young subject that a triangle be equilateral and that its base be parallel with the edge of the table. When these conditions are not met he perceives an impossibility: any other figure cannot be a triangle. Similarly, a square has to have two sides horizontal before it is deemed a square: when it stands on one of its corners it "cannot be a square," and the subject at this stage describes it as "two triangles." So strong, in fact, is the idea that a square so placed is merely a diamond that the four sides cannot be perceived as equal—only pairs of opposite sides are so perceived.

Within such "pseudo-impossibilities" or "pseudo-necessities" it is possible to distinguish two reactions, although these are actually indivisible and in a sense logically interdependent. The first reaction conflates the habitual and the necessary: the fact that a triangle or a square is usually shown with its base horizontal induces the idea that this is a necessary feature and that its negation or neglect is an impossibility. The second reaction fails to differentiate between factual and normative; because something is "this way" the subject concludes that it "has to be this way," proceeding according to a sort of obligation that is at once logical and value laden. In such instances the reaction of "subjective impossibility" seems to occur whenever something that is being dealt with or questioned is "not what you do" or "not done by the rules." In the ordinary way, however, such "impossibilities" are simply eliminated without reflection by the child, or to be more precise, they are stripped of the right of entry to the sphere of the possible.

Such exclusions are very illuminating with regard to the difficulty observed when the earliest openings on to new possibilities are occurring for the child. By virtue of their very newness, these openings violate the prohibitions imposed by pseudo-impossibility or (and this is really the same thing) they abolish the limits set by pseudo-necessities. In other words, the difficulty encountered by new openings on to possibilities at this point does not stem entirely from the fact that new things are difficult to imagine, but also from the resistance put up by the child's stabilized reality to new possibilities in motion. In this light the increase in possibilities may also be seen to entail a triumphant but laborious struggle with previously established limitations.

To illustrate this gradual conquest of possibilities through the progressive removal of barriers, one case among many in our experiments shall be considered—the situation where subjects are asked to cut a square of paper into pieces and then place these on another square. Subjects in the earliest stages cut out significant shapes (apple, house, etc.) and neglect to treat the part of the paper they cut off as a "piece" in its own right. This pseudo-impossibility is related, of course, to the absence of any regular form in the discarded piece. At a second stage, realizing that the point is to reduce the square to smaller pieces, subjects start by cutting it exactly in half, then cut the halves also into two symmetrical pieces each and add one or two diagonal cuts, but always symmetrically. Eventually, however, the children override the limitation of symmetry, beginning to cut randomly but still confining themselves to straight lines. In time this restriction also goes by the board, as the subjects start using slight curves, then random variations, zigzags, and so on. A clear progression is thus visible. Initially, when the subjects refuse to treat discarded portions from graphic shapes as "pieces," we are seeing the effects of an explicit pseudo-impossibility. Later the increase in possibilities consists of an elimination of restrictions one by one, which gives the impression that subjective impossibilities are simply evaporating. In fact, though, such impossibilities remain implicit, and instead of manifesting themselves in the form of refusals, such as the early refusal to consider the discarded pieces of paper, their effects may be seen in the child's lack of imagination with regard to new shapes.

In short, subjective impossibility or pseudo-impossibility is a reaction important to our understanding of the global process that eventually leads to the proliferation of possibilities and to authentic "necessities." This reaction may be described simply as an overestimation of current reality, or of given factual states of affairs, either in the sense that the particular, and hence limited, characteristics of this reality can only be perceived as general and necessary (whence "pseudo-necessity") or else in the more simple sense that current reality is treated as the only possible one, thus inhibiting any opening up of new possibilities. It is worth noting, too, that, under the general heading of pseudo-impossibilities, one may include as specific cases those "pseudo-contradictions" that have been studied elsewhere (Piaget, 1974). For example, "If B is smaller than C, it cannot be bigger than A because it is small"—hence the uncoordinated pairs that precede empirical seriations. It is especially important to remember that the negation of pseudo-impossibilities and pseudo-contradictions does not give rise to necessities but simply to new possibilities.

Turning our attention now to logical impossibilities, which are the negation of necessities, one finds a very different situation. Here are three examples. In the paper-cutting experiment already referred to, a child at the first level believes that by making n cuts he will get n pieces; and when making a single cut, as has been noted, he only pays attention to one piece and ignores the other. If he is asked to make three pieces he makes three cuts and does not understand why he ends up with four pieces. Subjects discover sooner or later, however, that it is impossible to obtain n pieces by making n cuts, and this leads them to the discovery that n cuts $\rightarrow (n + 1)$ pieces. In the triangle experiment, the subject will eventually discover that with three sticks where $A > (B + C)$ he cannot make a triangle because the figure cannot be closed. He thus infers the necessity $A < (B + C)$ or $B < (A + C)$. In the experiment involving the possible routes of a toy car where the experimenter rules out reverse movements, the child concludes that a backward trajectory is an impossibility. In such true impossibilities, therefore, there is a factor that facilitates the discovery of possibilities, or at any rate of circumscribed possibilities.

There are two kinds of physical impossibilities. The first kind is deduced from simple observation, as, for instance, when a child understands that a pile of objects cannot retain its equilibrium if the highest objects are not properly balanced, even though he cannot explain the principle of equilibrium in detail. The second type may be illustrated as follows: the subject fairly soon realizes that a ruler poised on a table's edge will not retain a stable position once it overshoots by more than half its length, and he explains this fact in terms of relative weights, thus attributing to physical objects relationships conceived on the analogy of direct and inverse operations. Here the physical impossibility, derived lawfully now, not just empirically, depends on an "insertion of reality" into the framework of operational, and hence logico-mathematical, impossibilities and necessities.

NECESSITY

The third section of this chapter deals with the problems surrounding necessity. It may be useful to outline the context of these problems, inasmuch as they are bound up with the question of possibility and impossibility. Our initial hypothesis is that the necessary and the unnecessary do not stand in relation to each other in a simple dichotomous way, but that necessities vary in degree as a function of weaker or stronger forms of equilibrium, or, as present day mathematicians might put it, according to the relative "power" of structures.

When we consider that these two poles, necessity and non-necessity, are constituted on the one hand by the pseudo-necessities just described and on the other by formal hypothetico-deductive thinking, which from the age of 11 or 12 allows the subject to link pure possibilities (including hypotheses deemed false) in necessary relationships, one sees immediately that it must be possible to find any intermediate forms.

It should be noted that pseudo-necessity is not the only form taken by necessary relationships at the beginning of their development. In the early phases of childhood certain relations are perceived that are rightly judged necessary by the subject but that are nevertheless in some ways akin to pseudo-necessities. Among relations of this type are topological inclusions in cases of direct observation: if A is enclosed in B, and B in C, then A must also be enclosed in C. Just as in a pseudo-necessity, the factual state of affairs is seemingly indistinguishable from an "it must be this way" derived through a sort of obligatory connection analogous to implication by attribution of meaning (where connections are made between predicative attributions and not between propositions), so here it seems probable that the composition of these spatial inclusions—A in B and (A + B) in C—is arrived at by direct "perception" of a state of affairs and depends very little on inference. One is thus led to look upon the initial state of affairs as a mixture in which facts, necessities, and impossibilities (in the simplest sense: those things that are to be expected) are barely distinguishable, with the connections varying according to the circumstances, whether these are static or transformational in character.

It is only when the subject reaches the stage of transformations that these three modalities are clearly differentiated. A *state* can only be factual: the establishment of correspondences between such states calls, of course, for activity on the part of the subject, but this activity does not modify the states themselves. By contrast, transformations may be: (1) simply noted (described, etc.), like facts; (2) engendered (anticipated, etc.) as new developments; or (3) composed (or explained—but here explanation in any case presumes composition). If the production of transformations is a function of one or the other of the four kinds of possibilities distinguished at the end of "The Possible," above, the composition of transformations is the origin of necessity. A fact *per se* can never be necessary, and the relation of necessity as between possibilities can only arise as a result of composition. Therefore, because transformations are in a sense the common multiple of possibilities, which are their source, and necessities, of which they are composed, there should be nothing surprising about the fact that the development of necessities proceeds hand in hand with that of possibilities. This evolution is manifested in weak and localized fashion at first; then systems are instituted, though of limited scope; and finally one witnesses an explosive general expansion associated with the attainment of the level of hypothetico-deductive structures.

At the preoperatory level, where the generation of new possibilities seems so inhibited, one finds that the same is true of the development of necessary relations, although these present a number of problems at this stage. One of these problems concerns the demarcation between inferential necessity and what appears to be a form of necessity, that is, a kind of necessity based on compositions without which there can be no necessity in any real sense, evolving out of simpler interpretations such as pseudo-necessity. Consider, for instance, the experiment in which the child puts one bead with one hand into a transparent jar A, and another bead with the other hand in an opaque jar B. In this case all subjects agreed that n in A was equal to n' in B, but when it came to predicting whether $n + x$ would equal $n' + x'$ the youngest children refused ("Let's see first") whereas among those over five and a half there were some who appealed to the necessity of recurrence: "What happened at first will keep on happening forever." These older children had clearly arrived in this case at necessity through composition. Surprisingly, however, these same subjects failed elsewhere to show that they had grasped the principle of the conservation of number: in a test involving the arrangement on the table of a set of visible counters they were unable to manage composition with conservation. What is apparently happening here is an initial phase in the perception of inferential necessity, but one that is still localized, restricted to one situation: our subjects have made the step in the jar experiment but not in the counter experiment. How is one to characterize subjects who can express the fact that $n + x = n' + x'$ for completed actions, but cannot predict recurrence? It is not clear whether this response expresses a true composition of earlier actions or a mere interpretation of facts akin to that involved in pseudo-necessity.

In the spatial and physical spheres the problem is even more complex because of the confusion already mentioned between moral imperatives and causal necessity. A little boy was asked "Why does the moon light up the night and not the day?" His reply was "Because the moon is not in charge." This inability to distinguish between physical and moral laws is an index of the sort of difficulty one may expect to run into in attempting to draw the line between the comprehension of necessity due to the composition of actions and reactions still reminiscent of the "perception" of pseudo-necessity. In an experiment in which subjects could in principle deduce, by pulling on a string A, that another string B would get shorter, we were able to distinguish three levels in the development of the functions needed for this inference. At the first level subjects assumed a simple covariation of the lengths of A and B. At the second level they understood that the length of B was a function of that of A. And at the third level they conceptualized the fact that, in addition to B's dependence on A, the total length $A + B$ was conserved. It is thus clear that covariation alone is comprehended by lawful inferences in which necessity is not involved, while the perception of dependence with conservation (children 7 to 8 years old) is an instance of a necessity arrived at by conservation. How can one interpret the ability to see the fact of dependence but not that of conservation (children 5 to 6 years old)? All that can be said for the moment is that there are degrees of necessity, just as there are different levels in the development of possibilities and intermediate stages between empirical and lawful physical impossibility. In addition, the rate of increase of the perception of necessity is a function of the relative strength of the structures involved.

The first authentic, if limited, forms of necessity appear, then, along with the first elementary structures capable, as "groupings" are, of a certain degree of closure in their composition, for example, transitivity, recursivity, commutability, quantification, or inclusion, and all the compositions specific to the various groupings. A systematic limit is set on the extension of relations of necessity, however, in that they can only be conceived as such where concrete elements are involved, that is, objects, predicates, or relations that are directly observable. Thus they are not as yet perceived as holding between hypothetical propositions, especially where these are deemed false and where their necessary dependence serves to prove their falseness.

With regard to causality, by which we mean explanations or models that assign the quality of necessity to the content of lawful relations, our hypothesis is that in such cases the subject "attributes" his own operations to objects and thus treats these as "operators;" so it is not just a question of operations "applied" to reality, as when we describe or explain laws. It is our thinking at this time that necessity originates in the subject's compositions or coordinations of operations, while reality becomes the locus of necessary relations only on the condition that such causal "attributions" have first been made.

Our interpretation becomes clearer when it is applied at the level of formal operations. Here deducible necessity becomes generalizable to the case of verbally expressed hypotheses: reality is plunged into a universe of possibilities that as such, are susceptible to being linked by necessity. As a consequence, one sees in this stage a striking expansion in both causal explanation and logico-mathematical reasoning.

CONCLUSIONS

In conclusion, we look briefly at two problems. The first concerns the development of "the real," in the sense of an ensemble of recognized "facts," as it relates to the development of the possible and the necessary. The second is the problem of the striking special status enjoyed by "necessary" relationships between "possibilities."

With respect to the first problem, we know that transformations are the source of possibilities by virtue of their very existence, and that they are also, by virtue of the compositions they effect, the formative factor in the development of necessity. Transformations of reality should not be excluded from this formulation, for as we have described these are always comprehended thanks to the subject's logico-mathematical, and above all spatial, operations. From this dual role of transformations stems the parallelsim postulated between the growth of possibilities and progress in the perception of necessity. The fate of the real in all this, however, remains to be determined, and this both in the sense of those realities corresponding to each psychogenetic stage and in the sense of the reality constantly being uncovered by science.

In both these areas one general conclusion seems increasingly unavoidable. This is that "states" everywhere seem to be becoming subordinate to transformations. Transformations, in other words, appear to supply the key to knowledge. It has been a long time since Bachelard (1949) said "Tell me what you transform and I will tell you what you are." If one accepts this, and if what has been outlined above is correct, then it follows that reality, notwithstanding its immense and ceaseless enrichment through discovery, whether in the child's development or in that of the sciences, must become more and more integrated at its two poles with the possible and the necessary. To be more exact, it must increasingly intersect with these two areas. This does not reduce reality in any way; on the contrary, reality benefits greatly as a result. On the one hand, transformations of reality become a sphere of *possible* transformations, with only those that have been "actualized" falling into the category of reality. On the other hand, compositions of these transformations become *necessary*, although this does not remove them from the real realm. Thus knowledge of reality is forever being refined in these two areas, a fact that makes it even more difficult to reduce such knowledge to the terms of the preformationist thesis. By contrast, constructivism is well equipped, as has been noted, to deal with the totality of real "facts" itself, as well as with the subject's constant restructuring of these facts as a function of the two spheres of possibility and necessity.

The paradoxical aspect of the matter lies in the fact that possibility and necessity act on reality not independently but in concert. This brings us to the second question: why is it that in order to discover necessary relations within reality, reality must first be integrated into a system of possibilities? The answer is simply that before a transformation can be perceived as necessary it has to enter into composition with other transformations. In this way it is located as a particular aspect of the intrinsic variations of a structure; it is located, in other words, among "deducible possibilities." Thus the various forms of possibility that were listed at the end of "The Possible," above, already express a growing collaboration between possibility and necessity. This collaboration is inevitable in that the modalities of possibility all derive from the proliferation and coordination of transformations, that is, from the basic tools of knowledge. In summary, the general development whose outlines we believe we have uncovered (though we have yet to give close attention to the types of necessity) appears to have three phases: a first phase of undifferentiation in which reality appears as pseudo-necessity and possibilities are restricted to the most readily predictable developments; a second phase of differentiations in which possibilities and necessities are separated out from simple "facts," that is, states or transformations of reality, and in which both gradually increase in number and begin to refine "reality" in some ways; and a final stage of integration in which progressively constructed syntheses of the possible and the necessary subordinate and structure reality.

REFERENCES

Bachelard, G. 1949. Le Rationalisme Appliqué. Paris.

Inhelder, B., and Piaget, J. 1958. The Growth of Logical Thinking from Childhood to Adolescence. New York: Basic Books, Inc.

Inhelder, B., Sinclair, H., and Bovet, M. 1974. Learning and the Development of Cognition. Cambridge, Mass.: Harvard University Press.

Piaget, J. 1974. Recherches sur la Contradiction. Études D'Épistémologie Génétique, Vols. XXXI and XXXII. Paris: Presses Universitaires de France.

Poincaré, J. H. 1905. La Baleur de la Science. Translated by G. B. Halsted, 1907: The Value of Science. London.

Part II
Philosophy

chapter 6

Piaget and the Nature of Psychological Explanations

Theodore Mischel

Piaget's conception of the nature of psychological explanation is not only of intrinsic interest, but also bears on the way we are to understand his theories, on the one hand, and on the interrelations between philosophy and psychology, on the other. Both of these matters are controversial: critics doubt that the appeal to underlying logical structures, developed through a process of equilibration, can provide a psychological explanation of development (see Bruner et al., 1966; Kaye, 1974; Feldman and Toulmin, 1976), and there are arguments about whether the fact that psychological and philosophical issues come together in Piaget's work is a virtue or a fault.[1] Perhaps we can shed some light on the interrelations between philosophy and psychology, and also get clearer about the nature of Piaget's explanation of cognitive development, if we come to grips with his conception of explanation.

Piaget holds that scientific explanation requires more than the empirical establishment of laws—"the law in itself does not yet explain anything, since it is limited to verifying the generality of a factual relationship (succession, correlations, etc.)" (1968:159−160)—or the formalization of a system of empirical laws, as in Hull's learning theory (Piaget, 1968: 160; 1970b: 265).

---

[1] See the articles in Mischel, 1971, especially those by Hamlyn, Toulmin, Kaplan, and C. Taylor.

What is "essential" to explanation

> is the construction of a 'model' adapted to fit the facts them-
> selves—a model so constructed that deductive transformations can
> be made to correspond to real transformations, so that the model is
> the projection of the logico-mathematical pattern into reality, and
> thus consists of a concrete representation based upon the real
> modes of composition or of transformation that can be expressed in
> terms of the pattern. . . .In a word, the model is explanatory in so far
> as it enables us to give the objective processes a 'structure' which is
> itself isomorphous. (1970a: 49)

Piaget seems to think that the only alternative to this puzzling
view is "positivism," which asks us to stick to prediction and
forget about explanation because the latter can't do without
models of "real but still hidden processes" accounting for
observables (1970b: 265). But contemporary philosophy is not
positivistic, and few would quarrel with Piaget's rejection of the
notion that science is built up from observations of regular
conjunctions of event pairs, or with his insistence that scientific
explanation requires models of "real but still hidden processes"
that account for observations. What is puzzling is not Piaget's
rejection of Hume, but his contention that "the cause is a logical
co-ordination 'projected' onto a real co-ordination" (1968: 161),
so that the characteristics of scientific explanation are

> a) the *necessity* of relations between causes and effects, which
> arises from their deductibility; b) the *reality* of the causal tie
> underlying the measured phenomena. . .which is assured by the
> *model acting as a substrate* of the deductive argument. (1968:
> 161–162)

One hardly needs to be a positivist in order to think that
deductive relations hold between propositions in discourse, or
reasoning, and so find it hard to understand how "deductive
transformations can be made to correspond to real transformations," how a model of real processes in nature can be "a
substrate of the deductive argument." And one can acknowledge
that models of underlying mechanisms allow us to explain how
the cause brings about the effect, and so to recognize "natural
necessities," without identifying these with logical necessities.
A scientific theory that provides us with a model of underlying
generative mechanisms allows us to eliminate alternative sequences of natural events, all of which are logically possible, and
so to make claims about what "must" happen under certain
conditions. But this is very different from logical necessity,

which derives from the *form* of our statements and so is immune to experience. Natural necessity rests on factual rather than formal grounds; it depends on the *content* of the model, on what the underlying mechanism is, or is taken to be, so that claims about the conditions under which a certain effect "must" occur are not immune to experience. Of course, scientists may treat certain theoretical statements as unfalsifiable; but if they do, this is a choice that reflects their belief that, even if appearances seem to the contrary, the model they are using to explain the appearances is the right one. Models, no matter how fundamental, may be revised with further experience, while logically necessary truths are absolutely inviolable by experience.

In sharp contrast to this, Piaget seems to think that the "necessity" of causal explanations in science derives from the formal necessity of logico-mathematical arguments that are "projected" on reality in "the form of 'models' that are supposed both to represent the real processes and to express them in the form of deductive operations, the aim being achieved when the deductive operations are matched by the actual changes" (1970c: 234). I will return to this puzzling attempt to ground the "natural necessities" of empirical science in the formal necessity of logico-mathematical implications, an attempt that is connected with Piaget's claim that there is an "isomorphism between the implicative systems of meanings and the causal systems of the material world" (1968: 190).

For the moment, let us turn to Piaget's discussion of the models that have been used in psychology. The main thrust of his argument here is that all forms of reduction—whether of the psychological to the nonpsychological, or of the complex to the simple—must be rejected in favor of "constructive" explanations that deploy "abstract models" (cf. Piaget, 1968: 163 ff.; 1970b: passim). Piaget does not deny the relevance of the physical, organic, and social to the psychological, or the continuity between the higher and the lower—indeed, the continuity between mental (cognitive) functioning and biological processes is central to his whole approach. What he denies is that higher processes can be adequately understood by reduction to elements of exactly the same sort as are found at lower levels of organization. That is, Piaget objects to reductive atomism of the sort found in both modern behaviorism and classical empiricism, which tries to explain patterns of intelligent behavior in the adult in terms of the same sort of structures that are at work in the infant (or in lower animals), so that the higher and more complex forms are seen as incremental additions of homogeneous elements, and not as structures having a different form of organization. In Piaget's view there are different forms of organization at different levels, these structures being such that they cannot be explained as mere additions of homogeneous elements. The contrast is between reductive atomism, on the one hand, and constructive holism, or "structuralism," on the other (cf. Piaget, 1970: 479 ff.; Taylor, 1971).

Piaget draws two conclusions from his discussion of psychological models:

> It is essential that a) psychological explanation allows a certain reduction to take place from the higher to the lower, since its organicism provides an irreplaceable model (capable of leading to physicalism); b) in order to interpret the higher forms of conduct (including their characteristic of 'self-awareness') one resorts to a certain form of construction, with all its technical demands (abstract models). There cannot be any contradiction between these conclusions a) and b) and the best proof of this is that when the neurologist studies the nervous system he uses, as an active and intelligent subject, the higher forms of conduct and the deductive schemata whose logical necessity is not reducible to material facts. (1968: 182)

So the intelligent, self-aware logical activity of, for example, the scientist, though dependent on and continuous with his biological functioning, which in turn is dependent on his material nature, cannot be reduced to (i.e., cannot be adequately explained by) the structure of material organizations; in order to explain intelligent conduct we need a constructive, rather than reductive, explanation that relies on "abstract models." Such models, we are told,

> set a certain standard of legitimacy and precision to constructive explanations by stressing the activity of the subject. Whereas reductionist hypotheses subordinate the higher to the lower, the abstract schema, while not denying that links with the organism are important, reveals the uniqueness and the novelty of developments occurring at the level of behavior and conduct. (Piaget, 1968: 181–182)

But precisely what are the distinctive features of "constructive explanations" that bring out the uniqueness of intelligent conduct by deploying models that stress "the activity of the subject"?

Perhaps a concrete example will help. Piaget explicates the process of equilibration by reference to a series of four "strategies" adopted by the subject, such that the consequences of adopting one strategy increase the probability of his adopting the next, until he reaches the last strategy and succeeds in establishing a more stable and permanent cognitive equilibrium than was achieved by any of his preceding strategies. For example, in learning conservation concepts the child begins by reasoning on the basis of one of the two transformed dimensions (e.g., it's longer); after a time he is likely to shift to the other dimension (it's thinner); and after a period in which "he will oscillate between the two," it becomes probable that he will begin "discovering the interdependence of the two transformations." The child now "starts to reason about the transformations," and the probability increases that "he will discover that the two variations are inverse to each other. . .the child now finds a reversible system" (Piaget, 1967: 154—157). Piaget does not want to say that the child necessarily goes through conscious calculations in adopting these strategies, but he does insist that it is always the "failures or insufficiencies" of one strategy that lead to the adoption of another, more "equilibrated," strategy (1957: 58—59). Moreover, it seems clear that these failures must be seen from the subject's point of view, since Piaget explains the increasing probability of successive strategies by talking about "consideration by the subject," his "choice" of strategies, his "doubts" and "reasonings," what he "conceives," "asks himself," "imagines," "discovers," and the like (1957: 62—72).

Now this psychological process of equilibrating, that is, of repeatedly adopting a succession of strategies for coping in more and more effectively organized ways with cognitive perturbations or problems of increasing complexity, is Piaget's explanation for cognitive development. Beginning with the infant's earliest copings, "every schema tends to assimilate every object," but runs into the "resistance of objects to assimilation" (Piaget, 1959: 43). This produces "perturbations" that the child equilibrates by "accommodation" and "assimilation." As new structures develop the child can appreciate problems that could not arise for it before it had those structures, and in its efforts to cope with these problems it equilibrates new structures. "Logical structures" thus develop out of "pre-logical" ones, and all of cognitive development "consists of reactions of compensation to perturbations (relative to previous schemas) which make necessary a variation of the initial schemas" (Piaget, 1959: 50). Equilibration continues until the "permanent equilibrium" of formal (logico-mathematical) structures is achieved.

Clearly, this is an explanation of cognitive development that appeals to the activity of the subject. But it appears to be an explanation of an entirely different type from those provided by the physical sciences, because it appeals to the subject's developing understanding of various situations, and such an appeal plays no role in the physical sciences. Piaget, however, wants to minimize this difference by stressing the "links between biological structure and the structure of knowledge, especially between organic control mechanisms and the cognitive control systems with their gradual equilibrations" (Piaget 1970: 238). There is no arguing with Piaget's contention that intelligence is biologically adaptive and that cognitive processes have, in some sense, "evolved" out of organic ones, but the question is whether or not there is a significant analogy between Piaget's explanation of cognitive development as due to "compensation resulting from the activities of the subject in response to external intrusions" (1967: 101) and the homeostatic mechanisms that maintain biological equilibria by compensating for environmental changes. Three particular differences seem important.

First, the "external intrusion" to which the subject responds is not a physical stimulus; what he responds to, and whether or not there is anything at all for him to respond to, depends on the cognitive schemas to which the stimulus must be assimilated. Because equilibration depends, from start to finish, on the subject's cognitive schemas, it is not a biological process of compensation. What influences behavior is not feedback from physical stimuli, but the subject's cognitive assimilation of it; what he responds to is his construal of the external intrusion, and he is also the one who interprets the outcome of his compensatory activities.

Second, at the operational level, the intrusions to which the subject responds "can be imagined and anticipated by the subject. . .the compensatory activities will also consist of imagining and anticipating the transformations" (Piaget, 1967: 113). So we are not talking about any interaction between internal mechanisms and actual occurrences in the environment, but about "virtual" rather than "actual" intrusions and the subject's "precorrections for anticipated errors" (Piaget, 1967: 108), that is, his "logical" (operational) thinking about the situation confronting him.

Finally, there need be no "external intrusions" at all in order for there to be equilibration. For example, the acquisition of conservation concepts is, in Piaget's view, due to "internal factors of coherence. . .the deductive activity of the subject himself" (Piaget, 1959: 32). Equilibration is here a response to *internal* conflict between the subject's conceptual schemas, rather than a response to any disturbance from outside.

The differences come to this: in biological self-regulation both the external intrusion and the operations that compensate for it can be specified in terms of physical concepts whose application is external to any point of view; we don't need to see things from the system's point of view, we don't have to ask about the way the system understands the intrusion, in order to understand the workings of a homeostatic mechanism. But in order to understand why a subject abandons one strategy in favor of another, we do have to understand the situation from the subject's point of view—we have to understand the meaning that the intrusion, or conflict, has for him and the point of his compensatory activities. Because the cognitive equilibrations to which Piaget appeals can only be understood by taking up the subject's point of view and interpreting the meanings things have for him, while accounts of the workings of homeostatic mechanisms are external to any point of view, an explanation that appeals to the "activity of the subject" seems to differ in type from explanations in the physical sciences.

Piaget might reply that it is a mistake to think that explanations in the physical sciences are external to a subject's point of view. He argues that though the human sciences have "man both as their subject and their object. . .this situation is not entirely novel and can be paralleled in the natural sciences" (1970a: 16). Even though physical objects can be known only "through perceptions, which have a subjective aspect," objectivity, the relative independence of the object from the subject, becomes possible through "decentering." "The whole history of physics," Piaget tells us, "is about decentration, which reduced to a *minimum* the deformations introduced by an egocentric subject and based this science to a maximum on the laws of an epistemic subject" (1970a: 16). Although the fact that the object of the human sciences "is a subject endowed with speech and multiple

symbolisms. . .makes objectivity and its prerequisites of decentration all the harder to achieve" (1970a: 17), Piaget sees no
difference in principle.

But then the point about the "activity of the subject" is an
epistemological point that applies to physics as much as to
psychology. Because Piaget believes that "the work of the
Geneva school on the development of mental concepts and
operations in children also succeeds in showing the part played
by the activities of the subject in the elaboration of knowledge"
(1970b: 227), he rejects any sharp distinction between the
natural and the human sciences. He argues that the natural
sciences are "exact" only because they explain in terms of logico-
mathematical structures, but these in turn arise out of activities
of the subject that are studied in developmental psychology (cf.
Piaget, 1970a: 42–45), so there can be no explanation external
to the epistemic activities of a subject.

But this point has nothing to do with the claim that
psychological explanations differ from explanations in the physical sciences because they deploy concepts that can only be
understood by taking up the subject's point of view. For the
subject here is the actual rather than the epistemic subject, and
the distinction in question is not between subjectivity and
objectivity, but between physical characterizations, whose concepts are extensional, and psychological characterizations that
employ intensional concepts.

The notion that intentionality, or "direction toward an
object," is the distinctive feature of psychological concepts goes
back to Brentano (1874), who attempted to distinguish mental
from physical phenomena on the ground that the former are
always directed toward some content. A thought, or perception,
is always *of* something, a desire is always *for* something, etc.,
and whether or not what is thought of, desired, etc., exists, it will
still be true that this is what is desired, thought of, etc. Because
thoughts, desires, etc. can thus be individuated only in relation
to the object intended, or meant, while physical objects can be
individuated without reference to what someone intends, Brentano thought that this "intentional inexistence" of the mental
provides a criterion for distinguishing between mental and
physical phenomena.[2]

---

[2] The discussion of intentionality here is greatly simplified and abbreviated;
for a more detailed account see Mischel, 1976.

In a very similar way, we characterize actions in relation to what the agent intends. "He is looking for his glasses" is a description that individuates an action in terms of an intention the subject is taken to have, and not in terms of his bodily movements. It matters not which of the indefinite range of bodily movements that may be involved in looking for one's glasses occurs, and the only thing that can individuate whatever bodily movements do occur as the act of "looking for his glasses" is the agent's intention. He may move his hands, etc., in indefinitely various ways with the result that his glasses turn up, but one could not characterize what he is doing as "looking for his glasses" unless that was what he intended—for he might, for example, be looking for his keys, or just nervously shuffling papers on his desk, and in the process accidentally turn up his glasses. Because actions are normally individuated in relation to the agent's intentions, they share the characteristic of "intentional inexistence" by which Brentano sought to distinguish mental and physical phenomena: looking for Shangri-la is just as much an action as looking for one's glasses.

"Intentionality" thus distinguishes not two different kinds of phenomena, but two different ways of individuating and describing phenomena. Bretanos' insight pertains not to the difference between physical and mental phenomena *qua* "things" of a different sort, but to the different sort of concepts deployed in physical and psychological descriptions of behavior, whether these be intentionalistically characterized bodily acts like "looking for one's glasses," or such "mental acts" as thinking of, hoping for, etc. Psychological characterizations always presuppose a subject, they appeal to what he means or intends, and they describe situations and behavior from his point of view.

Applying this to Piaget, it seems clear that characterizations given in relation to a subject's cognitive "schemas" are characterizations in terms of something like his schemes, beliefs, desires, etc.—they are intentionalistic characterizations. And the systematic, conceptual interconnections between a subject's aims, beliefs, desires, and actions make it impossible to understand such psychological characterizations, or to grasp the connections between them, from outside, i.e., without taking up the point of view of the subject to whom they are ascribed and interpreting the meanings that situations and behaviors have for him. This makes psychological explanations, which deploy intentionalistic concepts, different from physical explanations, which employ extensional concepts whose application is independent of any point of view on the part of the phenomena under investigation: because they employ intensional rather than extensional concepts, psychological explanations cannot satisfy Hume's atomistic requirement that the evidence for an effect must be specifiable in a way that is logically independent of the evidence for the cause. Because we characterize a psychological state in relation to its intentional object, we can individuate it as, for example, a desire for X, only by taking the point of view of the subject to whom the desire is ascribed and grasping the non-contingent connections between that desire and the actions that, in light of his beliefs, etc., he is disposed to perform because of it. Thus, our evidence for saying that he desires X will consist of the things he does, says, daydreams about, etc., but all this is evidence only insofar as it can be regarded as an expression of that desire—e.g., his talking about X would not be evidence if it were intended to deceive the listener, his daydreams about X would not be evidence if they are intended to avoid thoughts about some unpleasant family problem, etc. Our evidence for attributing a desire for X to the subject coincides with the evidence for attributing to him a disposition to act in appropriate ways, and because actions, in turn, are identified in relation to the subject's intentions, beliefs, etc., our evidence for saying that the actions in question are of the appropriate sort cannot by purely external, but requires interpretation in terms of his beliefs, aims, etc.

Thus the evidence for attributing, for example, a desire, to someone cannot be logically independent of the evidence for attributing actions of the relevant sort to him, because it is only by virtue of the noncontingent ("meaningful") links between desires and actions that are, from his point of view, in light of his beliefs, etc., *appropriate* to the desire, that we can have evidence for attributing to him both the desire and the (intentionalistically characterized) actions or action dispositions. Put another way, both the desire and the action can be characterized intentionalistically only by being interpreted so that their non-contingent connection is intelligible in relation to that same wider context of systematically connected aims, beliefs, etc., that constitutes the subject's point of view. This is why no logically independent characterizations of desires, beliefs, motives, emotions, and actions can be given at the psychological level; it is only insofar as we grasp these noncontingent links from the point of view of the subject to whom they are attributed that we can be in a position to individuate and explain his behavior intentionalistically.

As a number of writers have pointed out (e.g., Boden, 1973), intentionalistic explanations that account for behavior in terms of the complex interrelations between a goal and the hierarchically structured action plans a subject generates as appropriate for achieving it, in relation to his beliefs and values, his sociocultural constraints and opportunities, motivations, etc. (all of which are encompassed in Piaget's notion of "schemas"), are analogous to program-level explanations of a computer's behavior in terms of subroutines. Such action plans bring about behavior because they "guide" it, in much the same sense in which a program can be said to "guide" the machine that executes it.

In giving such explanations one assumes that a person has the power to act intentionally, without explaining what it is, in his biological nature, by virtue of which has has that power— much as program-level explanations tell us nothing about the hardware that makes it possible for the computer to execute subroutines. But just as program- and hardware-level explanations are perfectly compatible, so intentionalistic psychological explanations, which appeal to meanings for the subject, are compatible with there being extensionalistic, physical explanations, at a different level. Even if actions cannot be individuated without interpreting their meaning in relation to the subject's intentions, desires, etc., and these in turn cannot be individuated without reference to appropriate action dispositions, should it turn out that sufficient conditions for having a desire, intention, etc. can be specified at the neurophysiological level, and linked contingently to the motions performed when the system is in that state, then there would be physicalistic explanations, which satisfy Hume's atomistic requirement, at that level.

I expect that Piaget would agree with most of this, for he holds that

> the most general characteristic of states of consciousness is undoubtedly that they consist of 'meanings' of a cognitive nature (translated in terms of truth or falsehood) or an affective nature (values) or more probably, both, at the same time. So neither the connection between meanings nor the relation of the significant to the signified object arises from causality. (1968: 188)

The relation between meanings, we are told, is one of "implication in the broad sense" and we must "respect the uniqueness of
conscious necessity while ensuring that it will continue to reflect
its factual origins" (1968: 182). Again, Piaget contrasts psychology and neurophysiology on the ground that

> neuro-physiology is exclusively *causal* while psychology is based
> on *implication.* The reason is that the data of neuro-physiology are
> concerned with physio-chemical states which can be given purely
> causal explanations, while states of consciousness and mental
> behavior cannot be given causal explanations, but constitute only
> systems of significations or significant actions which are interre-
> lated by 'implications' in the broad sense of the term. A healthy
> psychology consists, in this case, in the replacement of the
> imprecise and incomplete implications of consciousness by logico-
> mathematical implications which constitute a coherent body of
> knowledge and which are adequate representations of experience.
> (1969: *xxiii*)

But the problem is how to understand Piaget's account of the
development of the systems of "implications in the broad sense"
that are operative in the adult. So far, we have distinguished two
possible readings of the story about the equilibration of schemas
that seem to be mixed together in Piaget: (1) it is a causal
explanation on all fours with accounts of homeostatic mechanisms in biology; and (2) it is an empirical explanation that deals
with activities actually performed by children, but one that
differs from physical explanations because it depends on intentionalistic characterizations. Because Piaget says the psychology
should replace the "incomplete and imprecise implications of
consciousness" with "logico-mathmatical implications," there is
a third possibility: the account of the relation between less and
more equilibrated schemas might be construed as an analysis of
purely formal relations between the logico-mathematical structures that we, as theorists, can use to characterize the conduct of
subjects at different developmental stages. In that case, the
"generation" of more equilibrated schemas will have to be
understood not as an analogy to the way homeostatic mechanisms
causally generate the restoration of a physical state when there is
a physical intrusion, nor as an analogy to the actual activity of
someone who *intentionally* generates a modification of his
conceptions when he recognizes that they conflict with his
observations or other conceptions, but rather as an analogy to the
way in which the premises of a logico-mathematical argument

may be said to "generate" its conclusion—i.e., they logically imply that conclusion, whether or not it is, in fact, drawn by a subject. Which of these is Piaget's view?

Elsewhere (Mischel, 1971) I have argued that Piaget's account of equilibration is best understood as a logical reconstruction in terms of which the developmental psychologist can order the stages leading to adult rationality according to such formal characteristics as coherence, clarity, reversibility, etc. Seen in this way, Piaget's stage-dependent account of the interests, conflicts, modes of conduct, and reasoning that are typical of children at different stages is empirical; but the stage-independent account of the development of more and more equilibrated structures is not an empirical theory because what Piaget says about cognitive "perturbations" and the restoration of "equilibrium" can be cashed only by applying our logical concepts of consistency, relevance, etc. to the subject matter with which the child is coping. One is inclined to think that Piaget would agree with this sort of interpretation when he says that he is dealing with the epistemic rather than the actual subject—it is not "a question of the processes and logic of the subject itself" (1968: 178). Talk about the "activities of the epistemic subject" does not refer to real activities performed by a subject: it is a way of talking about timeless, logico-mathematical relationships. The same is true when he says that it is "natural to use as a model the logical processes themselves, as is done systematically by the Geneva school" (Piaget 1970b: 268), or when he claims that there is an invariant sequence—i.e., a *logical* order—in cognitive development.

But there are other places where Piaget seems to think of equilibration as a mechanism that provides an empirical, scientific explanation. Because the mechanism is psychological, Piaget points out that it must be identified in terms of "characteristics that are not specifically 'physical,'" (1957: 40) and this requires "abandoning strict causality in favor of such a system of interpretation" as is involved in describing a particle's trajectory in terms of the principle of "least action" (1957: 31). But the fact that it is possible, and sometimes useful, to characterize the behavior of particles in quasi-psychological terms does not obliterate the distinction between intentionalistic and extensionalistic explanations, for the empirical content of quasi-intentionalistic characterizations of the behavior of material particles can also be expressed in extensional terms, while no such translation is possible for intentionalistic characterizations of human behavior.[3] Because Piaget holds that psychology is based on implications and meanings, and that meanings "do not arise from causality," one may be inclined to think that he must really intend his account of equilibrations as an intentionalistic explanation. But in still other places Piaget says it is a "form of causal explanation" (1968: 177)—"equilibration . . . is based on the active compensatory adjustments made by the subject in reaction to external changes, thus leading to a causal explanation of reversibility" (1970b: 262).

Some of us find it hard to understand why Piaget fails to recognize the differences among these three readings. Thus critics contend that *formal structures* or relations (i.e., operations like identity, reversibility, etc.) are timeless, logical representations of properties abstracted from actual behavior; they must be distinguished from *functional structures*, which are cybernetic, program-level representations of sequentially ordered activities actually performed by the child in time, and these in turn differ from the *material structures* of the neurophysiologist. Piaget, they hold, confuses formal and functional analysis when he tries to account for development in terms of logical relations, which are timeless; because psychological development is a temporal process, it can only be explained by a functional analysis of psychological activities that real children perform in time (cf. Kaye, 1974); "what is needed for psychological explanation is a psychological [rather than logical] theory" (Bruner et al., 1966: 3). Again, in the view of Piaget's critics, the theorists' ability to represent the child's behavior by means of formal structures does not, by itself, prove anything about the existence of corresponding structures in the child's mind. For the formal characteristics of theories in, for example, mathematical physics, are one thing, and their empirical reference an entirely different thing. The fact that physicists can represent their observations by means of certain formal structures and relations does not allow us to conclude anything about the real existence of corresponding physical structures and relations; for the logical formalism is only an instrument that the physicist decides to use in order to express his observations clearly and precisely, and that decision entails nothing specific about the

---

[3] For support of this claim see Mischel, 1976.

empirical world. The trouble with Piaget, the critics contend, is that he fails to distinguish between the logical features of his theoretical representations and empirical reality—the purely logical entities and relations of his theory get confused with actually existing entities, i.e., structures in the child's mind, and the empirical relations among them (cf. Feldman and Toulmin, 1976).

Piaget is aware of the charge that his approach "relates to logicism and no longer to pure psychology," but replies that "just as an experimentalist cannot be charged with 'dabbling in mathematics,' if he resorts to the calculus of probability or algebraic functions," so he should not be charged with "dabbling in logic" because his psychological theory resorts to logic (1970b: 268). This reply does not help, because it presupposes a view of the nature and role of logico-mathematical formalisms that is not shared by Piaget's critics. Where the critics hold that such formalisms do not imply anything about empirical reality, Piaget holds, as we have seen, that logico-mathematical systems are "adequate representations of experience" and that causal explanation in any science is the "projection" of these logical relations on reality. Discussing the relation between neuro-physiology and psychology, Piaget says that

> there need be no conflict between physio-chemical causality and psychological implication any more than between physical or material experience and the logico-mathematical deductions used to explain it: there is an isomorphism between causality and implication. . .and the future harmony between causal physiology and analyses based on implication should be sought on the basis of the relations now existing between experimental or causal, and mathematical or implicative, physics. (1969: *xxiii*)

Elsewhere he maintains that "causality is an assimilation of material actions between objects to the operations of the subject-theoretician" (1968: 190) and that "abstract deduction can also be applied to the real substrates by virtue of the principle of isomorphism" (ibid).

This is not an easy view to understand, but I think it may amount to something like this: the logico-mathematical systems, which make causal explanations in the experimental sciences possible, are rooted in the activities of the human subject; these systems of implications are "structures of thought resulting from the gradual interiorization of actions," but the subject "though having constructed them by his very activity, is not conscious of their existence as structures" (1970b: 228)—or, at least, his consciousness of them is "imprecise and incomplete." These logico-mathematical structures are not just formalisms that tell us nothing about the world, they are "adequate representations of experience" because experience must conform to them. We can arrive at a causal explanation of experience, whether in physics or physiology, only by "projecting" our logical coordinations onto material substrates. Causal experimental sciences, like physics or physiology, have the job of finding models that can be "matched by the actual changes," i.e., empirically checked by predictions. But the structure of reality revealed by the explanatory models of experimental physics, or physiology, must be isomorphic with the structure of our own thought because, as Kant would say, it is not derived from, but prescribed to, experience.[4] Because causal explanations can be developed only by assimilating interactions between material objects into the logical operations of the subject theoretician, our logico-mathematical representations and the empirical realities they represent will be isomorphic.

Logicians may, for their own purposes, treat these systems of logico-mathematical implications as timeless, but the "logic of the logician" is only a "formalized and highly enriched extension of the logic behind the subject's activities" (1970a: 43). And psychology studies the way these activities develop into "systems of implications in the wide sense." In so doing, the psychologist, like any other scientist, will use logico-mathematical representations and these will be isomorphic with the actual activities of children—the real, sequentially ordered activities of functional analysis—for much the same reason that there is isomorphism between the formal structures and relations of "mathematical or implicative physics" and the material structures and processes that they represent: the explanation of actual activities in time becomes possible only insofar as they are assimilated into the operations of the theorist and so made isomorphic with our logico-mathematical structures. There is always "isomorphism between the implicatory and causal systems" (1970a: 50), because the latter are "projections" on reality of the former.

---

[4] Piaget says that "if we keep to the spirit of his pronouncement rather than to the letter, Kant was undoubtedly right in claiming that perception is organized from the outset. . .and that the same subjective sources which underlie the categories of understanding underlie perceptual organization" (1969: 361–362).

But then it is clear that what is at issue between Piaget and his critics cannot be settled in terms of considerations pertaining only to developmental psychology; it requires getting into much broader issues about the nature of human knowledge. If one believes that physical explanations assimilate the behavior of material objects into the activities of a subject, then the distinction between intentional and extensional explanations may not seem very important, nor would there be much point in insisting that formal, functional, and physical structures and relations must be carefully distinguished, if one believes that they are all isomorphic. But why should we accept these claims?

In science, claims about isomorphism can be established by showing that the laws governing two sets of phenomena—e.g., the flow of current in a wire, and the flow of a fluid in a pipe—have the same syntactic structure. But nothing like this comparison of the structure of systems of empirically established laws is involved in Piaget's claim of "isomorphism between the implicative systems of meanings and the causal systems of the material world" (1968: 190). That claim, as the context makes clear, is Piaget's alternative to parallelism and interactionism as solutions to the mind-body problem (cf. Piaget, 1968: 182–190; 1970b: 49–51), and that problem is surely philosophical rather than scientific—it is a conceptual problem that no amount of empirical investigation can solve. Piaget gets entangled in that problem because his theory of cognitive development is embedded in a philosophical theory about the nature of human knowledge.

There is considerable irony in this, for Piaget's continental background leads him to identify philosophy with speculative systems—the characteristics of philosophy, according to Piaget, lie in "not dissociating questions one from another" and in "evaluation and commitment, which excludes the possibility of any general meeting of minds" (1970a: 13). The sciences were detached from philosophy, we are told, "not because their problems were established once and for all as scientific" but because scientific progress "requires that problems should be identified and that those on which no agreement is possible at a given moment should be set aside" (1970a: 13). That makes philosophy "speculative" by definition, and leaves problems that can be solved to the sciences. This in turn may incline Piaget to think that we must separate scientific from philosophical epistemology, that "genetic epistemology" should be part of scientific psychology rather than speculative philosophy. But his appeal to the isomorphism of meaning and causality is in itself an instance of purely speculative philosophy.

In light of Piaget's work, there is a sense in which it is plausible to hold that "in order to understand man we must know something of epistemology, and in order to understand epistemology we must have a knowledge of man" (Piaget, 1970c: 525). Piaget's psychological investigations lead quite naturally towards the epistemological issues that interest him, and there is, in fact, much recent work in Anglo-American philosophy that seems relevant to these interests—not speculative expressions of "evaluation and commitment" that fail to sort out different questions, but detailed conceptual analyses dealing with the nature of functional explanations in psychology, the sense in which a reduction of psychology to physiology may be possible, the nature of intentionalistic action explanations and their relation to causal explanations in the physical sciences, and the like. But one finds no reference to that work in Piaget. This is unfortunate, because such analyses might obviate the need for his purely speculative appeal to the isomorphism of meaning and causality. Philosophers and psychologists can, after all, bring very different skills to bear on the sorting out and solution of problems at the intersection between epistemology and the psychology of cognition, and such cooperative investigations might well be more fruitful than either the purely experimental psychologist's "hard-headed" attempt to ignore epistemology, or Piaget's attempt to make it part of empirical psychology.

REFERENCES

Boden, M. A. 1973. The structure of intentions. Journal for the Theory of Social Behavior 3: (1).

Brentano, F. 1973. Psychology from an Empirical Standpoint. O. Kraus and L. L. McAlister, eds., A. O. Rancurello et al., trs. New York: Humanities Press.

Bruner, J., et al. 1966. Studies in Cognitive Growth. New York: John Wiley & Sons.

Feldman, D., and Toulmin, S. 1976. Logic and the theory of mind: Formal, pragmatic and empirical considerations in a science of cognitive development. In W. J. Arnold (ed.), Nebraska Symposium on Motivation, Vol. 23. Lincoln, Nebraska: University of Nebraska Press.

Kaye, K. 1974. Formal structures do not develop. Paper presented at the first meeting of the Society for Philosophy and Psychology, October, Massachusetts Institute of Technology.

Mischel, T. (ed.) 1971. Cognitive Development and Epistemology. New York: Academic Press.

Mischel, T. 1971. Piaget: Cognitive development and the motivation of thought. In T. Mischel (ed.), Cognitive Development and Epistemology. New York: Academic Press.

Mischel, T. 1976. Psychological explanations and their vicissitudes. In W. J. Arnold (ed.), Nebraska Symposium on Motivation, Vol. 23. Lincoln, Nebraska:University of Nebraska Press.

Piaget, J. 1957. Logique et équilibre dans les comportements du sujet. In L. Apostel, D. Mandelbrot, and J. Piaget (eds.), Logique et Équilibre. Études d'épistémologie Génétique, 2. Paris: Presses Universitaires de France.

Piaget, J. 1959. Apprentissage et conaissance. In P. Gréco and J. Piaget (eds.), Apprentissage et Conaissance. Études d'Épisténétique, 7. Paris: Presses Universitaires de France.

Piaget, J. 1967. Six Psychological Studies. D. Elkind (ed.). New York: Random House.

Piaget, J. 1968. Explanation in psychology and psychophysiological parallelism. In P. Fraisse and J. Piaget (eds.), Experimental Psychology: Its Scope and Method. New York: Basic Books.

Piaget, J. 1969. The Mechanisms of Perception. New York: Basic Books.

Piaget, J. 1970a. The place of the sciences of man in the system of sciences. In Main Trends of Research in the Social and Human Sciences. Paris and The Hague: Mouton, UNESCO.

Piaget, J. 1970b. Psychology. In Main Trends of Research in the Social and Human Sciences. Paris and The Hague: Mouton, UNESCO.

Piaget, J. 1970c. General problems of interdisciplinary research and common mechanisms. In Main Trends of Research in the Social and Human Sciences. Paris and The Hague: Mouton, UNESCO.

Taylor, C. 1971. What is involved in a genetic psychology? In T. Mischel (ed.), Cognitive Development and Epistemology. New York: Academic Press.

chapter 7

Radical Constructivism and Piaget's Concept of Knowledge*

Ernst von Glasersfeld

Unlike the majority of contemporary psychologists, Piaget has never dodged the epistemological question that the study of human behavior, and especially of cognitive behavior, inevitably raises. In fact, in almost everything he has written he touches upon the problem of knowledge and how we acquire it. Nevertheless it is not easy to come to a clear understanding of Piaget's theory of knowledge. This chapter attempts to show that his genetic epistemology entails a drastic break with the traditional conception of "knowledge" that can be interpreted from a "radical constructivist" point of view. This constructivist approach is "radical" because it embodies not only the view that cognition must be considered a process of subjective construction on the part of the experiencing organism rather than a discovering of ontological reality, but also the belief that there can be no *rational* access to any world as it might *be*, prior to, and independent of, our experience.

After a short exposition of the traditional view of cognition and the concept of interaction between organism and environ-

* The work that led to this paper was supported in part by the Mathemagenic Activities Program, Follow Through (C. D. Smock, Director) under Grant No. OEG-8-522478-4617 (287), HEW, Office of Education, and the Department of Psychology, University of Georgia. The opinions expressed in the paper, however, do not necessarily reflect the position or policy of the U.S. Office of Education, and no official endorsement by the U.S. Office of Education should be inferred. Comments and criticisms by C. D. Smock, John Richards, and Stuart Katz are gratefully acknowledged.

ment, the epistemological ideas that have recently been developed in the field of cybernetics are outlined. The emerging radical constructivist model is then applied to the Piagetian concept of knowledge and it is suggested that this interpretation, though rarely explicitly stated, is implicit in Piaget's genetic epistemology and is, indeed, necessary in order to make it an internally consistent theory of knowledge.

THE TRADITIONAL APPROACH TO COGNITION

In the main stream of philosophical tradition, ever since the pre-Socratics, the questions "What is knowledge?" and "How do we come to have it?" are inextricably tied to the concepts of truth and of reality. Whether or not it is explicitly stated, "knowledge" is conceived as the knower's representation of things and events "in themselves" as they are supposed to exist in a "real" world, i.e., a world that is thought to "be" prior to and independent of the knower's cognizing activity. This was the general view before Kant, and, in spite of his well-founded reservations, it still is the general view among psychologists and the bulk of other scientists. The one significant exception are the great physicists who, during the first third of this century, demolished the naive realism of classical science and revolutionized the physicist's picture of the universe.

The traditional view of cognition, as Maturana (1970) says, begs the basic epistemological question, because it tacitly presupposes both a reality to be known and the knowing organism's possibility of discovering it. Inevitably, any view that conceives of "knowledge" as a representation, image, or replica of structures that *are there* prior to the knower's act of cognizing runs into an unsolvable problem: how could the knower's representation ever be said to reflect, or correspond to, or approximate, reality if the only access he can possibly have to it is his very own activity of "knowing"? To establish the "objective truth" or "validity" of such a representation, some form of *non*cognitive comparison or match with that supposed independent "reality" would be indispensable. Such a comparison, however, is doubly impossible, first because there can be no way of comparing what we have experienced to what we have *not* experienced, and second because—whatever else it might mean—"to know" means to cut up experience into repeatable, recognizable segments (cf.

Brown, 1969), and again, there can be no way of comparing these segments, and the structures we build out of them, to the uncut and, therefore, unstructured whole of our experience.

EXPERIENCE AND SUBJECTIVITY

Many scientists—just as craftsmen, engineers, and technicians in general—can carry on with their jobs perfectly well without ever asking a question concerning the relation between the perceiver and the perceived, or between the knower and what he comes to know. They can do so as long as the items and events they are concerned with are all contained in their fields of experience. In that case, items, and the relations between them, can be considered the "causes" of other events or states, which then become their "effects." Both the causes and the effects will be accessible to experience, at least in principle. That is precisely what is required by theories of "verification" or "falsification" as they have been advanced by logical empiricists[1] and by Karl Popper (1934/1965:33). Inferences drawn from experience are confirmed or disconfirmed by further experience. From an epistemological point of view, it is important to stress that confirmation may make an inference or hypothesis more plausible, or valid, or even more useful, in that it shows it to have held over a larger population of experiences. This may lead us to make some other inferences about how we structure our experience, but it cannot possibly justify inferences about the ontological status of the experienced items and the relations we have posited between them.

If existential inferences are proposed, they are always, explicitly or implicitly, *causal* inferences. What we experience, they suggest, is to be considered the effect of something that "exists" prior to our experiencing it. The causal connection, in this case, is posited on the basis of "analogy" to what we do *within* our experience. In order to systematize experience and to make predictions about it, we are constantly inferring causal links between segments of it, which, after Hume, we may call events A and events B. An existential inference, however, requires that we consider the elementary segments of our experience as Ds, i.e., as effects caused by Cs that are prior to our

---

[1] Cf., for instance, Quine (1953/1963:41): "The factual component of statements must, if we are empiricists, boil down to a range of confirmatory experiences."

experience and, therefore, lie outside it. Clearly, this is *not* the kind of "generalization by analogy" that scientific methodology sanctions. Analogy can be invoked, if we believe that C is like A and D is like B (Kaplan, 1964:107). In this particular case, we never have been, nor will we ever be, in a position to say what an item of that supposed pre-existing reality is or is not like, *before* we have actually experienced it, and because, afterwards, all we can possibly know is what we *have* experienced, the generalization of the causal connection is wholly illegitimate. Thus, though we may intuitively believe in a structured ontological reality, to invest it with the power to "cause" our experience is no less an act of mythical faith than to invest it with the power to punish or reward us or to protect us from the things we happen to dislike.

ORGANISM AND ENVIRONMENT

When, however, a scientific investigator *does* ask the question concerning the relation between the perceiver and the perceived (or, more generally, the relation between the experiencer and what he experiences), he introduces an element that wholly changes the situation. If he observes an "organism," i.e., an item that he invests with the capability of perceiving and "behaving," he has already discriminated that item from the rest of his, the observer's, experiential field. Thus, he can meaningfully speak of the organism's "environment" when he wants to refer to all that part of his own experiential field that is *not* the organism. The relations he then sets up between the organism and its environment will still be relations between parts of his, the observer's, experiential field. Anything he then says, or might want to say, about the *organism's* experiential field must necessarily be in terms of (or derived from) his own experiences as an observer. This does not mean that the organism's experiences must always be in every way the same as the observer's. They may be composed of different coordinations of elementary segments of experience and/or they may be made up of a smaller set of segments; but, as far as the observer is concerned, he cannot meaningfully include in his analysis or description of the organism elements that are not bits of his own experience.[2]

---

[2] We may observe an organism and conclude that it is "color blind," i.e., that the elements in our own experience that we call "color" are not part of the organism's experience. Or we may conclude that an observed organism *directly*

This limits the observer's explanation and understanding of an observed organism to what Maturana (1970) has called their "domain of interaction," a limitation partially foreshadowed in Klüver's (1965) doubts concerning "stimulus equivalence." Within the domain of interaction, however, the observer may speak of causes and effects, placing the causes in the observed organism's environment as "stimuli" and attaching the effects to the organism as "observable responses." By and large, that is what behaviorism has led psychologists to do, and insofar as they have tried to stick to the rigid program, they have striven to remain "technicians," i.e., to limit their explanations and interpretations of "behavior" to the linear cause-effect pattern of mechanics.

But because, in mechanics, there is no room for the transformation of energy into information, nor for inferential processes, their analyses of behavior could not come to terms with the very factors that make behavior essentially different from mechanical action and interaction. In virtually everything a psychologist may want to investigate, perception and/or cognition are involved, and the reason why we want to set these processes apart from the processes covered by mechanics is precisely their "informational" aspect. In cybernetic terms, that means that we want to specify relations between events not as energy transformations and by means of energy equations, but semiotically as signs and their interpretation (Rosenblueth, Wiener, and Bigelow, 1943; Haldane, 1955). In other words, the process of coding, which is a prerequisite wherever we speak of information, inference, or cognition, involves the institution of a connection (semantic nexus) that is quite independent of the physical or mechanical characteristics of the items that are being connected.

THE INTERACTIONIST VIEW

The various "interactionist" theories start with the explicit assumption of two types of entities: organisms and environments. An environment impinges on everything in it and thus provides

---

experiences elements that to us are accessible only indirectly via transformation from one sensory mode to another by some instrument, e.g., some of the sounds auditorily perceived by bats or dogs. But we cannot conceive of elements of experience to which we cannot accede either directly or indirectly.

for "selection." Certain items will last, others will not. Living organisms are seen as a product of this principle. They have been "selected for" because, whatever it is we call "to live," it constitutes a specific way of dealing with certain aspects of the environment. What is alive is not only "adapted" as a category or species, but also has some capability of *individual* adaptation. In this view, then, perception and cognition are, on the one hand, capabilities that have resulted from adaptation by phylogenic selection and, on the other, instruments of ontogenic adaptation. If this is granted, we would seem to be justified in inferring that an adapted organism "reflects" its environment—at least in the sense that the organism's biological structure, being one that has manifestly survived, gives us some clues as to the structure of the organism's environment. Similarly, the results of perception and cognition, insofar as they can be shown to enhance an individual's adaptation, could be said to "correspond" in some sense to the structure of the environment. In short, with regard to the basic problem of epistemology, we would seem entitled to say that, though our knowledge of the existing world may be limited and somewhat distorted by our specific characteristics as organisms, we *can* acquire some knowledge of the real world.

There are two snags to this generalizing conclusion. The first we have dealt with above: what we conclude about organisms and their environments, when both are within our experiential field, can in no way be generalized to our own position, since *our* environment, i.e., an independently "existing" world, is not accessible to us except through *our* experiencing it. Hence, whatever we say about organisms we observe cannot serve as a logical analogy to ourselves *qua* organisms in an intuitively posited "real world" environment. It can be no more than a mythical metaphor.

It does not help either, to present the problem in crisp terms and then to say, as Attneave (1974) recently did, that its solution is the business of epistemologists and that he, the psychologist, prefers to go on believing that knowledge *does* reflect an "existing" reality. Such an act of faith is a rationally unfounded assumption and will sooner or later interfere with the investigator's logic of theory construction and, hence, also with his interpretation of "data."

The second snag is that the terms "selection" and "adaptation" are somewhat misleading. The theory of evolution from which they originate is essentially a cybernetic theory, in that it is based on "restraints" rather than on causation (Bateson, 1972:399 ff.). "Selection" means no more than the elimination of the nonviable, and an "adapted" organism is merely one that comprises no feature, biological or behavioral, that would significantly increase the probability of the organism's elimination (prior to its having procreated others). Adaptation, therefore, can never be said to reflect the structure of the "real" world, because, even if it did, we could not possible *know* it. Similarly, from maladaptation and extinction we can at best infer some organismic features that seem *incompatible* with the extinguished organism's environment as we see it. That is, we may gather indications as to what that environment does *not* allow. But a description in negative terms cannot be turned into a positive description, because the exclusion of some possibilities, in a field of infinite possibilities, does not make that infinity finite.

The trouble with the "interactionist" view is that, in fact, it presupposes much more than the two explicitly made assumptions. The generalized separation of organism and environment takes for granted an objectively existing *space* in which the two can be separated. Any assertion of action, by the environment on the organism or vice versa, takes for granted the objective existence of *time* in which these actions and their "selective" effects take place. Even if we are not prepared to follow Kant to all his conclusions, we cannot avoid admitting that he has successfully deprived time and space of ontological reality and turned them into characteristics of our particular way of experiencing (Anschauungsweisen). This is corroborated, on the basis of very different studies, by the physicist Schrödinger[3]: "The space-time continuum must not be assumed to be conceptually prior to what has been considered its contents; just as the corners of a triangle are not there, before the triangle." Hence, if space and time are prerequisites of "interaction," an interactionist view or theory can never legitimately prove the existence of an environment or of a "real" world, because it has a priori posited the spatio-temporal framework without which the separation of organism and environment, and their interaction, are meaningless.

---

[3] Schrödinger (1956:24): "Das Raum-Zeit-Kontinuum darf nicht als begrifflich früher angesehen werden als das, was bisher sein Inhalt genannt wurde; so wenig wie etwa die Ecken eines Dreiecks vor dem Dreieck da sind."

THE CONTRIBUTION OF FEEDBACK AND CONTROL THEORY

The birth of cybernetics as a discipline in its own right can be collocated with the publication of the paper by Rosenblueth, Wiener, and Bigelow (1943) that supplied a scientifically usable and, indeed, useful definition of "purpose." Future historians may explain why, for 30 years and more, the behavioral sciences disregarded that formidable conceptual conquest, while the builders of mechanical and electronic control devices, who adopted it at once, proceeded from one empirical success to another.

In the context of this chapter, the relevant aspect of feedback theory is the epistemological one. The heart of the theory is the concept of *negative* feedback. A system is considered to incorporate a control device if it serves a homeostatic function in that it is capable (within certain practical limits) of keeping a sensory "input" signal quantitatively close to a pre-established reference value. Thus it must comprise a comparator (the material implementation of this is irrelevant) that "compares" the sensory signals to the reference value. If this comparison yields a difference (negative feedback), this difference generates an error signal that, in turn, activates an "output" function, i.e., triggers an activity apt to result in the modification of the sensory signal (adequation to the reference value).

Such a feedback control system is a highly successful and versatile model for the analysis of the behavior of living organisms (Powers, 1973). It differs from the stimulus-response model in that it posits a circular rather than a linear cause-effect chain. While S-R theory attempts to link an organism's responses to specific stimuli, in the feedback model, on the one hand, it is the difference between a sensed quantity and the reference value that "causes" an active response and, on the other, it is this response that "causes" a change in the sensed quantity and, thus, the elimination of the error signal.

For an analysis of cognitive processes, this development of feedback theory has several important implications. If behavior can be seen as directed towards the adequation of sensory signals or percepts rather than aimed at the modification of an "outside" environment, the process of learning and the structures (motoric or cognitive) that result from it, are no longer dependent on any match with an "outside" world, but only on the experientially "correct" association of effector functions with subsequent changes in sensory signals. In other words, the logically impossible match with an objectively existing *ontological* reality is no longer necessary and the organism can now be seen and described as operating wholly *inside* its own field of experience, i.e., operating towards internal equilibration.

In this model, the concept of "knowledge" is in one important respect radically different from the concept of knowledge in traditional philosophy, science, and common sense thinking. It explicitly excludes any idea of "reflection of" or "correspondence to" an independent objective reality supposed to "be" or "exist" in itself and awaiting a perceiving and/or cognizing organism to discover it. Instead, "knowledge" now designates any structure, i.e., any coordination or association of individually recurring elements of experience, that an organism uses in the ordering and systematization of its experience. Genetic epistemologists should have no difficulty in agreeing with this. Piaget has said it often enough: knowledge is whatever an organism holds invariant in the changing flow of experience.

THE CONCEPT OF KNOWLEDGE
IN GENETIC EPISTEMOLOGY

In Piaget's view, a living organism begins its intellectual or cognitive career with *some* genetically determined "reflexes." A reflex, by the observer's definition, is made up of a stimulus and a response, both of which recur contiguously and in that sequence. From the regularity of their recurrence, the observer infers a "fixed" connection between the two. But what would it look like from the organism's point of view? The stimulus, simply enough, would have to be a sensory signal or, more accurately, a constellation or pattern of sensory signals. The response, analogously, would be a signal or constellation of signals going to an effector function, i.e., a kind of signal that even the most introspectively inclined organism does not claim to be aware of. Again Powers (1973) has supplied an extremely insightful formulation: to the cognizing system *everything is input*. This means that an acting system can register, record, or define its activities exclusively in terms of signals from proprioceptive or kinesthetic sources and their experiential coordination (Hume's contiguity) to subsequent changes of sensory signals. Important though this point is, it is not what interests us here. The point is that, although the terms "reflex" or "fixed action pattern" focus attention on the coordinated or patterned character of the activity, they do not make equally clear that the stimulus that triggers the activity usually also has the character of a coordination or pattern. Thus it would perhaps be better to define a reflex as consisting of a fixed connection between a specific perceptual pattern and a specific motor pattern (i.e., a scheme).

This detail is essential if we want to understand the Piagetian terms of "assimilation" and "accommodation" in an epistemologically consistent way.

> Any new acquisition consists of assimilating an object or a situation to a previous scheme by thus enlarging it. . . . the thumb stimulus releases the sucking response only if it assumes a significance as a function of the scheme of this response, that is, if it is assimilated as a sucking object. (Piaget, 1974:69–70)

Assimilation of the thumb as a "sucking object" means no more and no less than this: there is a pattern of sensory signals that, owing to a genetically fixed connection, triggers the sucking activity in the infant; *from the observer's point of view*, this pattern, although first elicited by the nipple of the bottle or the mother, is now elicited by the infant's thumb as well. At that level, and with reference to the scheme we call "sucking reflex," there is, for the infant, *no* difference between nipple and thumb. A difference can be made only when some other sensory signals, for instance the taste of milk, are coordinated with the original sensory pattern—and such a novel coordination, resulting in a more comprehensive recurrent pattern of sensory signals, would constitute an *accommodation*. If we ask *how* this accommodation comes about, we can at once say it is induced by the very fact that, when the sucking response is triggered by the thumb, it does *not* lead to perception of the taste of milk, while if it is triggered by the nipple, it does; i.e., it creates a mismatch or "disturbance." The disturbance can be eliminated either by cutting the link between the "thumb" percept and the sucking scheme, or by differentiating two sucking schemes: one that leads to perceiving the taste of milk, and one that does not. In either case, what has to occur is another accommodation. Accommodation can thus be seen as the result of discrepancies or disturbances that arise from acts of assimilation when the assimilated item in some way modifies the outcome of the scheme into which it was incorporated. In the above example, the perceptual "thumb" pattern will eventually be coordinated with other perceptual signal patterns from tactual, visual, and proprioceptive sources, and will thus come to constitute a "permanent object," i.e., an item that is accessible and constructible in more than one sensory mode.

Although the observer of all this can meaningfully speak of "inside" and "outside" with regard to the observed organism, because he can separate the two in his own field of experience, the organism itself "assimilates" and "accommodates" and, quite generally, operates and acts *exclusively* on and with the signals that constitute its experience. The organism has no way of matching these signals or coordination patterns of signals with any outside reality, nor does it need anything beyond the sufficient availability of signals in order to continue with its construction.

"At eighteen months to two years this 'sensorimotor assimilation' of the immediate external world effects a miniature Copernican revolution" in the infant, and, as Piaget (1967:9) goes on to say:

> at the termination of this period, i.e., when language and thought begin, he (the infant) is for all practical purposes but one element or entity among others in a universe that he has gradually constructed himself, and which hereafter he will experience as external to himself.

Piaget's meaning seems perfectly clear in this passage. The "Copernican revolution" that leads to the child's *externalization* of his sensorimotor constructs, which include not only "permanent objects" but also the sensorimotor basis for the construction of the concepts of space, time, and causation, is Piaget's key to the adult's belief in an external "prefigured" reality. This act of externalization has to be constantly kept in mind if a logically consistent epistemology is to be gleaned from the Piagetian theory of cognitive development. Whenever we read, for instance, that the organism's cognitive activity is "to assimilate the external world into the structures that have already been constructed, and secondly to readjust these structures as a function of subtle transformations, i.e., to accommodate them to external objects" (1967:8), we must remain aware of the fact that this "external world" and the "external objects" it comprises are the sensorimotor constructs that we ourselves have externalized when we underwent the Copernican revolution at the age of 18 months.

CONCLUSION

If this interpretation is not altogether mistaken, Piaget's concept of knowledge is one that in no sense involves the idea of *getting to know* an ontological reality that would have to be imagined as a prefabricated, fully structured world, existing by itself and waiting to be "discovered" by a cognizing organism. The concept of knowledge he has developed in his genetic epistemology seems wholly compatible and congruous with what a cyberneticist would call "knowledge" in a control system. In the feedback model it is the structures or coordinations of signals—neuronal events, if you will—that the system has come to coordinate recurrently in its effort to eliminate "disturbances," i.e., negative feedback that creates error signals because it is different from the reference value. For Piaget, as well as for the cyberneticist, the structures or coordinations may consist of sensory signals in perceptual patterns, of effector signals in motor patterns, or of both in complex action patterns or schemata. Assimilation and accommodation, thus, take place when inconsistencies or contradictions arise through the interaction of different levels of constructs; for instance, externalized objects and specific action patterns. This interaction of cognitive constructs is, of course, not at all the "interactionist's" interaction because it does not involve a "real" outside world. Although the observer of an organism can place that organism into an "environment," he cannot derive ontological conclusions from this way of organizing his experience, because both the organism and its environment are parts of his own experiential field and this can contain no more than he himself has constructed and externalized.

In another paper (von Glasersfeld, 1974), using a cybernetic metaphor, it is argued that from the experiencer's point of view, ontological reality is like a "black box," in that he has no way of discovering what "is" and how it might be structured. Here it should be stressed once more that radical constructivism does not deny the existence of *a* world, but it does deny the possibility of rationally describing such a "real" world. The cognizing organism would have no way of determining or deciding whether or not its constructs in any sense reflect the structure of a "real" world, even if it could come up with structures that are not dependent on its concepts of space and time. The fact that our perceptual and conceptual structures are repeatable and seem at least to some extent dependent upon the availability of elementary segments of experience (out of which they are composed) in no way justifies the assumption that our structures reflect, or correspond to, "existing" structures; it merely shows that these structures have a relative degree of viability given the way in which *we* happen to have segmented our experience. If three dots are made on a blackboard in front of a person, an opportunity is created within a domain of interaction for the person to experience three "bits" that, in this context, may be called "elementary segments of experience." The person is free to use these three bits in order to construct what we call a "triangle", i.e., to connect them by performing a set of specific operations. But he is equally free, if he happens to be in a "poetic" mood, to construct out of them a horizon and the morning star. Neither of these constructions can be said to "exist" on the blackboard. Indeed, the three dots could be coordinated into innumerable other structures, and each one of them would be determined by the operations the person, the experiencer, performs, and only in a trivial sense by the three dots that, in this metaphorical example, constitute the raw material.

More complex and better examples are found in the history of physics. It is there that radical constructivism fully agrees with Kuhn's idea of paradigm shifts (Kuhn, 1970), interpreting paradigm shifts as "change in the habitual way of constructing." The more often a construct is repeated and the greater the number of larger structures in which it is involved, the more indispensable it becomes and the more "given" or "objective" it seems. If this is the case on the level of the natural sciences, it is a thousand times more so on the level on which we construct and externalize our everyday environments.

Finally, then, it has to be stressed that radical constructivism, like any other theory in science or common sense living, is a product of inductive inference. It does not purport to supply a model of the "world of being;" it merely hopes to develop a model for the rational organization of our experience that may make it a little easier (than do traditional models) to sort out what we can know and what must remain the unfathomable mystery of the world in which we find ourselves living.

REFERENCES

Attneave, F. 1974. How do we know? American Psychologist 29(7): 493–499.

Bateson, G. 1972. Steps to an Ecology of Mind. New York: Ballantine.

Brown, G. S. 1969. Laws of Form. London: Allen and Unwin.

Haldane, J. B. S. 1955. Animal communication and the origin of human language. Science Progress 43: 383–401.

Kaplan, A. 1964. The Conduct of Inquiry. Scranton, Pennsylvania: Chandler.

Klüver, H. 1965. Neurobiology of normal and abnormal perception. In Hoch and Zubin (eds.), Psychopathology of Perception, pp. 1–40. New York: Grune and Stratton.

Kuhn, T. S. 1970. The Structure of Scientific Revolutions. 2nd Ed. Chicago: University of Chicago Press.

Maturana, H. R. 1970. Biology of Cognition (Report 9.0). Urbana, Illinois: Biological Computer Laboratory, University of Illinois.

Piaget, J. 1967. Six Psychological Studies. New York: Random House.

Piaget, J. 1974. The Child and Reality. New York: Viking.

Popper, K. 1965. The Logic of Scientific Discovery. New York: Harper Torchbooks. (Originally published in German, 1934.)

Powers, W. T. 1973. Behavior: The Control of Perception. Chicago: Aldine.

Quine, W. van-O. 1963. From a Logical Point of View. New York: Harper Torchbooks. (Originally published 1953.)

Rosenblueth, A., Wiener, N., and Bigelow, J. 1943. Behavior, purpose, and teleology. Journal of Philosophy of Science 10: 18–24.

Schrödinger, E. 1956. Die Natur und die Griechen. Hamburg, Germany: Rowohlt.

von Glasersfeld, E. 1974. Piaget and the radical constructivist epistemology. In C. D. Smock and E. von Glasersfeld (eds.), Epistemology and Education (Report 14). Athens, Georgia: Mathemagenic Activities Program, Follow Through.

Part III
Psychiatry

chapter 8

Piaget and Mental Health*

Peter H. Wolff

Many people when speaking of mental health in fact mean mental illness. Given such an interpretation, it might be appropriate to examine how the Geneva studies can increase our understanding about the psychological forces contributing to the genesis of mental illness, or to consider how our current formulations about the nature and treatment of emotional illness might be broadened if they encompassed the functional categories of cognition, as they have been formulated, for example, by Piaget. At a presentation to the American Psychoanalytic Association, Piaget suggested how some internal contradictions of the psychoanalytic theory of the unconscious might be resolved if phenomena in question were analyzed as aspects of cognitive development (Piaget, 1973). Professor Inhelder (1963) and her colleagues have studied the de-differentiation of cognitive structures in patients with presenile dementia, and the thought processes of mentally retarded children have been examined from a similar perspective. Odier (1947) attempted to reconcile the phenomenon of clinical anxiety with a structural view of intelligence; and Anthony (1956) has analyzed in some detail possible intersects between child psychiatry and developmental studies from the Geneva group. Over the past 15 years, Piaget's discoveries have been applied to such a wide range of topics in abnormal psychology that the potentially productive applications of his work to clinical problems cannot be catalogued in a brief summary statement. Nor would a lengthier exposition be pertinent to this discussion of how Piaget's formulations and discoveries might improve the mental health of children rather than how they increase our understanding of mental illness.

* Work for this report was completed with support from USPHS Carrer Scientist Award MHK3461 and USPHS Research Grant MH1833206.

When discussing the factors that contribute to the mental health of children from this point of departure, emphasis must be placed upon the climate of prevailing intellectual traditions, ethical values, and political-economic realities to which children are covertly or overtly, but inevitably, exposed during their formal education, and how this initiation into the society at large affects their capacity for adaptation to a complex world. The liberties taken with the conventional meaning of mental health are done in the belief that the ability to cope in the broader social context is as essential to the well-being of children as the course of their psychosexual development, and that it is in the domain of intellectual development and the growth of ethical responsibility rather than any direct application to clinical problems that the Geneva studies will make their greatest contribution to the mental health of our children.

A member of the Harvard Faculty of Education recently recounted how his graduate students as part of their field work had undertaken to experience directly what going to high school is like when one is no longer involved in the day-to-day struggles of survival as a high school student. The high school in question has a good academic reputation. Each graduate student accompanied one pupil for the entire school day, and they were all shocked to discover that going to school consisted of six hours of unrelenting boredom, that the teachers were so overwhelmed by the mere task of keeping order they had little energy left to serve up even the programmed curriculum packaged for them at some institution of higher learning, and that teachers had no time whatever to find out what their students might be thinking. Therefore, all potentially embarrassing intellectual encounters between teacher and pupil were assiduously avoided; and the hours ground on until the final bell of the day released both parties to this struggle from their tedium. In another high school—this one enjoying a national reputation for academic excellence—a recent follow-up study revealed that only those pupils who had been in advanced placement for mathematics showed any progress in mathematics over the entire four years of instruction, whereas all the others upon graduation were by standard achievement measures exactly where they had been when they started high school.

The descriptions of these conditions are not meant to be startling revelations, and the examples were deliberately chosen from good school systems. For 10 years the paperback book trade has depended for its survival almost as much on the sale of well-reasoned critiques of public school education in general as it has on the sale of sex manuals. Yet the conditions that provoke such critiques will not change substantially unless we as former high school pupils, as parents, as academics, and as teachers combine our efforts to alter a system of education that makes it possible for a 13-year-old high school student to write: "A kid threw up today. Every year at least one kid throws up. No one ever throws up in camp or in any other place I've been to" (Hauben, 1972).

High schools are not the same everywhere. In every industrialized society, exceptional teachers can engage their students in a meaningful exchange of ideas, because they do not fear for their authority. At least in middle-class communities, the elementary schools do not appear to be quite as desperate or as dreary. Children are still alert—perhaps because they are still eager to discover something interesting in the classroom, or because their questions are not sufficiently differentiated to threaten the established lines of authority. Our limited experience, however, suggests that the process of attrition begins very early in elementary school, especially for vulnerable children. In a small study to test the effects of the Kodaly music program on cognitive style in first grade students from a ghetto school, we discovered quite by chance that children in the "control group" had made almost no academic progress during the year and had actually lost ground on our cognitive measures—in other words, that they were worse off after a year of schooling than when they started. Yet the law demands that all children must spend 12 years in the public school system on the assumption that the exposure will prepare them to become responsible and thinking individuals. As professionals who have agreed to take some responsibility for the mental development of children, we must ask at what cost to their mental health children are initiated into the society through formal education; and as citizens of an open society we are obligated to challenge the assumption by action.

Seasonal changes in the fashions of curriculum innovation will remain an empty exercise as long as the reforms are undertaken independent of the central issue, that is, for whose benefit the schools are designed. Is the purpose of public education to foster the intellectual and ethical growth of children, and to develop an independence of mind that will equip them with the means and the courage to challenge falsehood or social injustice, even when that challenge means making trouble? Or are schools in fact designed to socialize, train, and indoctrinate the young to fit in with the status quo? And if the social status quo that determines what will be taught does not serve the interests of its citizens—if, for example, the raising of intelligent children who ask embarrassing questions is viewed as incompatible with the intentions of the state—which of the conflicting goals of education are sacrificed and which assume priority? The reader is sufficiently familiar with the documented indictments of contemporary public education, articulated by Goodman (1960), Holt (1964), Kozol (1967), Illich (1970), Henry (1972), and others, to know their view that the intellectual vitality of children is often sacrificed to preserve the established order of things.

Yet, given the enormous capacity of the naive human mind to learn, adults will always teach their young; and in organized industrial societies this training will almost certainly take place in schools, no matter what the political realignments. The question is therefore not whether or not children should go to school, but how the goals of an established industrial society can be coordinated with the intellectual needs of children, at a minimum cost to children's welfare. At least in theory, a society that aspires to an ideology of political freedom, social justice, and respect for the rights of the individual should be able to define the overall goals of education with sufficient precision to identify the current contradictions between that ideology and classroom realities. In the belief that the discoveries by Piaget and his co-workers can best serve the mental health of children and of their society when applied to the process of education, the major contradictions that currently exist between the psychological concepts as they might be inferred from Piaget's genetic epistemology and classroom arrangements are briefly explored.

Schools seem to operate on the premise that learning is an inherently painful, odious task, and because natural children will reject knowledge and discovery as they might cod liver oil, they must be forced, coaxed, and seduced. Therefore classroom teachers are obliged to spend such a disproportionate effort *making* their pupils remember answers, *forcing* them to pay attention, and *controlling* their behavior that they have little time in which to help the children think and learn. How else are we to account for the emphasis on discipline and behavior modification, competition, and punishment and reward, as if teacher and pupil were adversaries locked in a perennial struggle that no one can win? Such arrangements evoke a vast and lucrative technology of education that has no apparent relation to thinking and knowing as Piaget might define these terms, but is guaranteed to drive the teacher up the wall and the pupil up against the wall.

Any view of education starting on the premise that children must be *forced* to exercise their minds fundamentally contradicts everything Piaget and his collaborators have written about the psychological forces that motivate acting, knowing, and thinking (Wolff, 1963). The harassed teacher and the pupil who is sophisticated by 6 years of school experience will consider it ingenuous of anyone to suggest that at least at the beginning of their school careers children might actually like to learn, or that the discovery of novelty through personal effort is its own reward, or that intellectual activity does not require extrinsic reward or the fear of punishment and public humiliation. Evidence to support the romantic view that children are self-motivated to explore and master intellectually challenging problems is formidable and can be found in many contexts. While studying the conditioning process in young infants, Hanus Papousek (personal communication), for example, observed that the infants could be trained to go through complex maneuvers of head turning when reinforced by intermittent swallows of milk. Once their hunger was partially satiated, however, the infants became more interested in the problems set up by the experimenter than the reward, and behaved as if they had to give an occasional perfunctory suck on the bottle in order to be presented with more problems. The intrinsic motivation of children to invent and discover is evident when preschoolers explore how the door bell rings and what makes a firefly glow. It is implicit in all the observations of young children Piaget has recorded so meticulously, even though hard-nosed psychology might quibble that Piaget was in fact reinforcing his children. The motivation is apparent in schools designed to foster intellectual curiosity and in the traditional school when pupils encounter an exceptional teacher who respects the child's intellect and treats learning as an active process. When such motivation is no longer evident in the classroom, it may still resurface after school, since the need to know does not die easily. Yet it can be crushed, and crushed with great efficiency, by an educational technology that substitutes behavioral manipulation and control for the encouragement of children's spontaneous exploration, on the assumption that the motivation for knowing is extrinsic to the process of knowing.

In an essay prepared for the UNESCO International Commission on the Development of Education, entitled "The Structural Foundations for Tomorrow's Education," Piaget (1974) proposed some prerequisities of a rational program of education for the future:

> The first of these conditions is, of course, the use of active methods which give broad scope to the spontaneous research of the child or adolescent and require that every new truth to be learned, be rediscovered or at least reconstructed by the student and not simply imparted to him. Two common misunderstandings, however, have diminished the value of the efforts made in this field up to now. The first is the fear (and sometimes hope) that the teacher would have no role to play in these experiments and that their success would depend on leaving the students entirely free to work or play as they will. It is obvious that the teacher as organizer remains indispensable in order to create the situation and construct the initial devices which present useful problems to the child. Secondly, he is needed to be provided counterexamples that compel the reflection and reconsideration of over-hasty solutions. What is desired is that the teacher cease being a lecturer satisfied with transmitting ready-made solutions; his role should rather be that of a mentor stimulating initiative and research.

In this essay Piaget proposes what must be done to make schools places that serve children, places where children can ask questions, think, and if necessary upset the established order of things; he implies what must be done to prevent schools from becoming laboratories for the cloning of automatons that serve blindly; and by implication he diagnoses what happens today in most school systems in the name of education, which is so damaging to the mental health of school children.

It is probably superfluous to review the many studies from the Geneva group converging on the conclusion that knowing does not grow from the accumulation, storage, and retrieval of predigested facts no matter how elegantly they may be presented or how effectively reinforced. Yet when one reads in learned journals about the use of behavior modification to teach children the concept of conservation, one may be justified in wondering whether the enthusiastic assimilation of Piaget's discoveries into the public school curriculum is merely a sham, another fad or curriculum innovation, in other words, a failure of accommodation. Unless children are encouraged to ask questions and given the freedom to experiment and test the limits of their discovery under the guidance of teachers, they will become those sterile information storage devices that are likely to result from the uncritical application of computer jargon to the process of education. A spirit of free inquiry in the classroom cannot flourish in an environment constructed on the a priori assumption that thinking and learning must be externally reinforced.

Piaget's recommendations to teachers and educators are not empty academic phrases. They come, as the reader knows, from a lifetime of work with the International Bureau of Education, which is of necessity concerned with practical realities. Moreover, the recommendations have been translated into concrete guidelines, for example, in Furth's letters to teachers (1970), that suggest many alternatives for introducing central concepts of Piaget's epistemology to classroom work without ever mentioning one-to-one correspondences or binary operations. And they have been put into practice in countries that have far less money to spend on education than the United States. In an elegant essay, Eleanor Duckworth (1972) has reported how intelligent teachers translate Piaget's ideas into organized class work by creating an intellectual climate that encourages the having of wonderful ideas. Nowhere does the report mention children pouring liquids into beakers or rolling plasticene balls.

To Duckworth's essay on the having of wonderful ideas, one should add one feature about Piaget's discoveries that may not have been sufficiently stressed, but is vital to the mental health of children and of the society in which they grow up. The uniquely human disposition to pose questions and to challenge prior belief systems probably is our most precious guarantee against intellectual decay and ethical stagnation. A few chimpanzees notwithstanding, no evidence exists to indicate that other species ask questions or challenge the validity of what they have been taught when they encounter contradictory evidence. No child, however, is ever taught to ask questions. It may, in fact, be impossible to teach children how to ask good questions; and programmed instructions have certainly not succeeded until now. Yet all children everywhere acquire this intellectual competence and motivation to ask, and the intrinsic need to find answers that will satisfy them—at least until they enter school.

Only children who are encouraged to continue asking questions in the classroom and given the support and guidance to explore solutions actively will ever discover that clay does not change its mass by being rolled from a ball into a sausage, that the earth is not flat, that the sun does not rotate around the earth, that American presidents are not necessarily honorable men, or that current public education may not be designed for their best interests.

From the beginning, Piaget was less concerned with right answers of children on the Binet task than with finding out why some children gave the far more interesting wrong answers. The clinical method so central to Piaget's discoveries is essentially the asking of good questions:

> We may thus state the first rule of our method. When a particular group of explanations by children is to be investigated, the questions we shall ask them will be determined in matter and in form by the spontaneous questions actually asked by children of the same age or younger. It is also important before drawing conclusions from the results of the investigation to seek corroboration in the study of spontaneous questions of children. It can then be seen whether the notions ascribed to them do or do not correspond with the questions they themselves asked and the manner in which they asked them. (Piaget, 1929:5)

What happens to the natural gift of children for asking difficult questions once they have entered school? Because teachers are given neither the time nor the training to take good questions seriously, they are in no position to find out what or how their children think, or how they could cooperate with children in the discovery of wonderful solutions. Behavioral objectives, programmed instructions, achievement tests, and teaching by behavior modification actively discourage the asking of questions.

The child who asks the teacher why 2 + 2 equals 4 is certainly a pain in the neck, all the more so when the teacher does not have the faintest idea what the child is talking about, and when the answer seems self-evident, because the teacher has lost touch with the importance of naïve questions. Moreover, because asking difficult questions threatens the established order in the classroom and undermines the teacher's right to teach on the presumption of authority and superior knowledge, it will be actively suppressed in a classroom designed for measured achievement, control, and efficiency.

When there is neither time nor inclination to encourage children to ask, work in the classroom becomes the witless digestion of facts that are justified to the child not by reason or evidence but by appeal to self-evidence; and it is inconceivable that children should have any stake in such facts unless their behavior is scientifically controlled by rewards and punishments. An intellectual climate that stifles good questions by appeals to self-evidence is the road to intellectual mediocrity and moral stagnation. It is also a direct threat to the mental health of children. It cripples their spirit of inquiry, indoctrinates them to accept revealed truth on the basis of authority, and humiliates those who once thought that their own ideas were wonderful. Children who stop asking good questions because they are afraid to make trouble have fallen mentally ill and are vulnerable to the lies and demagoguery of authoritarian pronouncements, whether these comes from the White House, the Pentagon, or the university pulpit. Children who accept the proposition that they must go to school in order to compete more effectively against their classmates and to earn better grades or salaries will later become the victims of a perverse society that equates democracy with property, profit, and power, and with the exploitation of those who do not compete as successfully or as obsessively.

The consistency of these remarks with Piaget's recommendations concerning the future of education is evident in this closing quotation from his essays to UNESCO:

> On the whole, whether it is a question of education of the mind and of intellectual functions or education of the ethical conscience, if the right to educate implies that it envisions full development, the human personality and the strengthening of respect for human rights and fundamental freedoms, it is important to understand that such an ideal cannot be attained by any of the common methods. Neither the independence of the person which is assumed by this development nor the reciprocity that is evolved by this respect for the rights and freedoms of others, can be developed in an atmosphere of authority and intellectual and moral constraints. On the contrary, they both imperiously demand a return by their very makeup to a lived experience and to freedom of investigation, outside of which any acquisition of human values is only an illusion. (Piaget, 1974)

REFERENCES

Anthony, E. J. 1956. The significance of Jean Piaget for child psychiatry. British Journal Medical Psychology 29:20–34.

Duckworth, E. 1972. The having of wonderful ideas. Harvard Educational Review 42: 217–231.

Furth, H. G. 1970. Piaget For Teachers. Englewood Cliffs, N. J.:
    Prentice-Hall.
Goodman, P. 1960. Growing Up Absurd. New York: Vintage.
Hauben, D. 1972. Diary. In R. Gross and P. Osterman (eds.), High
    School. New York: Simon & Schuster (Clarion Books).
Henry, J. 1972. On Education. New York: Random House (Vintage).
Holt, J. 1964. How Children Fail. New York: Dell.
Illich, I. D. 1970. Celebration of Awareness. New York: Doubleday.
Inhelder, B. 1963. Le Diagnosis du Raisonnement Chez les Débiles
    Mentaus. 2nd Ed. Neufchatel, Paris: Delachaux et Niestlé.
Kozol, J. 1967. Death at an Early Age. Boston: Houghton-Mifflin.
Odier, C. 1947. L'Angoisse et la Pensée Magique. Neufachatel: De-
    lachaux et Niestlé.
Papousek, H. Personal communication.
Piaget, J. 1929. The Child's Conception of the World. New York:
    Harcourt-Brace.
Piaget, J. 1973. The affective unconscious and the cognitive uncon-
    scious. Journal of the American Psychoanalytic Association
    21:249–261.
Piaget, J. 1974. To Understand is to Invest. New York: Viking Compass.
Wolff, P. H. 1963. Developmental and motivational concepts in Piaget's
    sensorimotor theory of intelligence. American Academy of Child
    Psychiatry 2:225–243.

chapter 9

How the Child Understands Social Institutions

Hans Furth

The exploration of children's understanding of social roles and institutions seems such an obvious topic for investigation that one is astonished to find hardly any relevant data in the psychological literature. The bulk of work on children's socialization concerns their practical or theoretical knowledge of how to *behave* in social-personal situations. In contrast, our interest is the child's *understanding* of the child's social world, particularly the more impersonal aspects of it, such as the educational system, shopping, and occupations. This is fully within the cognitive area, but it is also fully within the social area insofar as the social world is the content of what the knowledge is about.

As children grow up they begin to develop understanding, that is, they construct theories and interpretations about the physical world on which so much has been written by Piaget. But equally important, children develop theories, interpretations, and explanations about the social environment; including the institutions with which they are in daily contact. My colleagues and I interviewed children on this topic, much the same way as Piaget some fifty years ago started interviewing children about physical phenomena. He now considers these early investigations as exploratory and marginal, as if he had to apologize for them. Nevertheless, they are among his best books. The reason for Piaget's apparent uneasiness with the purely verbal interview method and his neglect of the social area follows logically from his endeavor to pinpoint children's developmental acquisitions at their best:

> Today verbal thinking appears to me to be marginal to real thinking which though verbalized remains centered on action until about

11-12 years. Thinking detached from action is not at all operatory below the level of formal or propositional operations (11-12 to 15 years). Exclusively verbal thinking does therefore no longer seem to be adequate for an exploration of the child's thinking: it provides us with various instructive signposts which, however, must be linked with results obtained elsewhere by means of truly operatory experiments. (Piaget: Preface to Pinard and Laurendeau, 1962)

What is stressed here by Piaget is the well-known fact that children know more than they can put into words. Children are best in concrete situations that they can handle and play with. Take a pencil and note how many different actions a child can perform on it. Consequently the child will acquire all kinds of advanced and theoretical knowing about weight, shape, and physical comparisons and transformations. But take an institution like money, a job, or the educational system and you realize at once the tremendous difference between physical and social objects.

Thus the reader should not be surprised to find that, relative to physical thinking, children may seem behind in social thinking. However, if this state of affairs continues into adulthood, this can be a bad situation indeed for the proper functioning of a democracy. In any case, if we want children and adults to take an intelligent interest in society and show enlightened concern about social events, it is of paramount importance that we pay attention to their acquisition of social knowledge.

In interviewing the children, we made it a point, as did Piaget, not to stress factual knowledge. Rather we attempted to get at the basis on which children understood, explained, or related certain observations. We started with social situations with which children are in daily contact (the family at home, their school, where they shop, etc.), and we were trying to find out what the children think about them in terms of explaining or relating the observed events. This focus on familiar events differentiates our research from a number of studies on children's knowledge of aspects of the political system. Naturally, one cannot expect young children to have any useful knowledge about politics and what they tell us on this topic hardly enlightens us as to their social thinking. But it is different with the events children cannot help but observe. Here some level of thinking beyond "facts" is almost inevitable. Because our focus was precisely on these interpretations of observed facts, five categories of understanding of social institutions are proposed and examples from our interview data given. The data are from some 200 children of primary school age, ages 5 to 11. The interviews were conducted in Southern England in three different schools and localities.

In the first category there is simply no attempt to explain beyond the observed facts. Asked about the source of money, the children frequently refer to the change they observe being given when they or adults are paying by cash. They consider that a shop has two functions: one to get food or other things, the second to get money. These two functions are not related in the child's mind. To get at the children's thinking we ask questions like: "Where does the teacher get the money from to buy his dinner?" Of course, knowing that the teacher has to buy food is already an inference about something a child has probably not personally observed. But taking this knowledge for granted—all our youngest children knew that a customer has to buy food with money—we asked a girl, age 5;11 (years; months) about the source of the money: "Where does she get the money to buy food?" The child answered: "She pays some rent." This child mixes up paying and getting money. She may know that her parents pay rent and this is a money event, just as is the buying of food. Thus the two events are linked. So then we ask her: "Where does she get the money from to pay the rent?" We get the answer: "Well, she gets the money. . .for paying the rent," which indicates again how this girl mixes up giving and getting money. But then she continues: "Well, she goes to the shopkeeper and she thinks, ah, the shopkeeper's got much more money than me. She has a fiddle about in his book-drawer, she takes the money and says, 'Could I have this, so-and-so pounds or two pounds'."

Of course, this is but one child's thinking, but we have observed many children around age six expressing themselves in similar terms. Some children even add a systematic quantitative relation and hold that in order to *get* a lot of money you have to *buy* a lot. Asked how the school gets money to pay for the chairs, one child refers to the buying of something presumably more expensive: "When you buy the table you get the money for the chairs."

There is fantasy in these examples, but actually these comments were merely variations on the theme "you get money from change in the shop" that the child has observed and accepts as a fact not in need of further explanation. Paying for services is quite a difficult concept, even more than paying for goods. Take an age 6;2 boy, asked about what happens when he rides on the bus. Here are some extracts from the interview: "People. . .pay the driver. . .and then the bus conductor takes it and pays them some money back, not the money back that was paid them." In other words the child knows that some exchange is taking place, not a literal giving and returning of the same coins.

"Why does he pay the money?"
"I don't know."
"Who decides how much the passenger pays the bus driver?"
"Well, I think they just pay any old money."
"They just give whatever they want?"
"Yes."

These examples also indicate the children's tendency to understand everything in personal and voluntaristic terms: the idea of an objective price is quite alien and an all-pervasive voluntarism ("people do what they do because they want to do it") and personification (impersonal rules are seen in terms of arbitrary decisions of specific persons) characterizes the early levels of thinking about social institutions.

A second category consists in explanations that appear to us as imaginative elaborations. Piaget (1963) calls it "romancing," and our first reaction to these inventions could be to dismiss them as silly verbalisms. But then two funny things happen. When one child says something apparently silly you can call it empty talk, but if you find ten or more children saying roughly similar things, the talk loses its emptiness. These children were not discussing these issues with each other and live in different parts of the country, so probably the speculations are not so wild after all. They may be founded, as Piaget has eloquently argued, on a common characteristic of children's developing intelligence. The second observation is that even the most idiosyncratic elaborations can be found to have some reasonable basis. So concerning these we can admit that they do not show the highest level of thinking a child is capable of at the time of the interview (for this, we would have to study physical thinking). On the other hand, they are genuine attempts at explaining the puzzling facts of social institutions and they do show a beginning in logically connecting different observations.

Here is the thinking of the girl, age 5;11, cited earlier, in response to the query, "What happens to the money in the cash register?": "She (the cash lady) gives it to the manager of the shop who counts it out at night and gives it to different people." Such a scene of distributing money occurs in several interviews. Asked about the different people, the girl continued:

"Well, like the mayor, or the king or somebody like that."
"That's interesting. Tell me a bit more about that. Where is the mayor?"
"Well, he's in London. . .He spends the money on jewelry and stuff for himself. . .Some of the money goes to the queen. . ."

The interview then turned toward the origin of the school that the child attends and the girl commented that somebody like the mayor or the queen must have decided to build it. "And where do you think the money comes from to build the school?" "Well, really some of the money goes to school and then they can pay the money to other schools to make buildings." Here we are back at the idea that you get money by paying money. And the girl completes the circle by saying that the money comes from tills in the shop. "Who gave it to the school?" "The shop manager." So here you have some imaginative elaborations, but also some beginning logical connections.

A third category of social thinking shows inferences with some functional basis; in other words, the child is beginning to understand the social function of a particular role or institutions. These inferences are at first quite limited and narrowly applied in one direction, but still in themselves they are valid and correspond to what will eventually be an objective understanding of the social world. An apt example of this category occurs in the rare instances when a child during the interview corrects an already initiated train of thought. In this way one observes an apparent jump from a lower to a higher level and there is at least the possibility that we are in fact witnessing what can be called a "developmental" experience, and what Piaget refers to by the forbidding term "logico-mathematical" experience.

Consider a 6-year-old boy with whom we talked about the bus driver, how he split the money he collects between himself and the conductor. That is fair enough for the child. "And what does the driver do with the money?" "Keep it, buy things for him." And the conductor? "The same thing." The interview continued and mention was made of petrol. The boy said that the driver buys it. "And where does he get the money from?" The answer corresponded to earlier levels: "He gets it when he buys it for petrol. The petrol man, he gets. . .the petrol man, he gives them petrol." Notice the child's difficulty in disentangling the giving and getting of money and of goods. The interviewer asked: "So, where does he (the driver) get the money from?" Answer: "The petrol man. The petrol man gives them some money and the money. . ." The child did not complete the sentence, which could read "and the money buys the petrol." This is our familiar money circle, not unlike what Piaget had observed about physical causality when children thought the flying ball is pushed by the wind and at the same time it is the flying ball that creates the wind.

But now we asked the child why the petrol man should give money to the driver. And then, putting two and two together, the child had an insight and corrected himself: "Oh no, the man gives him money." Interviewer: "The driver gives the man money?" Child: "Oh, I get it! The driver. . .the people who go on the bus give the money to. . .the people. . .the people who go on the bus give the money to the man and then the man can buy petrol." The child's rapid language, and the triple start to complete the thought, betrayed his apparent excitement over the insight. He benefits from the corrected insight about the source of money and transferred it to people in general. Interviewer: "Where do the people get the money from to get on the bus?" Child: "From their home money, they saved it up." After this apparent reference to pocket money, he continued: "They find a work. They find a thing to do and then they get the money." This episode neatly shows a breakaway from the earlier notion that money comes from change, and ushers in the first functional understanding that you get money for work and that the money given to the occupant of a role is used in the service of that role.

An illustration of categories one and two thinking can be provided in another area—the acquisition of a role. Many young children equated wanting to do a job with acquisition of the appropriate role. This is voluntarism taken to an extreme. You want to become a teacher; that is what makes you a teacher. If you want to become a postman, then you are a postman. This type of thinking would correspond to level one where there is no need for explanation. This view implies that for young children the adult world is a harmonious place where everybody does just what they want to do. So we noticed that personal choice is emphasized in starting a job, but at the same time something unexpected happened when several children spontaneously referred to job permanence. This is all the more interesting because we never asked a direct question on this point. Here is an example related to a person's position when off the job:

"Is he still a bus driver when he is at home?"
"Yes, they never give up."
"Never?"
"Once they choose, they have to do it."

Obviously the child misunderstood the question and therefore what he said was all the more noteworthy. This is "conservation" of roles. You are free to choose, but once you have chosen, you'd better stay in it. The child continued:

"Yes, they just go on."
"Until when?"
"Well until the end of their life."
"And the bus?"
"Well perhaps it still rides and somebody else can choose it."

So here you have the successive filling of a job, its free choosing, and the permanence attached to it. Such a system helps the child to understand the social world as stable and what the child observes as happening—namely, the fact that most adults stay in their niche for a long while—is assimilated to a moral imperative: "Once they choose, they have to do it."

On the level of imaginative elaboration there are some children who depict the government or the queen or the law personified as the supreme employment agency. Here is a boy, age 7;7: "The law is in charge of the whole world and he takes care of it." He then continued, "Only the people who want to buy a job or something" come to see him. Gradually, on the level of functional understanding, the children begin to recognize constraints on voluntary choice, job-specific training, and psychological prerequisites. Such an understanding is eloquently indicated in the following interview, which is given in its entirety not only in order to illustrate other areas of the social world mentioned in our inquiry, but also to show how one particular child's social thinking covering many different areas is interrelated. In its strengths and weaknesses it is surprisingly self-consistent.

Emma, a girl age 8;8, has an understanding of social institutions that is well beyond the first two categories of unexplained observation or imaginative elaborations. In many areas she is well beyond the mere beginning of functional interpretations that we have illustrated above as category three. For this reason it may be possible to postulate a fourth category where functional understanding is differentiated and extended beyond the narrow confines of simply relating personal experience. As we shall see, Emma's understanding of role acquisition and of the shop's business in particular is quite advanced. It already implies a system with an embedded social structure that is impersonal. But at the same time, along with this positive advance, notice that her system is still full of holes and contradictions. Emma understands a lot about how to become a doctor; yet basically her personal values and predilection are of paramount importance insofar as her desire to become a doctor colors her entire view of the social world. This personal desire limits the references by which other roles (mother, child, teacher) are evaluated. Similarly, although she seems to understand the basic mechanisms of money exchange between customer, shop, and factory, note that she assiduously avoids the question of how the owner of the shop gets money—she first brings in the local government and the council, then corrects herself on this point; in other words, the difficult concept of profit is not within her repertory. Even more revealing is her ignorance of taxes as the origin of public money. In general, therefore, Emma's interview illustrates what could be tentatively referred to as level four: a differentiated and extended functional understanding that has not yet reached a degree of overall structure and impersonalization that eliminates contradictions. Such an advance in overall logical consistency would characterize a fifth category that was only rarely observed in any of our more than 200 children from age 5 to age 11.

"And you are?"
"Emma."
"Emma. How old are you, Emma?"
"Eight."
"When were you eight?"
"May the 5th."
"Oh, you had a birthday not long ago."

"Yes."

"Emma, what can you tell me that you know about people who you think it's important for us to have because of the jobs they do? What people do jobs that it's important to have?"

"Doctors, dentists, and people who work in the shops, because we wouldn't get our food otherwise."

"Yes."

"And teachers to help us learn things. I can't really think of anything else."

"Perhaps you would like to tell me what you know about one of those. How does somebody decide whether to be a shop-keeper, or a doctor, or a dentist?"

"If somebody wants to be a doctor, when they are at school they sort of, when somebody falls over, rush to it and say—I'll wash it up for you. You wash your leg, and they enjoy doing that mostly and they are very intelligent at their work, and they try to pass the tests for a doctor, and they pass it and are very happy to pass it."

"And that's how you become a doctor?"

"Well, I don't know much about becoming a doctor, but I want to become a doctor—I want to try and become a doctor."

"Do you?"

"Yes."

"What do you know about being a doctor, what else can you tell me about it? What do you need to be able to be a doctor, what things do you need to have?"

"Thermometer. Water in dishes, and a bed to put people on, injection."

"Anybody can become a doctor, can they?"

"No, not anybody. You have to try hard to become a doctor, and work hard."

"Does a doctor wear special clothes?"

"Yes, they wear a white overall."

"Why do you think they wear special clothes?"

"To keep them clean, and so it looks sort of white like doctors are."

"Why do you think it's white?"

"Well, white is clean, and you must keep your leg clean."

"Why do you have to keep clean?"

"Well, you might get poison stuff, and germs."

"Where does the doctor get the thermometer and all the equip-ment he needs from?"

"I don't know. I wouldn't know that."

"Does he have to pay for it? Does somebody give it to him?"

"Does the Council give it to him? Or somebody who sort of runs all the doctors. . .in one place like Lewes, give it to him?"

"You think there's one person, do you, that runs all the doctors?"

"Yes, that runs all the doctors, and they provide all the thermometers and the beds."

"Does anybody pay the doctor for being a doctor?"

"Yes."

"Where does he get his money from?"

"The man—the Council."

"What can you tell me about the Council? What do you know about it?"

"Well, the shops are run by the Council mostly. People buy them, but they sort of get paid by the Council or the shopman who owns the shop."

"He gets paid by the Council?"

"Well, no, they pay the Council for the electricity and everything."

"Well, that's very interesting, you know a lot of things. Can you explain to me a bit more about it? What can you tell me, Emma, about the Council, where do you find it?"

"Well, mostly in a town, in a great big house, or something."

"Yes. In every town, or in one town?"

"Not every town has got a Council, I don't think."

"Has this town?"

"Yes, I think so."

"And is it one person, or a group of people?"

"A group of people."

"And what do they do?"

"I don't really know—I've got no idea really, but just guess things sometimes."

"Yes. You said that the Council pays the shop?"

"No, the Council pays the doctors and dentists, but the people who own the shop, I think, pays the people who sell things to people in it."

"So where does the Council come into it with the shop?"

"He brings the electricity—the man who owns the shop pays the Council for electricity."

"The Council have electricity, do they?"

"No. I think the switchboard, some place."

"How about the electricity that comes into your home, or the school here—do you pay for that? The electricity that comes to your house, for example?"

"Yes, we do."

"You do. Who do you pay?"

"I don't know—I don't hear my mother [talk ?] about the pay."

"Do you have to pay for it?"

"Yes. Because we get loads of bills, saying it's time to pay the electricity, and we send off the money to the person who says it."

"How does the electricity get to your house?"

"Through wires."

"And where do the other end of the wires go? Where do they come from?"

"They come sort of into the switchboard, where there are knobs, and you can turn the switch on to the wires, and the light comes through the wires and comes into your house, I think."

"How about something like the school—do you think the school's always been here?"

"No, it hasn't always been here."

"Who decided that there was going to be one?"

"I don't know."

"What do you think it was like before there was a school, can you tell me?"

"What, what it was like here on this ground?"

"No, what it would be like if there wasn't a school? Can you imagine some places where there aren't any schools?"

"Pakistan, I think, and some places like that."

"What happens—what's it like?"

"Well, they just work in the village. They just don't go to school, they work in the villages, and carry straw to make the houses, and eat food, and work everyday, and go to sleep, and it goes on like that."

"Does it make any difference having a school?"

"Yes it does, because you learn things. You learn to be a doctor or something, what you want to be. If you work hard at school you'll get to be what you really want to be, like a doctor. If you don't work hard and you just sort of laze about and muck around, you'll be just like a shopkeeper, I'd expect, or just stay at home like a mother."

"Do you think mostly people who are mothers, it's because they've mucked around at school, and haven't worked hard?"

"No, not really, they don't want to be a doctor or anything, because they don't fancy seeing all the blood, and that's why they're a mother sometimes, or a shopkeeper."

"You told me how you get to be a doctor and a shopkeeper—how do you get to be a child?"

"What do you mean?'

"Well, you told me how you get to be a doctor—how do you get to be a child?"

"What, an intelligent child, or just. . .?"

"A child."

"Well, you work at school and go home every night or you go to boarding school, or you just muck around, and then you'll be not an intelligent child, or if you just work hard you will be an intelligent child."

"How do you get to be a friend?"

"Well, you're kind to everybody else, and to a new girl at school, and if you've got a new girl at school and she's just looking lonely, I usually go up to her and say—Excuse me, what's your name, would you like to come and play with us?—and take her over to play with us."

"And how do you get to be a mother?"

"Well, when you are at home you look after your sisters, sort of, like if you were a big girl like my sister, she looks after me when my mummy goes out, and she looks after us, and we have a drink and biscuits sometimes, sit and watch television, and if the sun's shining we play out."

"And then she's the mother when she's doing that?"

"Yes, well I think she is. And then sometimes, the next door neighbours, they've got two children, David and a little boy called Dylan, and we take them down to the park and look after them, and push them in a pushchair and take them for walks. That's how I feel you can be a mother."

"Yes, by looking after people. Do you need to do anything or be anything professional to do that?"

"No, not really."

"Anybody can do it?"

"Well, I wouldn't say anybody could do it."

"What sort of person?"

"Somebody who doesn't—sort of be stupid and doesn't take notice of anything, and just mucks around and does silly things, they couldn't be a proper mother, I don't think."

"Talking about the—oh, I know, I was asking you about the school—Emma, who do you think pays for all the things we have in the school? The new things in the school?"

"The Council, I think, or the newsagent, or whatever."

"What do you mean—or the newsagent? What do the newsagents pay for?"

"I don't mean them—just people, I don't know, somebody pays for the things. I think the Council or somebody would."

"Where do you think the Council get the money from?"

"I've no idea—no, I couldn't say that, I don't know."

"Tell me about the shops, Emma, that you know—what happens when you go shopping for your mummy? What do you do?"

"...shopping basket and just walk up the road, and we ask for what we want, or we take a shopping list, if it's for ten or eleven things we take a shopping list. If it's one or two things like a bag of sugar, you say—a bag of sugar please—and we pay for it and we go home."

"Who do you give the money to?"

"The person who's serving in the shop."

"Yes. And what does she do with the money, or what does he do with the money?"

"Put it in the till."

"And does it all stay in the till?"

"No, it goes to the man, and he pays for all the electricity and the things he buys for the shop, and it pays for their wages as well."

"That's a very good answer, very good. Where do all the things come from, for the shop?"

"Factories, for all sorts of things. They make things and just send them there."

"When a shopkeeper goes home, is he still a shopkeeper?"

"Yes, he is."

"How about the teacher, when your teacher goes home?"

"She's still a teacher, because she'll come back the next day and teach."

"And where does she—what does she do when she goes home?"

"Well, she goes home like most of the mums do after work. They just go home and put their feet up, and mark all your work, but mums don't do that—mark all your work and put what you've got to do for the next day—and do all sorts of things, watch television sometimes."

"Where do you think the teacher gets the money from to buy the television and pay the rent?"

"Somebody—I think it's somebody who owns the school."

"There's somebody who owns the school, is there?"

"I don't know, but I just think there's somebody who owns it and all the teachers, all the dinner money went for all the things they buy, and I think sometimes the Council buys some things for it, sometimes the teachers buy something for it, buy something for the classroom or something to make it look a bit gay."

"So who pays the teachers, then?"

"Well, I think all the dinner money goes to the man who owns the school, and he sort of divides it out, and leaves about half of it to go to all the stuff, and the teachers sort of divide it out—well, he divides it out and gives it to them and they keep it for their wages."

"It's just the dinner money, is it?"

"I don't know, I couldn't say."

"How do you think somebody gets to own a school?"

"Well, they pay for all the bricks and everything, and say—could we have it built please—and pay for the building."

"It's an awful lot of money—I wonder where they get all the money from?"

"I think not always just one person does it."

"And how about the headmistress? How do you get to be a headmistress?"

"I couldn't say really, but I'll have a go—I daresay you wouldn't have to be so strict or anything, you just—you work sort of hard at school, or you could just muck around and you won't be an intelligent. . .well actually, you would have to work hard, because you have to mark things and send off bills, things like that."

"So what sort of person becomes a headmistress?"

"Somebody who's sort of middle, like they can write well, and do maths well, not marvelous."

"If you could do maths marvelously what would you become?"

"You could become a doctor, or you could become a headmistress if you wanted to become one, I would think."

"Do you know how you become one? What you have to do to become a headmistress?"

"A teacher?"

"Yes, or headmistress."

"I think I should know that because my mum's going to try and be a teacher, now she doesn't want to. Well, you have to go to sort of, if you wanted to be a teacher you'd have to go to, well, college, you do maths there, and you do English, and when you've learnt to be a teacher and you've passed the tests, then you can be a teacher or whatsoever in the sort of—column of teachers or something like teachers, or something which sort of goes with it, which is the same kind of work, and you'd learn maths there as well as English, because you'd have to write children's sums out, and then when you know and you can become a teacher, you could go to the college and you could ask for the things you needed for your class."

"How do you decide which school you're going to?"

"I think—the class you would like."

"So you'd choose the one that you'd like?"

"Yes, I would."

"And are some more important than others?"

"What, some teachers?"

"Yes."

"Yes, I'd say so."

"How do you become more important?"

"Well, you could work at a boarding school, they're still teachers, but they are very important."

"Why are they very important?"

"I wouldn't say they were important, but they are just a bit higher than the others."

"Are they?"

"Well, I wouldn't—I would—well they work at an importanter school, boarding school, a bit for cleverer children. People in the school are clever, but they're sort of people who are going to pass the tests; you don't have to pass the tests to go to this school."

"That's fine, thank you very much, Emma."

Besides taking the opportunity to interpret Emma's view of social transactions, note her reply to what a community needs. She mentioned four occupations and related them functionally to personal needs. Although the reply contained more occupations and a better awareness of their function in the community than was found at earlier age levels, it certainly does not imply any overall inferences from the general needs of the community to the particular. Her view on a country without schools is revealing: when you have schools, you learn—you learn primarily to be a doctor!—with no school, you just work. The theoretical and socially baneful split between working and thinking is already firmly established in this young child. (One may wonder where she acquired this notion.) In addition, Emma seemed to comprehend well the role/person distinction, at least when an individual is off duty, and she distinguished occupational roles from more personal roles, such as a child, friend, or mother. Her remarks in this personal area indicate perhaps a greater immaturity than in the more impersonal occupational roles. Finally, the clinician will observe strong personalized values in this child, a spirit of competition and hard work that is rewarded.

So far four categories of understanding social institutions have been proposed and a fifth category is implied where a consistent overall political and social system is beginning to be worked out and gross logical inconsistencies—the typical children's errors—are avoided. It has been our experience that category one and two thinking is often found in the same child and probably characterizes a substage that could be called "egotypic," corresponding to preoperatory thinking in the physical sphere. Categories three and four would still be preoperatory, albeit at a somewhat more advanced substage, and could be referred to as "intuitive." Only with category five would something like consistent operations appear, and we could call this stage—corresponding to concrete physical operations—the stage of "consistent" or "systematic" social thinking. Finally, there would be a "formal" stage in understanding social institutions that would require a formal capacity to understand abstract systems. In the final analysis our major social institutions are abstract systems and one could not really expect an adequate understanding of these in children of primary school age.

To illustrate the actual distribution of these levels in the children interviewed, consider Table 1, which is based on 122

Table 1. Description of buying and selling in a shop and shopowner's profit by 122 children (percentages for each age)

Developmental categories	Goods & profit	Percentage for each age (number of children)						
		5(7)	6(28)	7(18)	8(16)	9(24)	10(21)	11(8)
1 and 2[a]	Goods not paid	100	61	22				
3[b]	Goods paid		25	34	56	29	14	
4[c]	Profit ignored		14	44	38	67	62	63
5[d]	Profit described				6	3	24	38

[a] Children describe change as main source of money or goods as free to shop.
[b] Children don't relate their own paying for goods to the shopkeeper's paying.
[c] Children consider shopkeeper's own money as deriving from extraneous source.
[d] Profit of shopowner described and also, with one exception, tax to government mentioned.

children commenting on buying and selling. Some of the comments belonging to categories one and two have been mentioned earlier and are largely characterized by an almost complete lack of understanding about the function of payment. At the more advanced level of category three, the children understood that the payment of the customer is for the goods and that in turn the shopkeeper has to pay for the goods. However, these payments were not coordinated: it was not obvious to these children that the customer's pay is the source of the shopkeeper's money for goods. Nevertheless, this is a beginning of a functional understanding of payment, albeit not really an understanding of buying and selling. It is only in category four that the children, like Emma above, related the money paid by the customers to the money needed to buy the goods for the store. But what these children primarily failed to appreciate is the fact that goods have to be bought for less than for what they are sold. This became particularly clear when the children were asked where the shopowner gets the money for personal use, such as for a car or television. To overcome these conceptual difficulties, children in this category frequently had recourse to an external source that provides the shopowner with money. In Emma's transcript her first spontaneous remark—later corrected—about the council (which is the local government) was that "the shops are run by the council mostly." If that were the case, she wouldn't have to worry about the concept of profit. In contrast, the children in category five clearly expressed the notion of buying for less and selling for more and consequently had no difficulties with the concept of profit.

In summarizing our discussion, seven characteristics of how the social world "out there" may appear to a 5- to 6-year-old child are proposed. It appears: 1) undifferentiated; 2) personalized; 3) rule-dominated; 4) conflict-free; 5) with easy access to money; 6) ego-typical; and 7) focused on external aspects. Undifferentiated refers to the children's lack of awareness of differences in institutional roles and between persons. To the child everything an adult does—apart from the immediate family circle—is probably very much the same. We have stressed the child's tendency to see real persons behind each social event insofar as the event needs any explanation at all. The sufficient reason for any particular event is then simply a personal decision. Somewhat opposite to this extreme voluntarism is a pervasive sense of rules and permanence. The social world is seen as static, a-historical, morally necessary. Together, points 2 and 3 should result in conflict—the conflict between personal decision and impersonal rules. But to the young child these two poles are miraculously harmonized. Adults do what they do because they want to do it and therefore they must. Insofar as money is recognized as needed in social transactions, children would think it is easily available, and just as its use is not related to any particular value, the getting of it is not related to definite preconditions. By egotypical is meant the spontaneous tendency of young children to consider their personal experience as typical of all similar events. Thus the particular teacher of a child becomes this child's notion of what all teachers are, do, and look like. Finally, as Piaget has amply documented, a child's thinking develops from the outer superficial characteristics of an event to its inner relevant mechanism. In this interpretation, for a young child a uniform or a building creates a role: e.g., to become a doctor you only need builders to make the hospital and when you are in it you are a doctor.

Five years later each of these characteristics has radically changed. An 11-year-old child is frequently capable not only of clear differentiation of specific roles and functions but also of recognizing individual differences. Above all, the notion of an "impersonal" role and the difference between a personal and an impersonal attribute (e.g., strictness in a teacher) is observed and understood. Hence, just as there are constraints on personal freedom, there are also constraints on rules. Not everything that happens *must* happen. Historic contingency is accepted and rules are detached from personal whims. A network of subsystems takes the place of the apparently pre-established harmony, and the adolescent becomes capable of relating them without creating unsolvable conflicts. The use of money is set against an overall system of exchanges, and personal experience can be weighed against what is necessary or relevant from what is contingent or superficial in a social context. Finally, social institutions are seen as fulfilling certain functions that make sense within the overall social structure.

How the child changes from the earlier to the later view is, of course, the $64,000 question. The "developmental" experience is the source of growth in understanding, and it is implied that, in spite of obvious differences in content, social thinking develops no differently from the way Piaget has described physical thinking. Hence children do not understand social institutions simply because "they have been told." Too many youngsters have no occasion to have been told and yet appear to be passably intelligent. For example, consider profoundly deaf children, the vast majority of whom grow up with hearing parents apart from what can be called the deaf community and therefore not exposed to the Sign language of this community. On the other hand, their fruitful exposure to the spoken language of society is very limited; even with intensive educational efforts, their knowledge of society's language is quite poor, so that at the age of 11 or 12, corresponding to the oldest age in our sample, they would not be able to comprehend or construct written sentences and paragraphs that could explain social institutions. Hence if they understand anything at all beyond observed events, they must have acquired it by a means other than verbal language.

Unfortunately, the extent of their social understanding is not known. A method of investigation that would not entail a verbal dialogue is difficult to imagine. Perhaps as a consequence of this research with hearing children it will be possible to devise some nonverbal procedures—such as constructing a model of a social scene or playacting—through which some aspects of social understanding could be explored. These procedures would be a necessary requirement for deaf children and also of great benefit for hearing children in that it would supplement the admittedly imperfect procedure of verbal interviews.

From our research with many hundreds of deaf children and adults and hearing persons who relate to them as parents, teachers, or other interested persons, we are aware that deaf children frequently lack knowledge of specific social facts that they do not encounter. It is doubtful that in their general understanding of social events with which they are in personal contact, they are substantially behind their hearing peers: they do not behave like social idiots. They seem to put sense and logical coherence into the social world, so that the question arises as to how they do it.

Deaf children without language acquire social understanding no differently from the way hearing children with language acquire it. However important language may be for personal, social, and emotional communication, and for the transmission of particular information, it is not a suitable mechanism nor even an appropriate occasion for creating understanding in the mind of children. In Piaget's terminology, understanding is the result of an internal feedback—developmental experience—through which the child relates and transforms given input according to psychological schemes that this feedback is constructing. In developmental experience, the child experiences the self as a logical thinker in comparing, relating, interpreting, and explaining observed social events. This goes on in all children, sometimes on a fully conscious level, more often half unconsciously; sometimes during verbal interaction (as in the example of correction cited above), most often unobserved and not fully verbalized. As an example, the children's observation that one pays when one buys things in a shop does not automatically give them knowledge that the money is used by the shop to pay for goods. This insight is an interpretation, the result of relating two states— buying with money and possessing goods—and it is doubtful that this relating ability on the part of the child is the learning and memorizing of what an adult had previously said, if only for the simple reason that adults do not commonly say the things that our children spoke about.

In conclusion, a description of the developing understanding of social thinking in the child appears as a natural extension of Piaget's developmental approach, an extension that is long overdue. The present research program is, of course, only one small part of social thinking; other aspects, more closely related to personal relations, are under active investigation in our research center at Catholic University in Washington as well as in other places. There is a need to integrate various approaches both theoretically and empirically and to describe the process of the developing child as a whole, that is, the child's growing understanding of the physical and biological world, social institutions, personal relations, emotional reactions, moral values, art, music, etc. If this is not a handful of work for a lifetime, one can add the behavioral side of the coin, that is, the child's actual socialization, actions, behaviors, emotions, and moral decisions within the concrete life of the social world.

The practical implications of this research are more manageable and should have immediate relevance to any school activity designed to teach children about the society they live in. As teachers of primary school children, we can probably do no greater service to the children and to the well-being of our society

than to give these children the repeated and continuing experience of being thinkers—what I have called "developmental" experience or, in another context, "high-level thinking" (Furth and
Wachs, 1974)—and to expose the children to the whole gamut of
life areas to which they can apply their thinking. In other words,
an atmosphere of thinking is indispensable for the child's intellectual health, and the child should not—as did the girl in our
interview—make a split between a narrow area of learning to
which thinking is applied and a broad area of work apart from
thinking. As Piaget has cogently stated, thinking at all levels is an
activity or an action: rules of actions, that is, aspects of thinking,
are present in all human behavior. A child who uses his or her
intelligence vis-à-vis an object brings this object under mental
control and feels related to it. Conversely, not thinking about
something means not being concerned with it and not having
control over it. Apply this to social institutions and you see at
once that intelligent concern for society's institutions can have
its most natural and most important origin in the thinking atmosphere of a primary school. And just as Piaget's developmental
theory has made a decisive difference in the planning of school
activities for mathematical and physical knowledge, so it is obvious that an analogous developmental theory of social thinking
would have a similar impact in the much more vital area of social
relations (Furth, Baur, and Smith, 1976).

REFERENCES

Furth, H., Baur, M., and Smith, J. 1976. Children's conception of social
    institutions: A Piagetian framework. Human Development 19:351–
    374.
Furth, H., and Wachs, H. 1974. Thinking Goes to School. New York:
    Oxford University Press.
Piaget, J. 1963. The Child's Conception of the World. Patterson, New
    Jersey: Littlefield Adams and Company.
Pinard, A., and Laurendeau, M. 1962. Causal Thinking in the Child.
    New York: International Universities Press, Inc.

Part IV
Education

chapter 10

The Impact of Piaget on Early Childhood Education

Millie Almy

CURRENT STATUS OF PIAGETIAN THEORY

In considering the contribution that Piaget has made to early childhood education, one is reminded of the 6-year-old girl whose mother, having just been introduced to *The Early Growth of Logic in the Child*, said to her, "Sally, suppose I had four geraniums and six orchids, would I have more geraniums, or more orchids, or more flowers?" The mother was quite pleased when the child responded, "More flowers." Several days later, however, when the mother remarked that the geraniums were dry and in need of water, Sally said, "Oh! I didn't know that *those* are what you call geraniums."

The analogy should not be pushed too far, but it seems that the immediate intuition that the addition of Piagetian theory to early childhood education has resulted in a new and superior kind of education should be tempered. Like the child who did not know what geraniums were, one is dealing with a field (early childhood education) that lacks clear definition, and with a theory that is dynamic, not standing still to be appraised. Furthermore, the evidence on when and how the field and the theory have come together is to be found in a variety of places, many of them not readily accessible to a researcher with limited resources.

Definition of Early Childhood Education

The Encyclopedia of Education defines the age range for early childhood education as from 2-to-3 years to 8 years. From the viewpoint of Piagetian theory this clearly encompasses the preoperational period and the beginning of the transition to operational thinking. Sometimes, however, early childhood education is thought to cease at age 6 and to extend downward to include programs for infants.

Another problem of definition arises from the fact that early childhood education, particularly for children under the age of 6, is so diverse. A majority of 5-year-olds attend public school kindergartens, and an increasing number of 4-year-olds are also in public school. Other children attend play groups or cooperative or parent participation nursery schools; some youngsters are involved in home-based programs where instruction is provided by visiting teachers or parent education workers. An increasing number of children are in programs whose primary purpose is care rather than education. Despite this the program, except for the length of its day, sometimes closely resembles that of a nearby nursery school. And, of course, television brings Sesame Street and The Electric Company to most of these and to many others who have no other exposure to deliberate early education.

Although it is clear that Piagetian theory has had considerable influence on programs for infants, the main focus of this chapter is on programs for 2- to 8-year-olds. It will also deal primarily with what might be called the "mainstream" of early childhood education, those programs that receive public funding. Most of these are in the public schools but some of them, like certain Head Start and other innovative programs, are not. To give less emphasis to cooperative, private, or proprietary schools does not mean that they are less subject to the influence of Piagetian theory, but rather that information about them is, with some exceptions, less accessible.

Piaget's Theory

If the field of early childhood education is difficult to define, the relevant elements of Piaget's theory are no more clearly delineated. This is not only because Piaget's writing (as he himself has been known to admit) is difficult, but also because the theory is dynamic and subject to revision. Piaget, although not altering the basic grand design of the theory that he began to sketch some 50 years ago, has continually explored new problems, made discoveries, modified some of his views and strengthened others. He is, as he has noted, the "chief revisionist" of the theory (Piaget, 1970a). Furthermore, investigators in this country and around the world have conducted research, some of which strongly supports the theory and validates Piaget's findings and some of which calls certain elements into question. To further complicate matters, many of Piaget's American interpreters, particularly those interested in educational applications of the theory, have assimilated his ideas into the essentially behaviorist theories in which they were trained. Thus one finds Piaget described as a maturationist or discussed as a "learning theorist" despite the fact that his basic concern is not with learning, seen as changes in behavior attributable to external stimulation, but rather with the underlying mechanisms of intellectual development (Piaget, 1970a).

One cannot hope to analyze the influence of Piaget's theory on early childhood education without coming to terms with the theory not only as it is set forth by Piaget, but also as it is understood in the field. Before attempting this, it seems appropriate to consider the nature of the evidence that can be used to reveal such influence.

Sources of Evidence   Flavell (1963) notes that Piaget's early studies, conducted in the 1920s and early 1930s, were quickly translated into English, but the rate of translation of his later work was much slower. Accordingly, for some time, the references to Piaget in most child psychology texts, which influence early childhood teachers to some extent, were largely limited to the early studies.[1]

Certainly Flavell's work, providing a comprehensive view of Piaget's theory and his research, had considerable influence on the rising interest in Piaget, especially among psychologists. Books by two other authors, appearing somewhat earlier, may have more directly affected the field of early childhood education. The first of these, *The Process of Education* by Jerome Bruner (1960) called attention to the relevance of Piaget's ideas for curriculum revision and initiated a period of elementary school curriculum reform in which Piaget was often cited. The second, *Intelligence and Experience* by J. McV. Hunt (1961),

---

[1] The widely used *Child Psychology* by Arthur T. Jersild, (Prentice-Hall, New York, 1954, and Englewood Cliffs, N.J., 1960, 1968, 1975) in its 1954 edition, made four references to Piaget, all dealing with the early work. The 1960 edition has nine references, mostly dealing with the early work but including *The Origins of Intelligence* and *The Growth of Logical Thinking*. The 1968 edition has 19 references citing 14 different books and articles. In the 1975 edition the number of citations has grown to 36.

dealt more directly with the early childhood period and influenced the direction that federal programs for young children, initiated in the mid-1960s, took. Although both of these volumes represented some degree of assimilation of Piaget's theory into their authors' intellectual predilections, they stimulated the growing interest in the implications of the theory for education.

One source of evidence of this interest is provided by an examination of the periodical literature listed in the *Education Index* under the topic heading, "Jean Piaget."[2] In the quarter century spanned by the years 1934–1959 one finds 15 articles, eight of which appeared in 1959. In contrast, the next decade provides 62 articles and the proportion of them dealing with applications of the theory increases steadily. In the 1970s the number of articles dealing specifically with application varies from as many as 12 to as few as three.

"Research in Education," the journal of the Educational Resources Information Center (ERIC) system, is a comparable and perhaps superior source of evidence. It includes curriculum guides, speeches, and conference proceedings, as well as research reports that may or may not find their way into publication. A count of the citations from 1968 to 1974 shows an increase from an average of two prior to 1971 to an average of 17 since 1970.

Books about Piaget's theory directed to teachers are more and more available. They vary widely in their readability, their focus on education, and the faithfulness with which they adhere to the theory. Perhaps the ultimate in attempts to write simply and to focus most directly on insights and practical suggestions for teachers is the 60-page *Teacher's Petit Piaget* (Charles, 1974). The author in his introduction confronts the problem of all such volumes when he notes that "because (the ideas) are greatly distilled they cannot, of course, convey the full aura of meanings found in Piaget's original works" (Charles, 1974: *iv*).

Books explicating Piaget's theory are paralleled by the current spate of textbooks dealing with early childhood education. Few, if any, of these fail to give some attention to Piaget. However, the range of sophistication regarding the theory varies widely. Some authors cite only explications of Piaget's work,

---

[2] Della Perreti, seminar paper, School of Education, University of California, Berkeley, March 1973.

others make direct reference to it. Some present several aspects of the theory, others deal with only one or two concepts. These texts are usually eclectic, drawing on other theorists and points of view, and occasionally raising questions regarding certain aspects of Piaget's work. Without any doubt, however, Piaget's ideas have permeated these current textbooks in a way that contrasts strikingly with the relative lack of mention of even his name in such texts a decade ago.

Books and articles may provide less support to the teacher who becomes interested in Piaget than do conferences and workshops. In these, reciprocal exchange with peers may lead to a clearer understanding than is derived from merely reading about the theory. There should be some way to assess the number of such events that have been devoted to Piaget's work. Perhaps the first were the 1964 conferences on cognitive studies and curriculum development held at Cornell University and the University of California, Berkeley, with Piaget as the principal speaker. No doubt Piaget knows how many times he has come to the United States since then to present his views on some feature of the child's development or education. He may also know the number of trips taken by other Genevans to attend single conferences or those that have been held annually since 1970—the meetings of the Jean Piaget Society on the east coast, and those focusing on Piagetian Theory and the Helping Professions on the west coast. Such large conferences may attract individuals who are already somewhat knowledgeable about the theory. Workshops such as those sponsored by the Jean Piaget Society and Glassboro State College and focused on Piagetian applications to curriculum probably have greater direct impact on classroom practice. How many similar workshops have been held across the country? How many in-service courses for early childhood teachers have focused on Piaget? How many college and university courses make substantial reference to his work? Some enterprising historian may some day find a way of answering such questions.

The number of early childhood curricula that have been developed around the ideas of Piaget constitute further evidence of his influence. Such curricula range from those that have been published and implemented with manipulative materials, such as Lavatelli's (1970), through those that have been described in considerable detail in various publications, such as Weikart's

(Weikart et al., 1971) and Kamii's (1972), and on to those that
have been developed for specific school systems or specific research projects. Some of the latter are available through the
ERIC system. Some provide a rationale, or include tasks that
clearly identify their Piagetian origins. Others, although they
may stem from a developer with Piagetian interests, are not so
clearly differentiated from the more traditional curricula.

The best place to gather evidence regarding the extent to
which Piaget's ideas influence the practice of early childhood
education would seem to be the classroom. Because teachers,
particularly at the early childhood level, may relate on a purely
intuitive basis to the activities of the children in ways that are not
incomparable with Piaget's theory, observations of classroom
behavior may be less informative than interviews with the
teachers and the children. The critical factor in distinguishing a
Piagetian from a traditional classroom rests not so much with the
activities of either the children or the teacher as with their understanding of what they are doing.

The limitations of time and resources have not permitted an
adequate presentation of all the sources of evidence of Piaget's
influence. However, from personal experience I can testify to the
fact that their exposure to Piaget has led many teachers to inquire
about the meaningfulness of the activities they are providing the
children. Not all the teachers I meet have reached that level, but
all seem to have some knowledge of Piaget. This is different from
the situation when I first began to talk about Piaget. Then I could
always predict that the first question would be, "How do you
spell Piaget?" To the best of my recollection it is at least five
years since I have heard that question. Now most teachers know
how to spell Piaget and many have some notions about what
putting his theories into action might mean!

A Closer Look at the Theory   The early childhood teacher
who confronts Piaget's theory with trepidation joins company
with many other American educators and psychologists who
have found it difficult to grasp its scope. How can anyone trained
in a single discipline, such as psychology, come easily to understand the theory that has evolved as a biologist, concerned with
"the problem of the relation between the organism and environment," has extended that problem "into the realm of knowledge"
(Piaget, 1952: 245). Using the methods of psychology to answer
epistemological questions, Piaget "attempts to reach knowledge

mechanisms at their source and development" (Piaget, 1971: 21). Furthermore, it is not the knowledge of any one individual that is the focus of his theory, but rather the larger problem of how knowledge is increased. "By what process does a science pass from a specific knowledge, later judged insufficient, to another specific knowledge, later judged superior by the common consciousness of adepts of this discipline?" (Piaget, 1971: 26, 27). This is the kind of question Piaget's genetic epistemology addresses.

Such questions seem remote indeed from the play that has so long been nurtured in the nursery school curriculum, the so-called readiness activities of the kindergarten, and the beginning reading, writing, and arithmetic that typify first grade. Yet as everyone who has read even a little Piaget or a little about Piaget knows, Piaget's observations of children and the clinical interviews he and his staff have conducted with them reveal much that seems pertinent to their classroom experiences. This is true despite the fact that Piaget has not investigated school learning.

Nor, it should be added, has he attempted to formulate a theory of instruction. From those books (Piaget, 1970b; 1973c) and speeches in which he has discussed educational matters, his views on what constitutes good education are clear. There can be no doubt that he places a high premium on those methods that stress the spontaneous activity of the child. On the other hand, he also espouses an "experimental pedagogy," the systematic study of educational methods and programs of instruction. Many of the questions that arise regarding such methods and programs can only be resolved by carefully controlled research.

One observer of the educational scene, noting both that Piaget's theory is difficult to understand and that various interpretations of it have influenced recent curriculum development, has pled for him to make a pronouncement regarding which are the correct interpretations (Gaudia, 1974). Any educator who has struggled to understand Piaget's theory and to derive implications for education may be forgiven the wish for the imprimatur. To ask for it, however, is to overlook Piaget's insistence that the answers to questions about the effectiveness of one method as compared with another are to be sought in pedagogical research.

That Piaget's theory is interpreted in so many different ways is hardly surprising. It illustrates the principle that new information is assimilated into already existing cognitive structures. One tends, if one does not reject the theory completely, to make it fit what one already believes. Moreover, further differences in interpretation appear to depend on the time at which interest in the theory has arisen and on the books that have been read. In the early 1960s, for example, many people say Piaget as a maturationist. They knew about his earliest studies, but little about his later work. Recently educators have begun to ask how intervention or training affects the spontaneous development of concepts. *Learning and the Development of Cognition*, by Inhelder, Sinclair, and Bovet (1974), suggests the direction the Genevan answers to these questions may eventually take. But if the history of the '60s provides any prediction, it is that these new ideas, like the earlier ones, will only gradually be understood.

At the risk of revealing a personal assimilation of Piaget's theory to fit my own intellectual predilections, an outline is presented of the elements of Piaget's theory that seem to be most accessible to early childhood educators, considering them first as they are derived from Piaget, and second as they seem to have been accepted in the field.

1. Knowledge is constructed.
2. Construction is an active process in two senses: the child acts directly on his environment and he is mentally active.
3. Construction is a step-by-step process, marked by three major periods. The first of these, the sensorimotor, lasting until around a year and a half, evolves with the onset of mental representation into a second period of concrete operations and that in turn evolves into the period of formal operations. The subperiod of major concern for early childhood education as defined in this chapter is that of preoperations, marked at its beginning by the formation of semiotic processes enabling the child to make one thing stand for another as in language or mental imagery. At the end of this subperiod the child is moving toward the more systematic, logical thought that is revealed in the ability to conserve and to handle class inclusion and seriation problems. It appears that both the research and the educational literature dealing with the preoperational period have emphasized this latter portion of the subperiod almost to the exclusion of consideration of its beginnings. This is true despite the fact that recent

Genevan studies have revealed the child's prior grasp of qualitative (as opposed to quantitative) identity and of functional dependencies (Piaget, 1973a:712; Sinclair, 1973).

4. "The affective, social and cognitive aspects of behavior are in fact inseparable" (Piaget and Inhelder, 1969). "Affect serves as a source of energy on which depends the functioning of intellect, but not its structure, just as the functioning of an automobile depends on gas, but the action of the engine does not change its structure" (Piaget, 1954).

5. Language is not the source of thought. Rather, its development stems from the formation of the semiotic processes. Verbal expression may mask as well as reveal the nature of the child's thought.

6. All areas of the developing child's knowledge are linked and have their roots in the sensorimotor period. Nevertheless, different kinds of knowledge can be distinguished and are derived from different sources. In developing physical knowledge the child abstracts properties directly from the objects he explores. In developing logico-mathematical knowledge the child abstracts characteristics from the coordination of his own actions on objects. As knowledge of this kind is constructed, it appears to permeate other areas so that not only cognitive but "playful, affective, social and moral reactions (are bound) into a whole" (Piaget and Inhelder, 1969: 128). A further distinction can be made between knowing that is "figurative" and knowing that is "operative." The former focuses on the static aspects of a given situation whereas the latter is concerned with transformations (Piaget, 1969).

7. Piaget and his collaborators have traced the sequence of the areas of content. Although the recent interest of early childhood educators seems to have focused mainly on mathematics and logic, other studies deal with the physical world and the child's conceptions of objects, space, time, and causality. Early studies dealt with the child's conception of the social world as revealed in his moral judgments, and with his understanding of language as revealed in his conversation, his explanations, and his questions. Piaget has also studied the development of representation through his observations of children's imitation and play. With few exceptions these studies have been cross-sectional rather than longitudinal.

They have shown comparable sequences of development in the various content areas. In general, longitudinal and cross-cultural studies have confirmed these sequences.

8. Four factors, three of them traditionally used to explain development and a fourth that Piaget regards as essential to the coordination of the first three, account for the transitions the child makes from one stage in the sequence to the next. The first factor is maturation. The second is experience of the physical environment. This consists of simple exercise in which action may be exerted on objects without any necessary extraction of knowledge, physical experience in which information is abstracted from the objects, and logico-mathematical experience in which the child abstracts relations from his own actions. The third factor is the influence of the social environment. Here Piaget suggests that the child's active collaboration with his peers, as well as his cooperation with adults, needs consideration. The fourth and most critical factor is equilibration, the self-regulating and self-correcting process of adaptation whereby the individual assimilates new information into existing cognitive structures or accommodates those structures in ways that modify them. It is the child's own activity, intrinsically motivated, that determines the transitions the child makes from one level of thought to another.

In addition to his theory, Piaget has provided a method for the investigation of children's thinking. Over the years he and his colleagues have designed a large number of tasks, or experiments, to elicit the child's thinking in a number of areas. The clinical interview, now known as the "method of critical exploration" (Inhelder, Sinclair, and Bovet, 1974), gives the interviewer who has a thorough theoretical background and mastery of the interviewing technique considerable latitude to formulate hypotheses about the cognitive implications of the child's responses and to devise ways of checking these within the interview situation.

This brief sketch of the tenets of Piaget's theory and some of the methods he has used takes no account of either the research that provides a bulwark for the theory, nor that which extends it or calls it into question. It does provide sufficient framework to discuss the ways that the theory, and the methods, appear to have influenced curriculum and instruction at the early childhood level.

RETROSPECTIVE ANALYSIS

Any attempt to analyze the impact of a particular theory on educational practice raises a number of questions regarding the ways that theory does contribute to practice. It also calls for some separation of the theory from the theorist (Ammon, 1974). In the present instance Piaget has not chosen to identify any particular program as a true application of his theory. On the other hand, he has not hesitated to make observations on the educational scene, nor to indicate his preference for some methods of instruction as compared to others. Despite this it appears that a stronger test of the impact of his theory comes when we look for evidence of the elements of his theory that have been influential, rather than looking for those methods he appears to like.

Despite the fact that the last decade or so has given considerable attention to curricula for early childhood education based on a specific educational philosophy, there are few guides for evaluating the extent to which a particular program exemplifies a particular philosophy. It appears, however, that there are three different ways in which a program may be influenced by a given theory.

The first way might well be termed an "opportunistic justification." For example, the sponsors of or the teachers in a program that has always provided a generous amount of time for spontaneous play, on discovering that play, as assimilation, has a specific place in Piaget's theory, may announce that their program is based on theory. Judging from the variety of kinds of programs I have observed for which Piaget is cited as authority, a considerable amount of such opportunistic justification can be found.[3]

A second way of using theory is more deliberate, and may be termed "using theory to inform practice." Here the choice of theory is more deliberate and it involves more reflection. It ap-

---

[3] Educators may be prone to use of this kind of justification. A colleague, trained in the physical sciences, who has also worked with educators, has noted that scientists, challenged about an idea or a procedure, cite theory or research; teachers cite an authority.

pears that this is the way the theory of Piaget has been called on in the modern British Infant School. Brearley and Hitchfield (1966) note, for example, "Each teacher learns, through daily observation of children at work, those laws of child development which adults must heed if they are to educate well . . . . Piaget helps us to see the developmental significance of a child's successes and failures in thought and action during everyday experience by breaking down each activity into separate mental components" (pp. *x, xi*). They draw on Piaget not to justify the fact that the teachers do observe, but rather to make their observations more meaningful.

A third way of using theory differs radically from the first two. Here the attempt appears to be to make practice conform to or exemplify the theory. In the case of Piaget's theory, which is epistemological, not pedagogical, this use demands its translation into pedagogy, prior to its use in the curriculum. Few, with the exception of Constance Kamii, have had the stamina and persistence to tackle this. Accordingly we should not be surprised to find relatively few programs that are consistently Piagetian.[4]

It seems reasonable to hypothesize that the elements of Piaget's theory that are most congruent with traditional practices and beliefs in early childhood education will have wider and earlier acceptance than those that are more novel. Thus the concepts of stages or sequence together with the emphasis on activity may be expected to have more impact than the equilibration factor. The early childhood education textbooks confirm this ex-

---

[4] Whether such programs would be educationally viable, were they to be found, is debatable. John Dewey, in *The Sources of a Science of Education* (New York: Horace Liveright, 1929), cautions, "It may conduce to immediate ease or momentary efficiency to seek an answer for questions outside of education, in some material which already has a scientific prestige. But such seeking is an abdication, a surrender. . . It arrests growth; it prevents the thinking that is the final source of all progress. Education . . . is an activity which includes science within itself. In its very process it sets more problems to be further studied, which then react into the educational process, to change it still further, and thus demand more thought, more science, and so on, in everlasting sequence" (p. 77). In a similar vein, Joseph J. Schwab, in *The Practical: A Language for Curriculum* (Washington, D. C.: National Education Association, 1970), comments that the "field of curriculum is moribund" and has "reached this state by inveterate, unexamined and mistaken reliance on theory," including "borrowed theories as principles from which to deduce aims and procedures" (p. 2). Neither Dewey nor Schwab denies the usefulness of theory but rather they insist that it take its place alongside the "arts of the practical." (Schwab, 1970: 27)

pectation. If they deal with Piaget, they tend to discuss the stages and to make some mention of the activity of the child. Other features of the theory receive less or no attention.

The Stages

The idea that development proceeds through a series of stages, each with its characteristic challenges and accomplishments, has been well supported in American educational thinking, despite the fact that certain psychologists have questioned the utility of the concept (Kessen, 1962). Rooted in the work of G. Stanley Hall, set forth as age profiles by Gesell, and implicit in psychoanalytic theory, the concept of "developmental tasks" was popularized for educators by Havighurst (1949). Erikson (1950), whose work contributed directly to the developmental task concept, also has had considerable direct influence on the thinking of early childhood teachers, particularly at the nursery school level.

To teachers oriented to developmental tasks, the sequences in Piaget's theory could be seen as a further refinement of something with which they were already familiar. This is not to say Piaget's stages are equivalent to those of Erikson. Indeed, the special subtleties of Piaget's stages were surely not grasped initially. The idea that the cognitive structures available to the child change as development proceeds so that thinking differs qualitatively from one stage to the next was difficult for most teachers to understand.

Recalling early discussions of Piaget's theory with teachers who taught children at the different grade levels from kindergarten through third grade, it was clear that some teachers intuitively grasped the idea of the shift in available structures that occurs around the second grade. They talked about the fact that before then the teacher, if she wants the children to carry out certain procedures in an orderly fashion, must take them through each, one step at a time. Older children are better able to grasp what is intended, hold it in their minds, and proceed accordingly. They also discussed the ways that changing the formulation of a task could confuse a child whose performance had previously been adequate. In reflecting on the examples they gave, it appears that they were beginning to explore the differences between figurative and operative knowing, and the significance of programs where the child receives maximal cues regarding correct responses, seldom needing to deal with transformations.

On the other hand, the teachers of younger children, who had had experience with a narrower age range, were somewhat less willing to come to terms with the meaning of the child's thought. They resented the negative aspects (lack of reversibility and conservation) that Piaget attributed to the preoperational period. They often reported examples of confusion in the children's thinking, but appeared to think of them as amusing instances of the child's lack of experience, not as evidence of the nature of the child's information-processing structures. The associationist psychology they knew best reinforced the conviction that the way to reduce the child's confusion must be to instruct him differently. A kindergarten teacher who was enrolled in a developmental psychology class in which the students were required to conduct some Piagetian interviews with children provides an extreme example of this point of view. She reported tearfully that she could not complete the assigned interviews because she could not bear to find out what the children did not know. She seemed to feel that she had not taught them properly.

It is not surprising that many teachers felt Piaget's theory necessitated giving young children more information. Certainly Piaget's theory of stages was cited in justifications given for many of the mathematics and science curricula that were developed and promoted from the end of the 1950s. However, the significance of the stages was treated differently in different curricula. Some accepted the inevitability of the preoperational predelictions of the kindergartener and even the first grader, while others were more concerned with structuring the lessons to facilitate the transition to operational thought. Whatever the stance of the curriculum, conservation was presented as the index of the transition and classification and seriation were seen as its forerunners. Since 1960, exercises involving sorting and ordering, then occupying a very small place in the curriculum, have increased steadily not only in first grade and kindergarten but in programs for younger children as well.[5]

Programs that emphasize what may be termed the vertical dimension of the stages, represented in the transition from preoperations to operations, sometimes do so at the expense of the horizontal dimension, represented in the breadth of the child's

---

[5] These statements are based on analyses made for our study, *Logical Thinking in Second Grade* (New York: Teachers College Press, 1970).

experience (Bussis and Chittenden, 1973). A full understanding of the active way knowledge is constructed implies a wide range of experience that draws on the child's ability to invent and test his own systems of grouping and ordering, his own explanations of the phenomena he encounters. Such experience may include dealing with the categories of color, size, and shape that are used so exhaustively in textbooks and workbooks but must also, if Piaget's theory is truly represented, include problems that are based in a reality that is more earthy and less schoolish.

Activity

Many educators interpret Piaget's emphasis on activity in the construction of knowledge to mean that the child must manipulate his environment. As far as it goes, this is a correct interpretation. It is also an interpretation that has influenced early childhood curricula at least as much as the concept of stages, perhaps more so. As in the case of the stages, the earlier theorists to some extent paved the way for its acceptance. To many educators, Jean Piaget, in this regard, has simply picked up where John Dewey left off. Beginning with activities that were similar to those engaged in in the home, the child in the Dewey school moved through an ordered progression that led by the age of 12 or 13 to projects in one or another of the academic disciplines (Cremin, 1961: 135–142). As Cremin points out, not all of those who saw themselves as Dewey's disciples understood that the teacher's thorough acquaintance with organized knowledge as represented in the disciplines combined with his or her awareness of the common experiences of childhood to make the activity curriculum effective. Thus, by the end of the 1950s the vestiges of activity that were the legacy of Dewey and progressive education had, in many instances, at the kindergarten-primary levels, lost their intellectual vitality. In the nursery school the curriculum still provided generously for activity, but often with little consideration for its cognitive implications.

To some extent, and perhaps largely by way of the modern British Infant School where the influence of Dewey came later and the influence of Piaget earlier than here, Piaget's theory has restored activity to its rightful place in the early childhood curriculum. Although the "look and say" program has by no means disappeared from the kindergarten and first grade, there seems to be little question that more and more youngsters have opportunities in school to observe, to explore, to experiment, to try out for themselves, to "mess about," as well as to watch the teacher, mark x's in boxes, and color within the lines.

One can only hope that the purpose of activity and its function in the intellectual development of the children will be better understood by the disciples of Piaget than it was by the disciples of Dewey. Piaget himself has questioned how thoroughly educators understand the role of actions in the development of children's intelligence and knowledge when they believe that the "mere fact of perceiving the objects and their transformations will be equivalent to direct action of the learner in the experience" (Piaget, 1973b). "Action," he adds, "is only constructive when it involves the spontaneous participation of the child himself with all the tentative groupings and apparent waste of time that such involvement implies." Furthermore, "it is absolutely necessary . . . that they form their own hypotheses and verify them (or not verify them) themselves through their own active manipulations."

"Messing about" eventually contributes to intellectual development to the extent that it is represented mentally. The importance of mental activity is highlighted by Inhelder, Sinclair, and Bovet when they write, "Being cognitively active does not mean that the child merely manipulates a given type of material; he can be mentally active without physical manipulation, just as he can be mentally passive while actually manipulating objects" (1974: 25).

Understanding of the relationship of physical activity to mental activity in Piaget's theory may be clarified by the distinction he makes between simple abstraction, in which the child abstracts a specific bit of information from an object, and reflective abstraction, in which he derives information not from the object itself but from the coordination of the mental actions he performs on the object. This is a distinction, however, that is rarely made in the early childhood education textbook descriptions of the theory (Hess and Croft, 1975).

When a curriculum provides a wide range of activities for the children, and encourages mental as well as physical engagement with materials, it is likely that it has been subject to the influence of Piaget. The heart of Piaget's theory, however, lies not in the elements so far discussed, the stages and activity, but in its dynamics, the factors involved in the transitions from one level of development to the next.

Factors in the Transitions

Of the four transition factors, the crucial factor, and the one that has given American psychologists and educators the most trouble, is equilibration, It is, however, the one that Piaget regards as pedagogically fundamental. The other three factors, maturation, experience of the environment, and action of the social environment, are coordinated by the fourth or self-regulatory factor, equilibration. The first three Piaget regards as the classical factors involved in development. From his view they are necessary factors but not sufficient. They are also factors that early childhood educators have customarily considered in planning programs.

The age of the children, taken as a rough index of their maturation, influences the planner's expectations as to what the children can or cannot do. Normative studies of young children, previously called on to provide a scientific base for such expectations, began to be questioned in the 1960s as certain psychologists proposed that with proper programming even very young children could learn in ways not previously believed possible. Despite this optimism, most would concede that planning for a 2-year-old differs from planning for a 4- or a 6-year-old, even if for no other reason than the obvious differences in the behavior of the children.

Particularly in planning for children under the age of 6, early childhood education has traditionally emphasized the importance of physical experience. The environments of both the classroom and the play yard attested to the teacher's conviction that the children need many opportunities to manipulate and explore. As the distinctions between physical knowledge and logico-mathematical knowledge are better understood, this conviction takes on new significance.

When it comes to the nature of the child's social experience, as it is planned by the early childhood educator, Piaget's theory provides justification of traditional practice and suggests new possibilities. Children influence their own intellectual development as their collaboration in mutual projects causes them to decenter and to become better able to take the viewpoint of the other. Piaget's work on moral judgment and his discussions on education also support the importance of a relationship between the teacher and the child that is based on "mutual respect" and the building of attitudes of reciprocity between them (Piaget, 1973c: 121).

The fourth and comprehensive factor, equilibration, is now being examined in the child psychology texts available to early childhood education students but appears in almost none of the early childhood education textbooks. Part of the reason for neglect of this essential feature of Piaget's theory undoubtedly relates to a failure to understand the distinctions that Piaget makes between learning in the narrow sense and learning in the broad sense. The nature and extent of the former, derived from something in the environment to which the child accommodates, is dependent on the latter. Learning in the broad sense results from equilibration, and includes not only accommodation but also the assimilative activity by which the child incorporates new information into old structures. Learning in this broad sense is practically identical with development. Thus, "the processes of development can explain certain aspects of learning while the laws of learning cannot explain all of development (Piaget, 1969: 238).

Development takes time. The child spends a major portion of his preschool years in play, a primarily assimilative activity. Only after he has constructed and tested many action schemes, practical concepts, and practical judgments does he begin to reflect on them and to consider their consistency.

Considering that the distinctions Piaget makes are not congruent with the typical American approach to learning, the lack of any extensive treatment of equilibration in the early childhood education literature should come as no surprise. However, it is interesting to note that in certain respects the traditions of early childhood education, particularly those that are connected with the development of the nursery school, encompassed a notion of self-regulation that is not incompatible with Piaget's equilibration.

Despite a readiness on the part of early childhood educators to allocate at least part of the educative process to the child's self-regulating tendencies, the equilibration facet of Piaget's theory seems to have been less well assimilated than other aspects. The explanation of this may not rest only in the epistemological predilections of American psychologists, although those clearly have had their effect. Two other related factors need consideration. One is that as those psychologists discov-

ered early childhood education and began mapping out programs for the children of the poor, they gave early childhood education new status. The theory they articulated was not the theory
the teachers had intuited, a fact that many of the teachers recognized. Nevertheless they found themselves caught up in a
movement that saw preschool education expand from a largely
private enterprise into what promised to be an integral part of
public education. Whether or not a teacher agreed with all the
tenets of the curriculum developers, it was exciting to be part of
the movement for innovation. Piaget's theory gave impetus to the
movement, but most programs were designed to program the
child's learning in the narrow, not the broad, sense.

A second factor may also have led to the neglect of the traditional concept of self-regulation. The field rapidly absorbed
many individuals with varying backgrounds. In the long run this
influx may have strengthened early childhood education, making
it more self-conscious about its theory. In the short run, however,
its effect seems to have been to negate some of the intuitive
wisdom developed in the preceding 50 years.

Apart from the external factors that influenced, or failed to
influence, the incorporation of the principle of equilibration into
the theory and practice of early childhood education, the principle does not lend itself easily to such incorporation. The principle is, from the viewpoint of the child, a "do-it-yourself" process.
Considering his own life history, he may at any given time need
much or little physical experience or confrontation with his peers
or questioning by his teachers in order to accommodate his existing cognitive structures to a new idea, and the way he assimilates
that idea is always a matter of what he already knows or believes.
In commenting on the educational implications of his theory,
Piaget does not suggest that because it is the child who is ultimately in control of his own cognitive development the teacher
is thereby freed from responsibility. Indeed, in reflecting on his
visit to Susan Isaacs' nursery school (a school that had considerable influence on the thinking of nursery educators in this country
and also on the development of the modern British Infant
School), Piaget remarks that "some form of systematization
applied by the adult would perhaps not have been wholly harmful to the pupils (Piaget, 1970b: 169). He also notes the "necessity for a rational, deductive activity to give a meaning to (the
child's) scientific experiment, and the necessity also, in order to

establish such a reasoning activity in the child, for a surrounding social structure entailing not merely cooperation among the children but also cooperation with adults."

Perhaps 30 years later Piaget writes, "In the realm of education, this equilibration through self-regulation means that school children and students should be allowed a *maximum* of activity of their own, directed by materials which permit their activities to be cognitively useful. In the area of logico-mathematical structures, children have real understanding only of that which they invent themselves, and each time that we try to teach them something too quickly, we keep them from reinventing it themselves" (Piaget, 1966:*vi*).

Although the direction of Piaget's comments on education seems clear, equilibration theory has little that is specific to say directly to teachers. Much more must be done to unravel the relationships between development and learning, as current researchers trained at Geneva (Pascual-Leone, 1970; Inhelder, Sinclair, and Bovet, 1974) and elsewhere (Olson, 1970; Case, 1974) realize. We need not only the results of studies in the laboratory, but also studies by those who are using Piagetian theory to inform practice and from those who are attempting to derive a pedagogy from it. We need, as Piaget observed regarding Susan Isaacs' nursery school, follow-up studies that pursue children taught according to the theory and other children "until the end of (their) secondary studies" (Piaget, 1970b). Only then will the teacher have a firm base for including some activities and not others in the curriculum, and perhaps more important, for intervening when the child gives certain clues regarding the nature of his thinking, and not intervening at other times.

Affect and Cognition

The interdependence of cognition and affect, a concept that, like equilibration, is rooted in biology, is less difficult to comprehend. Teachers who have given children the opportunity to be both physically and mentally active have seen evidence of the children's satisfaction and of their motivation to carry a project forward. They can understand the role of intrinsic motivation in intellectual development. However, there are teachers who, in the tradition of the nursery school, have developed a special sensitivity to the individuality of children, their concerns, their fears and fantasies, their unique ways of expressing themselves.

They do not find that Piaget's theory, except perhaps as set forth in *Play, Dreams and Imitation,* serves to illuminate the emotional life of the children they know. The theory, in fact, does not deal with the individual child, but with what might be termed the "common child." The child's development of logico-mathematical knowledge, based on species-common experience, is its principal concern (Furth, 1974).

The individual child who has reached a particular stage of development according to that projected by Piaget for the "common child" is likely to filter his experience in ways that are different from those of a child at older or younger levels. His emotional life is, to some extent, determined by the cognitive structures he has available. The educational significance of these relationships between cognition and affect has not been widely explored.[6] Accordingly, it does not seem surprising that so many attempts at Piaget-based curricula have drawn on other theoretical formulations to explicate the children's emotional development.[7]

The Role of Language in Thought

For the American psychologist and educator, language and thought are traditionally as inseparable and complementary as affect and cognition are for Piaget. For Piaget, thought takes precedence over language.

Piaget regards language as insufficient for the development of operational thought. Such thought is rooted in the child's actions. The child may repeat an answer that he has been given but probing may reveal that he really does not understand what he has said. The Genevans, as Sinclair indicates, do not deny that "language permits rapid coding and an efficient storing and retrieval of data" (Inhelder, Sinclair, and Bovet, 1974: 115), but they do not believe that verbal training necessarily leads to understanding. "On the contrary, it appears that it is the formation of the thought operation that leads to the use of appropriate terms" (1974: 270). In the case of conservation, "verbal training

---

[6] The books that have made such explorations and that teachers find useful are: Selma Fraiberg, *The Magic Years* (New York: Scribner and Sons, 1959), and David Elkind, *Children and Adolescents* (New York: Oxford University Press, 1970).

[7] Erik Erikson is frequently called on in this connection.

helps some children who have already acquired conservation but are unable to justify their answers to give clear explanations during the post-test" (1974: 115).

The obvious receptivity of the young child to language and an instructional tradition that relies mainly on verbal methods share responsibility for American opposition to the Genevan conclusions. Nevertheless, Piagetian theory in this regard has had considerable impact on practice.

Piagetian experiments are designed to reveal whatever lies beyond the child's verbal responses. The method of critical exploration confronts him with any contradictions between what he says and what he observes or what he does. It requires him to argue for his own view in different but related contexts.

Although there is no evidence that this method of inquiry abounds in early childhood education classrooms, there is reason to believe that some teachers have changed their questioning strategies as they have developed some familiarity with Piagetian theory and methods. They are more inclined to pose questions that enable them to see where the child is in his thinking before they start to provide instruction. They are less prone to using questions that provide the clue to the expected response.

The Role of the Teacher

Teaching involves more than the questioning strategies the teacher uses. At the preschool level, Kamii describes the teacher's function. It is "to help the child construct his own knowledge directly from feedback from objects and through his own reasoning with objects" (Kamii, 1972: 117). The teacher encourages the child's reasoning from his (the child's) point of view. Obviously, to do this the teacher needs to have a good grasp of Piaget's theory.

In some programs, particularly at the kindergarten and first grade levels, the teacher's role has expanded to include assessment of the children using a variety of Piagetian tasks. The assumption is that, guided by the results, the teacher will provide more appropriately individualized instruction. Again, the need for understanding the theory seems obvious.

The idea that Piagetian assessment might become an integral part of the early childhood curriculum has enticed many students of Piaget. However, those who understand the complexities of the classroom as well as the nature of the children's cognitive development question whether such continuous assessment with Piagetian tasks is either necessary or practical. Longitudinal data both highlight the length of time that is involved in moving from one level to another and reflect the individuality of the children's interests (Almy et al., 1970). The assessment tasks provide a rough index to the level of the child's thinking but offer little help regarding breadth of his knowledge at that level, or the nature of his motivation. These must be derived from observation of his activities.

Administering a battery of Piagetian assessment tasks may give the teacher some insights into the nature of child development and learning. It seems preferable, however, for her to have such knowledge in her head, as part of the frame of reference from which her teaching evolves, so that she can see the child as a being who is at once cognitive, affective, and social. She should be able to respond to him, to ask a question or refrain from asking it, to suggest a new approach or to encourage the one he is using, or to say nothing, in the light of her understanding of both his general cognitive level and where he is that day.

This is clearly a large order, one that imposes a heavy and unaccustomed burden on both teachers and teacher educators. How difficult it may be to fill is suggested by Robison, Jagoda, and Blotner (1974). They compared the performance of student teachers who received either competency-based or traditional instruction for teaching preschool children in either a Skinnerian or a Piagetian mode. They report that the Piagetian mode seems instrinsically more difficult for the student teachers to master.

There are, however, a few studies that show that the more individualized, flexible, and open teaching strategies associated with Piagetian theory can be mastered, and that show outcomes that differ from the more directive traditional strategies. They underscore the importance of the teacher, as contrasted with the particular curriculum. Weikart, following a study of the effects of three different preschool curricula, noted that in terms of the usual measures of effect, the crucial factor was not the curriculum content, but rather the support the teachers received (Weikart, 1972). Soar and Soar, in their study of Follow Through programs, reported that "higher amounts of teacher direction, control and narrow subject-matter focus have a destructive effect on complex-abstract growth" (Soar and Soar, 1972: 250). Stallings (1975), in an analysis contrasting classroom observations made in different Follow Through programs, found significant differences between models that emphasized drill, practice, and praise and those that were more open and flexible. The latter models have been, in varying degrees, influenced by the theory of Piaget. In these the children scored higher on nonverbal problem-solving tests of reasoning and had lower absence rates. Their scores on standardized reading and mathematics achievement tests were, however, lower.

Stallings' findings are interesting, not only because they show so clearly that what the teacher does, that is, what goes on in classrooms, does make a difference to the children's learning, and presumably to their development as well. At the same time they pose a variety of questions related to the content of the curriculum, and whether it is to be directed to academic achievement or to intellectual development or to development broadly conceived.

Curriculum Content

Piaget's theory and research have contributed to the content of the curriculum for early childhood education in at least two ways. Some programs have drawn on his experimental tasks for activities for the children. Others have tried to apply his theory to the teaching of a particular subject.

Many of the curricula that were planned for poor preschool and kindergarten children in the 1960s reflect Piaget's studies of number and the early growth of logic, and perhaps to a lesser extent his studies of space and time, and the earlier studies of the child's conception of the world. Classification, seriation, and one-to-one correspondence are common features.

Some curriculum developers, notably Kamii, eventually came to question the curriculum organized around Piagetian tasks. As she involved herself more and more deeply in Piagetian theory, Kamii moved from a curriculum organized around classification, seriation, numerical reasoning, and spatial reasoning to one in which the content is derived from three sources: daily living, the child-development (so-called "traditional") nursery school curriculum with more emphasis on physical knowledge, and group games plus a few Piaget-inspired tasks that are to be used with individuals or small groups (Kamii and deVries, 1977).

Piagetian research has contributed most directly to mathematics and science curricula. More articles have been written on the application of the theory to mathematics than to any other area, with science next in line. The effects of such application are not clear. Initially Piaget was cited at least to justify an earlier and more systematic approach to these areas. Some think that the new programs brought with them too much formalism and too rapid a pace. They also cite Piaget, suggesting that more account needs to be taken of the ways children construct new knowledge. A recent article in a popular teacher's magazine implies that there may be considerable tension in this regard (Glennon, 1974). The author calls attention to the "too heavy input of mathematicians to the comparative neglect of elementary school personnel and cognitive-developmental psychologists." He decries learning that is so difficult that most children are unable to master it. Nevertheless he also cautions against misunderstanding of Piaget's work that may lead to deferring or postponing topics in mathematics until the child has "genetically arrived at a certain stage of logical thinking."

The volume of Piagetian research devoted to the concepts underlying mathematics and science is much greater than that devoted to the concepts underlying other curriculum areas. However, the theory implies that the developing logical structures become more and more pervasive, and more widely applicable. Moreover, research dealing with moral judgment and social relations was translated prior to the bulk of the research in the mathematics and science areas. Accordingly, one might expect that the theory would have a major influence on other areas of the curriculum, particularly social studies. Examination of early childhood programs developed during the 1960s does not support the expectation.

The situation with regard to music and art is somewhat similar. Piaget's research has, of course, not touched either area directly, although certain inferences, particularly with regard to art, may be drawn from both the theory and the experiments. Despite the lack of experimentation, the periodical literature reveals more applications of the theory to music than to art.

In this connection, Elkind, Hetzel, and Coe (1974) provide a perceptive analysis of the role of aesthetics in the education of the young child. Noting that a distinctive feature of good practice in modern British primary schools is the recognition of the child's fundamental aesthetic propensities, they show how such practice accords with Piagetian theory. Piagetian theory distinguishes between representations that are acquired by imitation or copying on the part of the child, and the knowledge that is acquired by rational processes. An aesthetic judgment may be seen as a judgment of the adequacy or appropriateness of the relationship between knowledge and its representation. Such judgments have personal, social, and developmental dimensions. Elkind, Hetzel, and Coe (1974) suggest that such aesthetic judgments are necessitated by the principle of equilibration. "As the child matures intellectually, he must not only reconstruct reality but also the relations between his knowledge and his means for representing them. . . . The motivation for this reconstruction of meanings is aesthetic judgment."

This extension of Piagetian theory is particularly interesting because it deals with an area that has been largely neglected in most of the early childhood curricula purporting to be derived from Piagetian theory. This is not to say that music, art, and dramatics have not been included. Rather, they have either been accepted as traditional aspects of the curriculum or they have been analyzed from an exclusively cognitive view.

The area of curriculum content that, at least for kindergarten, first, and second grades, and increasingly for the preschool, receives the most attention from educators and the most concern from parents is that involved in teaching the child to read.[8] This is an area in which Piaget has specifically cautioned against extrapolations from psychological theory. "The best way of learning to read," he asserts, "is a question for experimental pedagogy to decide." "Only a patient, methodical research program using comparable groups of subjects for equally comparable periods of time, while taking care to neutralize as far as possible any adventitious factors (quality of the teachers and their preferences for one or other method, etc.) can permit a solution of the question; and there can be no question of seeking for a solution by means of deductive considerations provided by psychology, however experimental in origin itself . . ." (Piaget, 1970b: 21).

The fact that a number of studies (for example, Dimitrovsky and Almy, 1975) have revealed positive correlations between children's performance in certain Piagetian tasks and their performance on tests of early reading ability has led to an increasing interest in the applications of Piaget theory to beginning reading instruction.

---

[8] I am indebted to Barbara Foorman, University of California, Berkeley, for the review of this literature.

Those who find or read about positive correlations between concrete operational activities and reading achievement sometimes leap from correlation to causality. A number of authors prescribe programs without regard for Piaget's caveat against extrapolations unsupported by methodical research programs. With the exception of Elkind (1969), who has found that perceptual training facilitates learning to read, the research is limited.

Two kinds of studies are clearly needed before the implications of Piagetian theory for beginning reading instruction can be appropriately exploited. Most important are studies in which Piagetian theory is used as a structural backdrop for the building of a developmental model of the reading acquisition process. Also useful would be studies in which the reading acquisition and eventual reading achievement of children who have participated in Piagetian preschools are compared with those of children lacking such experience. Such studies have been anticipated by some of the evaluation studies of Head Start and Follow Through, but one would hope for a finer grained analysis of reading achievement than is possible with presently available reading tests.

Summary

In this retrospective analysis the impact of a dynamic theory on a field that is changing and poorly defined is analyzed. Although the theory is epistemological, not pedagogical, there is little question that it has had a major influence on early childhood education. It was suggested that the impact of the theory has been largely a matter of the assimilation of certain of its elements and that the rate of assimilation has depended on the extent to which the prior experience of early childhood educators has created a readiness for its ideas. At the same time, there exist many areas where more research regarding development and learning and instruction is needed.

LOOKING TO THE FUTURE

Piaget conceived the grand design of his epistemological theory some 50 years ago and has spent the intervening years filling in and transforming it. He continues both to elaborate it and to see new possibilities for its application and its modification (Piaget, 1973a). Considering his forward-looking orientation, one hesitates to conclude an analysis of the impact of his theory without some consideration of the future.

The extent to which Piaget's theory will continue to inspire and to transform early childhood education depends on three interconnected factors: the bureaucratization of early childhood education, the role assigned the teacher, and the collaboration of parents.

The more we strive for schools that promote thinking the more strongly we have to contend with those forces for bureaucratization that are inclined to treat education as the filling of so many boxes on an assembly line. As public schooling moves downward, early childhood education, unless it can mobilize its forces in ways that educators at more advanced levels have generally been unable to do, stands to lose the intellectual vigor that characterized its beginnings in the '20s and '30s and its renaissance in the '60s. To any who are skeptical of these results, I recommend Piaget's discussion of pedagogical developments between 1935 and 1965 (Piaget, 1970b: 25–41). It is clear that he sees bureaucratization as an ever-present danger.

Tied to this danger is that of the further downgrading of the status of the teacher. The teacher is the critical factor in the application of Piagetian theory to the teaching of young children and to be effective she must be intellectually active and inquiring. But, as Piaget notes, with the possible exception of Great Britain, "the schoolteacher is constrained to conform to a set program and apply the methods dictated to him by the state" (Piaget, 1970b: 13).

In discussing recent innovations in education, he underlines the importance of the "ethical and intellectual training of teachers," suggesting that they should receive full university training comparable to that provided doctors. This is especially important for the teachers of the youngest children, for "the younger the students are the more difficult the teacher's task" (Piaget, 1973b: 13). Clearly, early childhood education in this country has a long way to go toward establishing the teaching of the young as a true profession.

Perhaps, however, some impetus toward early childhood education that is designed to promote development, and teaching that understands the complexities involved in such education, can eventually be derived from a source that is too often neglected, the parents of the children. A hopeful trend in early childhood education today is the increasing involvement of parents. Although in many instances they have revealed that their immediate concern for their children is the acquisition of academic skills, there is no reason to believe that they do not also have concerns with long-term development. Furthermore, in many instances, their involvement in the schools has had a humanizing effect that has helped to broaden the sights of teachers and administrators.

It is questionable that early childhood educators who have been inspired by Piagetian theory have fully explored its implications for working with parents. Piaget writes that "a close relationship between parents and teachers . . . leads to much more than mutual information exchange: these exchanges are reciprocally advantageous and often lead to a real improvement in methods" (Piaget, 1973c: 84–85). If the educator believes that the relationship between the teacher and the child should be based on mutual respect and involve relations of reciprocity, it is curious that the relationship between the teacher and the parent is not also seen as one of collaboration, rather than one in which only the teacher is seen as having expertise.

It would be hazardous to predict that parents are going to assume greater responsibility for the education of their young children, or that in so doing they are going to insist on teachers who are responsive and open in their dealings with them, or that collaboratively they will overturn the bureaucracy that seems to threaten early childhood education. But there are those possibilities, and in some situations they will be realized. The implications both of Piaget's theory and of his views on education will be fully understood.

REFERENCES

Almy, M., et al. 1970. Logical Thinking in Second Grade. New York: Teachers College Press.

Ammon, P. 1974. Implications of cognitive theory for education. In W. D. Rohwer et al. (eds.), Understanding Intellectual Development, pp. 235–236. Hinsdale, Illinois: Dryden Press.

Brearley, M., and Hitchfield, E. 1966. A Teacher's Guide to Piaget. London: Routledge and Keagan Paul.

Bruner, J. 1960. The Process of Education. Cambridge, Mass: Harvard University Press.

Bussis, A., and Chittenden, E. 1973. The horizontal dimension of learning. In A. Tobier (ed.), Evaluation Reconsidered, The Workshop Center for Open Education. New York: City College.

Case, R. 1974. Structures and strictures: Some functional limitations on the course of growth. Cognitive Psychology 6: 544–573.

Charles, C. M. 1974. Teacher's Petit Piaget. Belmont, California: Fearon.

Cremin, L. A. 1961. The Transformation of the School. New York: Alfred A. Knopf. Inc.

Dimitrovsky, L., and Almy, M. 1975. Early conservation as a predictor of later reading. Journal of Psychology 90:11–18.

Elkind, D. 1969. Perceptual training and reading achievement in disadvantaged children. Child Development 40: 11–19.

Elkind, D., Hetzel, D., and Coe, J. 1974. Piaget and British primary education. Educational Psychologist 11 (1): 1–10.

Erickson, E. H. 1950. Childhood and Society. New York: W. W. Norton.

Flavell, J. H. 1963. The Developmental Psychology of Jean Piaget. Princeton: D. Van Nostrand.

Furth, H. G. 1974. Two aspects of experience in ontogeny: Development and learning. In H. W. Reese (ed.), Advances in Child Development and Behavior, pp. 47–66. New York: Academic Press.

Gaudia, G. 1974. The Piagetian dilemma. The Education Digest 4(3): 53–56.

Glennon, V. J. 1974. Too heavy input of mathematicians. Instructor 83: 45.

Havighurst, R. J. 1949. Developmental Tasks and Education. Chicago: University of Chicago Press.

Hess, R., and Croft, D. 1975. Teachers of Young Children. Boston: Houghton-Mifflin.

Hunt, J. McV. 1961. Intelligence and Experience. New York: Ronald Press.

Inhelder, B., Sinclair, H., and Bovet, M. 1974. Learning and the Development of Cognition. Cambridge, Mass: Harvard University Press.

Kamii, C. 1972. An application of Piaget's theory to the conceptualization of a preschool curriculum. In R. Parker (ed.), The Preschool in Action. Boston: Allyn & Bacon.

Kamii, C., and de Vries, R. 1977. Piaget for early education. In R. Parker (ed.), The Preschool in Action. Boston: Allyn & Bacon.

Kessen W. 1962. Stage and structure in children. In W. Kessen and C. Kuhlman (eds.), Thought in the Young Child. Monographs of the Society for Research in Child Development, Serial No. 83, Vol. 27, No. 2, pp. 65–82.

Lavatelli, C. S. 1970. Piaget's Theory Applied to an Early Childhood Curriculum. Boston: American Science & Engineering.

Olson, D. R. 1970. Cognitive Development: The Child's Acquisition of Diagonality. New York: Academic Press.

Pascual-Leone, J. 1970. A mathematical model for the transition rule in Piaget's developmental stages. Acta Psychologica 32: 301–345.

Piaget, J. 1952. [Autobiography]. In E. G. Boring et al. (eds.), History of Psychology in Autobiography, Vol. 4. Worcester, Massachusetts: Clark University Press.

Piaget, J. 1954. Les Relations Entre l'Affectivité et l'Intelligence dans le

Dévelopment Mental de l'Enfant. Paris: Centre de Documentation Universitaire (mimeo.)

Piaget, J. 1966. Foreword. In M. Almy et al., Young Children's Thinking. New York: Teachers College Press.

Piaget, J. 1969. Learning and knowledge. In H. G. Furth (ed.), Piaget and Knowledge, pp. 235–239. Englewood Cliffs, New Jersey: Prentice-Hall.

Piaget, J. 1970a. Piaget's theory. In P. H. Mussen (ed.), Carmichael's Manual of Child Psychology, pp. 703–732. New York: John Wiley & Sons.

Piaget, J. 1970b. Science of Education and the Psychology of the Child. New York: Orion Press.

Piaget, J. 1971. Psychology and Epistemology: Towards a Theory of Knowledge. New York: Viking Press.

Piaget, J. 1973a. Main Trends in Interdisciplinary Research. New York: Harper & Row.

Piaget, J. 1973b. Foreword. In M. Schwebel and J. Raph (eds.), Piaget in the Classroom. New York: Basic Books.

Piaget, J. 1973c. To Understand is to Invent. New York: Grossman Publishers.

Piaget, J., and Inhelder, B. 1969. The Psychology of the Child, p. 114. New York: Basic Books.

Robison, H., Jagoda, E., and Blotner, R. 1974. Competency-Based Teacher Training: Skinner vs. Piaget in Classification. Proceedings of the Fourth Interdisciplinary Seminar on Piagetian Theory and the Helping Professions. Los Angeles: University of Southern California.

Sinclair, H. 1973. From preoperational to concrete thinking. In M. Schwebel and J. Raph (eds.), Piaget in the classroom, pp. 46–49. New York: Basic Books.

Soar, R. S., and Soar, R. 1972. An empirical analysis of selected Follow Through programs: An example of a process approach to evaluation. In I. J. Gordon (ed.), Early Childhood Education, The Seventy-First Yearbook of the National Society for the Study of Education. Chicago: University of Chicago Press.

Stallings, J. 1975. Implementation and Child Effects of Teaching Practices. Stanford: Stanford Research Institute.

Weikart, D. P. 1972. A traditional nursery program revisited. In R. Parker (ed.), The Preschool in Action. Boston: Allyn & Bacon.

Weikart, D. P., et al. 1971. The Cognitively Oriented Preschool Curriculum. Washington, D.C.: National Association for the Education of Young Children.

chapter 11

Intellectual Growth and the School Curriculum

Kenneth Lovell

While we do not know the long term effects of an educational philosophy and general teaching strategy derived from Piaget's developmental psychology, his work does help us, here and now, to approach specific curricula in a way that enables us to better fit them to the pupil's intellectual structures and knowledge base, thereby helping him with his difficulties and maintaining his motivation. Accordingly, this chapter is divided into three parts. First, there is a bare mention of some of the problems that Piaget's work still leaves for the teacher. Second, there is a brief reference to the impact that Piagetian developmental psychology has had on educational philosophy and general teaching strategy. Third, there is, in the major part of the chapter, a review of the aid that Piaget has given the teacher in helping the latter to have a better grasp of pupil difficulties in coming to terms with aspects of the school curriculum.

PROBLEMS PIAGET'S WORK LEAVES FOR TEACHERS

Piaget's psychology alerts the teacher that it might well be the nature of the generalized thinking skills that the pupil has developed that is a major factor in determining the manner in which he can assimilate particular information. Long before teachers heard of Piaget they well realized that at school, individual pupils of a given age differed greatly in their understanding of, say, the role of hydroelectric power in the economic development of Quebec, even when they had the same opportunities for learning. But we had to await Piaget before we had clearer insight into the relation between the nature of the pupil's understanding of a topic and his intellectual growth, just as we had to await Piaget before we had a better understanding of pupils' difficulties in grasping the notion that tomorrow, that which is now known as today will be yesterday. The psychometric notion of IQ gives no such insights. Piaget and his colleagues have also shown the teacher the limited role of language in the growth of operational thought.

The conceptual framework that Piaget has provided does not, of course, answer all the questions that teachers want to ask about pupil learning, but it has given the teacher more insights into the relation between pupils' intellectual growth and the quality of their understanding of particular subject matter than any other group of workers. We are reminded by Rohwer, Ammon, and Cramer (1974) of some of the strengths and weaknesses of a cognitive theory vis-à-vis educational practice, so there is no need to pursue these issues to any extent here. There remain two problems that Piaget's work still leaves for the teacher, whether in elementary or high school. One is the defining characteristics of the stage construct. As is well known, by this Piaget (1956) postulates that mutual connections and reciprocal interdependencies exist between the logical operations; such interrelationships are said to create a unified system of logical operations that should permit related concepts to develop at about the same time, and tasks of related logical structure to be of equal difficulty. Alas, both in the classroom and in experimental situations, such things are not always found. Charles Brainerd of the University of Alberta at Edmonton reckons that his evidence suggests the developmental priority of ordination over cardination for the majority of, but not all, children, and that it is easier for the majority of preschool children to learn the ordinal meanings of the first five numbers than their corresponding cardinal meanings.

Such findings, it confirmed, would pose problems for the teacher in accepting Piaget's views on the nature of the number concept, for these combine a relational and classificatory view, and such findings would also challenge aspects of the so-called new math, where emphasis is placed on the cardinal meanings of number—the logic of classes or set theory. One may, perhaps, note in passing Toussaint's paper (1974), which might make some contribution to our further understanding of the stage construct. This study suggests that at the level of the elementary school and concrete operations, using tasks theoretically assumed to demand equivalent logical competence and equating for amounts of stimulus information and response requirements, it is the response measures that emphasize the operative rather than the figurative aspects—compared within each task—that have the highest intertask correlation.

Second, and still linked with the stage construct, there are gaps in our knowledge concerning the transition from concrete to formal operational thought. Lunzer (1973) drew attention to this in a paper very critical of the Piagetian construct of formal thought. He has suggested a number of intellectual skills that seem to be necessary but not in themselves sufficient for the full panoply of formal operational thought, although all these skills may not be involved in any one problem. Thus he drew attention to, among other things, the pre-adolescent's slow growth in the ability to handle unclosed operations, multiple interacting systems, and third level abstractions, and to the view that it now seems likely that formal operational thought as proposed by the Geneva school seems restricted to those problems where a causal and logical analysis coincide. Again, there is the problem of pupils not performing consistently across tasks—even when we are testing the same structure, say, proportionality reasoning as an element of formal thought. Many suggestions can be put forward to explain these inconsistencies; Lunzer's more extreme position was that there are a number of formal operations, such as proportionality reasoning, propositional logic, and so on, that are used by individuals according to motivation and cue.

IMPACT OF PIAGET'S WORK ON EDUCATIONAL
PHILOSOPHY AND GENERAL TEACHING STRATEGIES

Piaget has written *Science of Education and the Psychology of the Child*, in which he establishes the connection between genetic psychology and 'active' educational methods, the development of teaching methods, and the like. More recently, others have attempted to show in more detail the implications of Piaget's developmental psychology. A few papers refer to high school, e.g., Renner and Lawson's (1973) paper in respect of physics. But most writers have dealt with early childhood education, say, from 2 to 9 years. Hooper and De Frain (1974), in a search for a distinctly Piagetian contribution to education, reviewed among other issues the educational philosophy resulting from Piagetian theory, and some representative Piagetian-based programs. These programs differ somewhat among themselves, and some of the authors are critical of others.

In the United Kingdom the 'open classroom' owes more to Froebel in the first instance than to Piaget, but the implications of Piaget's work for the classroom fitted easily into the philosophy of the many British primary schools that had been influenced directly or indirectly by the work of Froebel. Professor Dowley at Stanford University has argued that Froebel had some influence in this country from 1870 to around 1914, but at the latter date denunciations of Froebel's educational philosophy began to appear, it being said that it led to an untenable use of the taxpayer's money, and the goals and purposes of Froebel largely disappeared in the United States. Thus in many, but far from all, British primary schools Piaget's work was, perhaps, more easily accepted than in schools in countries where Froebel had little or no influence.

In addition to the programs above, there are now a number of studies that have attempted to combine putting Piagetian theory into practice with short-term empirical evaluation—again particularly in respect of early childhood and early elementary education. The results, some of which have been reviewed by C. E. Meyers et al. (1974), seem promising although much more evidence is needed.

It is trite to say that there are many problems in the long-term evaluation of models of early childhood, or later, education, but it must be said. It is very difficult to evaluate a cognitive developmental type model, long-term, against other models. First, the educational goals must be clearly defined, and this is not always the case. Second, it is virtually impossible to allow for variations in teacher competence and enthusiasm, in discontinuities in type of program, in the beliefs, values, and aspirations of the home, in the *uses* of language by pupils, in the growth of the pupils' affective lives, in the pupils' self-concepts and the roles they feel they should play in school, and on other variables known to affect school learning. Matching children on the basis of socioeconomic status does not allow for these many variables. Before we shall have definitive evidence regarding the long-term effects of an educational program based on a cognitive developmental model such as Piaget's, we need to have:

1. A clear statement of educational goals
2. A longitudinal study of pupils over 15 years or so from nursery to the end of high school or beyond, with a serious attempt to assess the influence of the variables mentioned above
3. An educational philosophy and type of teaching strategy that remains constant throughout the school years
4. When evaluating, some supplementation of the methods used by the agriculturalist-botanist with the methods used by the social anthropologist: that is, some supplementation of the logical/psychometric type evaluation by illuminative evaluation

The relevant literature on the question of whether or not operational concepts can be taught by short-term training programs is extensive. Beilin (1971) has given a wide ranging and balanced review of the literature, the upshot being that in terms of criteria used by the experimenters, training was often effective, although whether or not operativity was increased remained more of an open question. Hooper and De Frain (1974), bearing in mind more recent studies, conclude that specific Piagetian concepts are generally modifiable, given enough time and effort and appropriate choice of concept and children, but whether or not far-transfer and permanent acquisition result is more questionable.

Inhelder, Sinclair, and Bovet (1974) have given the Genevan viewpoint on the learning and development of cognition. They argue (p. 244) that many subjects in the different training experiments made real progress, but such progress was dependent on the pupils' initial developmental level. But they also argue (p. 247) that we have little idea of the extent to which the early acquisition of a conservation concept speeds up the grasp of a more advanced concept later. Whether or not real progress under training has any long-term effect in relation to the growth of other concepts we simply do not know.

In Bearison's (1974) study, kindergarten children of an average age of 5 years, 10 months were divided into early natural conservers tested on one or more of a number of properties, trained conservers using quantity of liquid (superiority over controls lasting 7 months), and a group that could conserve no property. In the third grade these same children were administered the Otis-Lenon IQ Test and the Stanford Achievement Test (SAT). Bearison claims that the higher level of achievement attained by the early natural conservers as compared with the controls was not attained by the trained conservers.

The purpose in raising this issue of short-term training is twofold. First, long-term, systematically arranged, potential learning situations for the child is the message from Piaget and not short-term training. Second, no evidence exists that curriculum packages that involve direct instruction of conservation or other Piagetian concepts necessarily bring about improved understanding of, and performance in, school subjects. The pupils' thinking skills have been acquired independently of short-term attempts to induce them.

THE IMPACT OF PIAGETIAN THEORY ON THE APPROACH TO SPECIFIC CURRICULA

Piaget's work makes clear to the teacher the necessity of matching strategy and content to the level of pupils' intellectual development and knowledge base. Consider Piaget's influence in the sciences. Elsewhere (Lovell, 1974) much literature dealing with intellectual growth and understanding science both at the elementary and high school stages is reviewed. Shayer (1972) carefully analyzed the data in Inhelder and Piaget (1958) and categorized individuals' performance into investigating style, "the reason is," relationships, and model as theory. The work of Inhelder and Piaget suggests that in the early part of the concrete operation period the pupil:

Will investigate what happens in a haphazard way
Will argue that "this goes with that" (association only)
Will order a series (e.g., lengths or weights) but is unable to do so
    as part of a perception of a relationship in an investigation
Is unable to use any model as theory

During the latter part of the period, when the thinking is more flexible, the pupil:

Will find out what happens, including the use of seriation and
    classification as tools of perception

Can use ordering relations to partially quantify associative reasoning, e.g., "as this goes up, that goes down," "if you double this you must double that"

Can use seriation and the multiplication of two seriations as perceptual strategies

Understands the rules of a simple model but not in relation to the experiment at hand

Against this in the early part of the period of formal operations the pupil will:

Show more interest in looking for *why*

See the point of making hypotheses if simplified to one variable, but cannot perform the simplification systematically himself

Be able to establish causative necessity

Use or perceive metric proportion in a concrete situation

Make simple deductions from a model if the use of the latter is explained

Moreover, during the latter part of the period the pupil will:

Have an interest in checking a 'why' solution

Know that in a system of several variables he must "hold all other things equal" while investigating one variable at a time

Formulate general or abstract relations

Use direct and inverse proportionality for perceiving and formulating relationships

Actively search for an explanatory model or extend one that is given

Shayer and his colleagues have examined the British Nuffield GCE 'O' level science courses in physics and chemistry and classified the subtopics according to these criteria. He concluded that the courses as they stood in relation to age groups fitted only the top 5% of the high school intake. Teachers would have known that the courses were difficult without knowing of Piaget's work as such, but his work has enabled teachers to have far clearer insights into precise pupil difficulties. Moreover, Nuffield 'O' level chemistry has now been revised taking into account many of the findings. For example, the mole concept (gram atom) has been moved from year 3 to year 4. Piaget's work has also shown the science teacher why the mathematical side of physics, chemistry, or biology is difficult whenever proportionality is involved, as, for example, in problems of the ratio of surface area/volume in biology.

In some instances, of course, the curriculum has been greatly influenced by the work of Piaget from the start. Such an example is SCIS, developed under the direction of Professor Karplus at Berkeley. Again, in materials published by the American Association of Physics Teachers are seen the clear hand of Piagetian theory at work throughout.

Now consider a specific concept, momentum, and see how Piaget has helped us to understand pupils' difficulties. Raven (1968) indicated that approximately one half of 8-year-olds, admittedly with a mean measured IQ of 115, had an intuitive notion of momentum. Such an understanding depends only on first-order or concrete operations. But to have a good grasp of momentum at GCE 'O' level there must be an analytic understanding, with the concept related to other concepts, such as force and time, in a precise manner. Such a grasp requires formal operational thought. We have shown at Leeds that a good understanding of momentum at 'O' level necessitates the ability to tackle seven broad types of tasks that can be arranged in order of difficulty. In examining some 80 'O' level candidates, not one was found who could successfully work a harder, but not an easier, task. The first and simplest task involves no more than the ability to work $p = mv$ and simple calculation by rote. Only flexible concrete operational thought is required, because the candidate merely multiplies two variables that he takes as weight and speed—both first-order relations. Thereafter pupil performance falls off rapidly because the remaining tasks demand formal operational thought. For example, the third most difficult type of task involves "Σp = constant" type problems (excluding the class $\Sigma p = 0$) with the notion of inverse proportion, so that if mv = constant then $m \propto 1/v$. In the type seven task, the most difficult, the pupil must tackle vector p revealed as in problems involving Σp = constant in rebound and in calculations of Δp in rebound.

Piaget's development psychology also helps the science teacher to understand why the logical order in which concepts are introduced to pupils does not always indicate their relative difficulty. Consider the concept of temperature, which involves a first-order relation. A pupil of 10 to 11 years of age with flexible concrete operational thought has an adequate concept for everyday life because he understands measurement. But consider the concept of heat or thermal capacity. He certainly can have an intuitive notion of this related to concrete referents, but not a formal analytic concept unless he is outstandingly able. A formal concept involves $Q = m\theta$ or $mc\theta$. This involves a second-order relation devoid of concrete referent, and entropy $\phi = \int mc/T$ also involves a second-order relation but a more complex one than heat. But all teaching shows that the major move, the most difficult step, is from temperature to heat, from a first- to a second-order relation. Again, as Karplus (1973) has argued, some aspects of atomic theory have a language that can be used, providing it is learned, with concrete operational thought (e.g., the conservation of atoms in a reaction), whereas formal thought is required in applications of the ideal gas laws. Piaget has helped us again by providing a framework inside which we can see learning difficulties more clearly.

Next consider Piaget's influence in mathematics. An early book showing the clear influence of Piagetian theory was that by Johannot (1947); indeed, Piaget wrote the foreword. In this volume, which dealt with the mathematical reasoning of the adolescent, there is the clearest evidence of the many difficulties adolescents have in answering questions that would appear easy to an inexperienced mathematics teacher or one unaware of Piaget's work.

In Lovell (1972), much of the literature dealing with intellectual growth and understanding mathematics is reviewed. This review included a wide range of topics, for example, concepts of average, spatial, and geometric concepts in the elementary school, and concepts of point, limit, and mathematical function in high school. Throughout, the influence of Piaget's work is seen in helping the teacher to see that mathematical understanding is dependent on the growth of intellectual structures, aided, of course, by appropriate teaching, and that until such structures have been developed many errors will occur and many misconceptions arise; although in certain areas, such as the concept of proof, Piagetian theory is of less help than in many other areas.

Collis (1973) produced evidence that pupils likely to be thinking at the level of concrete operational thought tend to ignore a given defined mathematical system and reason by analogy with a familiar one. This involves a type of task now often set in British GCE 'O' level mathematics papers that pupils sit around 15 to 16 years of age. Suppose the definition of an operation is, say, $a°b = a + 2 \times b$. Pupils then had to indicate if statements like $a°(b°c) = (a°b)°c$ were true or false; if statements like $4°(3°5) = (4°3)°5$ were true or false; and if statements like $2687°(5924° 1753) = (2687° 5924)° 1753$ were correct or not. At 10 years of age pupils tend to substitute "+" and/or "×" for all °, while at 13 years pupils try to work according to the given conditions within the system, but they still cannot cope with the variables. But in Collis' sample of 17-year-olds, most students worked within the system even if only something over half of the examples worked were correct. The items involving numbers were generally worked correctly earlier than the more abstract items involving letters, but the real difficulty seems to lie in controlling the variables that define the operations allowable within the system. Such control requires formal operational thought, and Piagetian theory helps the teacher to see the considerable difficulties pupils have with such tasks until such thought is available.

There are many published studies of the growth of the scheme of proportionality both in Europe and the United States. Professor Karplus has developed a task in proportional reasoning that has been given to many hundreds of 13-year-olds in Europe and the United States. Moreover, he has indicated four broad stages through which pupils pass in handling proportionality. The percentage responses in each stage in the United States high schools and British Comprehensive schools are very close indeed—he has also given the percentage response in each category in selected British and German schools. If United States high schools and British Comprehensive schools contain a cross-section of ability, then only one in seven of 13-year-olds will handle proportionality successfully in this type of task. Karplus, as do many others, takes proportionality as an aspect of formal operational thought as it involves a second-order relation, and until the emergence of such thought the teacher will find proportionality remains a stumbling block in mathematics or science or wherever it is called for. This is not, of course, to deny that sometimes a problem involving proportionality, or indeed any type of problem, can be worked by means of an algorithm and not with understanding.

Piaget's developmental psychology also helps us to understand what ordinary or abler sixth grade pupils can understand with respect to probability. Such pupils can understand that in tossing a single coin we may expect one-half of the outcomes to be H and one-half T. The likelihood or probability of H is $\frac{1}{2}$. Again, in tossing a six-sided die whose faces are numbered 1 to 6, such pupils can grasp that all faces have an equal chance of falling uppermost, so that in a sequence of throws $\frac{1}{6}$ of the throws can be expected to indicate a 1, $\frac{1}{6}$ a 2, and so on.

Furthermore, if two coins are thrown these pupils can well understand that the possibilities are HH, HT, TH, and TT; Piaget's work has shown us that multiplicative classification is available to them. Thus they can appreciate that the chances of getting two heads is $\frac{1}{4}$ and the chances of getting a head and a tail is $\frac{1}{2}$. These pupils can also understand, using tree diagrams that in essence involve multiplicative classification, that if two dice are thrown there are 36 possibilities, and that the chance of a 2 and a 2 coming up together is $\frac{1}{36}$, or a 4 and 5 occurring, $\frac{2}{36}$.

But such pupils cannot grasp estimated probability because large numbers are involved, multiplicative classification no longer suffices, and there can be no concrete referents. The probability that an event will occur is defined as the relative frequency of occurrence in the long run; that is, if an event occurs x times in n trials, the probability that the event will occur again in a given trial is x/n. Such pupils may learn a rule for estimated probability but its understanding necessitates formal operational thought. The gulf between empirical and estimated probability is wide and deep; Piaget has helped the teacher to understand both the reasons for the gulf, and in what sense probability can be understood in sixth grade.

Now consider Piaget's influence in geography. Piagetian theory again helps the teacher to understand a number of issues. For example, it suggests why children in the 8- to 13-year age range can be taught to handle various aspects of map work like map symbolism, location, and direction, but not scale, unless the ratio is very simple (twice or one-half). Likewise it can suggest why pupils in the age range 11 to 13 years can, with appropriate experience, understand contour, but not isobar; why they can understand a chain of production in, say, food or clothing or shelter, but have only a vague idea of the relationship between the culture of an undeveloped community and its environment, or the extent to which such a culture can be greatly changed by modern economic and industrial development; why they can classify iron, wood, and wool as primary products—although they may not use these actual words—but cannot, even when using nontechnical language, classify subsidence and adiabatic heating of a high altitude air-mass, or rapid heat loss due to radiation at ground level on a clear night, as instances of temperature inversion.

Finally, consider Piaget's influence in three areas of subject matter—history, politics, and religious education—in which his developmental psychology has also illuminated problems of pupil performance. Although the applicability of formal operational thought in these areas may be more limited than in science, there are limitations even in the latter.

When we turn to history (Hallam, 1967; 1975), we find we can categorize pupil responses as preoperational, concrete operational, and formal operational. Thus in the latter stages of concrete operational thought the pupil has the ability to:

1.   Use the information provided, but limited to what is immediately apparent in the text or story
2.   Forecast a result from evidence but not form a mature hypothesis
3.   Move from one point of view to another but make no attempt to coordinate two or more points of view

Concrete thinking in history tends to persist somewhat longer than in, say, mathematics or science, coming at around a mental age of 16 to 16½ years. With the onset of formal thought we find the student goes beyond the information given, tries out his thinking in a systematic manner, reasons by implication at an abstract level, attempts to relate different variables, and realizes a multiplicity of possible links.

The work of De Silva (1969) shows much the same kind of picture. His work involved conceptual development in a historical context, e.g., taxation, and it suggests that the fourteenth year seems to mark the transition from immature to mature comprehension. If the work of Hallam and De Silva is considered together, it seems that the years 13 to 17 are the crucial ones for developing explanatory or formal thinking in history, the actual age depending on the intellectual development of the student.

Once again Piagetian theory has provided a conceptual framework inside which the teacher can assess the quality of the pupils' thinking with respect to the particular historical topic at hand, and adjust the level of difficulty of the material and the manner in which it is approached to fit their thinking. Increasingly in the United Kingdom the influence of the general ways of knowing on pupils' interpretation and understanding of history is being recognized.

The interesting findings of Connell (1971), concerned with the child's construction of politics, are illuminated by Piagetian developmental psychology. In the early years of the concrete operational period children (Australian) can make reference to a rise from a lower position in political order to that of Prime Minister. By the end of the period they can consider a series of positions through which politicians move and they begin to speak of 'leader' of the party. Since pupils are not taught about hierarchy itself in current affairs lessons, it seems that the concept of hierarchical role structures involves the growth of logical operations—the ordering of persons by means of asymmetric transitive relations and perhaps classification. Note that pupils can put sticks into such a relation before they can order social relations.

Or take the notion of political conflict: at 10 years of age the basis of conflict between politicians is but vaguely grasped, for the children seem unable to regard politicians as having opposing intentions. From 12 onwards, depending on the ability of the pupil and his experience, conflict over issues is a little better understood, but it awaits the onset of formal thought before there is a dawning awareness that conflict over specific issues is central to politics. Of course, conflict over issues involves a means-end relationship and in many instances formal thought, as such, may not be demanded. But if the pupil represents the differing views of politicians as one of logical incompatibility, or the means-end relation as one of reciprocal implication, then formal thought is necessary.

Here again we see that Piaget has helped the teacher to realize that certain thinking skills are needed before specific concepts can be grasped. In just the two concepts considered above—the concepts of hierarchy and political conflict—the importance of asymmetric transitive relations, and the capacity to represent logical forms of conflict relations, respectively, are seen. Of course, an expanding store of political facts is also required, but such facts themselves are assimilated in terms of the intellectual structures available. However, although Piaget's classic studies have given many insights, his model of cognitive development still leaves many questions unanswered with respect to the pupils' increasing conceptualization of politics.

The recent International Association for the Evaluation of Educational Achievement (IEA) Civic Education project, involving 35,000 children representing the 10-, 14-, and 18-year-old age groups in 10 countries and concerned with their perceptions of how society works, showed in some detail how a child's political outlook and awareness are linked with his stages of social and intellectual development. For example, it is the older child who is better able to understand adult conflicts of interest, and the contradictory functions of institutions; e.g., how trade unions can both help to settle disputes and create them.

In the United Kingdom, Piaget's developmental psychology, through the work of R. J. Goldman (1964), has greatly affected the approach to religious education. Using subjects aged 5 to 18 years, the older ones showed that their responses displayed the intuitive, concrete operational, and formal operational stages of thinking when questioned about Bible stories. The subjects also showed great change, with age, with respect to the concepts they hold of the Bible, God's nature, God's concern for man, Jesus, and prayer. His work clearly brought out the limits of understanding imposed by levels of operational thinking, and the great need to examine concepts involved in understanding the material chosen for any age group. As in science and mathematics such material, as presented, was found to be too difficult for many children. The changes in content and treatment in the United Kingdom following this research may have been too great, for many teachers failed to distinguish faith from logic in religious thinking.

Earlier it was suggested that there may be limitations to the applicability of formal operational thought when analyzing pupil responses in certain subject areas. In everyday life pupils and adults make assumptions about causal and temporal relationships that experience has taught them are sensible with respect to the given situation. That is, they are concerned with a causal and practical approach and not with true functional relations as such, although they may well be able to use such relations and formal deduction if pressed to do so. Perhaps formal operational thought better fits the individual's responses in those situations in which a causal and logical analysis coincides, as in the experiments of Inhelder and Piaget. Familiarity with content is also important. Yet even in science there are difficulties. Piaget's theory does not allow us to take into account the preconceptions with which a pupil approaches a problem and their effect on his thinking. When experimental results disagree with preconceptions, then the pupil puts his faith in his preconceptions rather than in logic. Indeed, the young adolescent often does put more weight on his preconceptions than on his scientific method (Driver, 1973). Not until he not only observes correlations but is experienced in seeing connections between phenomena will he reject a previous conceptual scheme.

Moreover, it seems that formal thought fits the responses better when the problem is clearly structured so that fewer assumptions or hypotheses have to be imported from outside the problem. There are fewer opportunities for importing misconceptions. This was indicated in Reynold's (1967) study of the concept of proof in mathematics.

Further light should be thrown on the question of the applicability of formal thought to history and social studies by a piece of work being carried out at Leeds by Mrs. Wellington. She is investigating the ability of students aged 12 to 21 years in evaluating historical evidence, or evidence in relation to current issues, e.g., pollution, with respect to: (1) the intrinsic veracity of the evidence; and (2) the conclusiveness of the evidence with respect to hypotheses that the pupil has formulated. Even if it is found that hypothetico-deductive thought is less applicable in some subject areas, it is Piaget's seminal work that has stimulated us to find out what other skills students need.

In summary, with respect to a number of disciplines, it has been indicated how Piaget's work is helping the teacher to pinpoint some of the difficulties that pupils have in coming to understand the deceptively simple material of the curriculum.

REFERENCES

Bearison, D. J. 1974. Is school achievement enhanced by teaching children operational concepts? In Proceedings of the Fourth Interdisciplinary seminar on Piagetian Theory and the Helping Professions. Los Angeles: University of Southern California.

Beilin, H. 1971. The training and acquisition of logical structures. In Rosskopf et al. (eds.), Piagetian Cognitive Developmental Research and Mathematical Education. Washington, D.C.: N.C.T.M.

Collis, K. F. 1973. A study of children's ability to work with elementary mathematical systems. Australian Journal of Psychology 25: 121–130.

Connell, R. W. 1971. The Child's Construction of Politics. Melbourne: The University Press.

De Silva, W. A. 1969. Concept formation in adolescence through contextual clues. Ph.D. Thesis, University of Birmingham.

Driver, R. 1973. The representation of conceptual frameworks in young adolescent science students. Ph.D. Thesis, University of Illinois.

Goldman, R. J. 1964. Religious Thinking from Childhood to Adolescence. London: Routledge and Kegan Paul.

Hallam, R. N. 1967. Logical thinking in history. Educational Review 19: 183–202.

Hallam, R. N. 1975. A study of the effect of teaching methods on the growth of logical thought with special reference to the teaching of history. Ph.D. Thesis, University of Leeds.

Hooper, F., and DeFrain, J. D. 1974. The Search for a Distinctly Piagetian Contribution to Education. Theoretical Paper 50, Research and Development Center, University of Wisconsin.

Inhelder, B., and Piaget, J. 1958. The Growth of Logical Thinking from Childhood to Adolescence. New York: Basic Books.

Inhelder, B., Sinclair, H., and Bovet, M. 1974. Learning and the Developments of Cognition. London: Routledge and Kegan Paul.

Johannot, L. 1947. Le Raisonnement Mathématique de l'Adolescent. Neuchatel: Delachaux and Niestlé.

Karplus, R. 1973. Opportunities for concrete and formal thinking in science tasks. Paper presented at the Third Annual Meeting of the Jean Piaget Society, Philadelphia.

Lovell, K. 1972. Intellectual growth and understanding mathematics. Journal for Research in Mathematics Education 3: 164–182.

Lovell, K. 1974. Intellectual growth and understanding science. Studies in Science Education 1: 1–19.

Lunzer, E. A. 1973. Formal reasoning: A reappraisal. Paper presented at the Third Annual Meeting of the Jean Piaget Society, Philadelphia.

Meyers, C. E. et al. 1974. A symposium of some unheralded parameters of Piaget in the schools. In Proceedings of the Fourth Interdisciplinary Seminar on Piagetian Theory and the Helping Professions. Los Angeles: University of Southern California.

Piaget, J. 1956. Les stades du développement intellectual de l'enfants et de l'adolescents. In P. Osterrieth et al. (eds.), Le Problem des Stades en Psychologie de l'Enfant. Paris: Presses Universitaires France.

Raven, R. J. 1968. The development of the concept of momentum in primary school children. Journal of Research in Science Teaching 6: 210–223.

Renner, J. W., and Lawson, A. E. 1973. Piagetian theory and instruction in physics. The Physics Teacher 11: 165–169.

Reynolds, J. 1967. The development of the concept of proof in grammar school pupils. Ph.D. Thesis, University of Nottingham.

Rohwer, W. D., Ammon, P. R., and Cramer, P. 1974. Understanding Intellectual Development: Three Approaches to Theory and Practice. Hinsdale, Illinois: Dryden Press.

Shayer, M. 1972. Some aspects of the strengths and limitations of the application of Piaget's developmental psychology to the planning of secondary science courses. M.Ed. Thesis, University of Leicester.

Toussaint, N. A. 1974. An analysis of synchrony between concrete-operational tasks in terms of structural and performance demands. Child Development 45: 992–1001.

chapter 12

Piaget and Education: A Dialectic

Irving E. Sigel

The history of psychology is replete with theories that have had their day and have disappeared into archaic and unused library collections. Other theories have been so assimilated into the everyday psychological perspective as to have lost their initial source and are now being viewed as part of the general psychological orientation. Such honored names as Wundt, Tichner, Ach, Brentno, and others are historical figures whose struggles and contributions to the development of psychology are not particularly familiar to many in this era.

The various theories have been collected at one point in a book called *The Seven Psychologies* by Edna Heidbreder (1933). About thirty years ago it was a best seller and familiar to every student of psychology. Today this book is merely a historical document. Not long ago, Hullian learning theory was a dominant perspective, behavioristic psychology was the psychology of experimentation, and Freudian psychology was the psychology of the clinician. These theoretical positions have lost their preeminence and to some degree their strong identity. In passing, of course, Freudian psychology is still vibrant in the fields of therapy, but as a psychological system actively inspiring further research, the Freudian concepts have lost much of their vitality as isolated systematic statements. Now we are in an era where the word and the concept of cognition has been reintroduced and placed in various contexts so that the cognitive components of human behavior seem to be preeminent. We have a journal entitled "Cognitive Psychology." We have cognitive approaches to psychotherapy; we have cognitive approaches to education, etc.

These variations and changes can lead one to suppose that psychology is a science of fads; a science where styles change with the winds, with charismatic leaders who impress upon searching students a perspective that may have little claim to science, and perhaps less claim to immortality. But if one were to stand back and review the field from 1879 to 1975, nearly 100 years, these roads and alleys are not all for naught. What we have is an increasing integration and set of interrelationships that help formalize and formulate the productive directions for psychological investigations. Of course, to the purist the last 100 years only define experimental psychology as we know it today, but there is no doubt that interest in man's mentation has been expressed virtually as long as man has had some self-awareness and consciousness of his own competencies.

At issue is what accounts for the survival of theories and what accounts for the death of theories. Simplistically, some theories die because they don't go anywhere. They deal with minutiae and do not begin to answer questions. On the other hand, some theories survive because of the dedicated devotion of orthodox individuals who insist on maintaining a perspective even in the face of various kinds of contradictory evidence. There is no doubt that in the history of intellectual thought, both ancient and contemporary, there is a constant dialectic between the given, the antigiven, and the emerging new synthesis. The changes that occur in response to the given are frequently based on new knowledge, new perspective, new environmental conditions, new social conditions; in fact, a new zeitgeist.

Thus the question is, what are the necessary and sufficient prerequisites for a theory to survive and develop? If we accept the proposition that today's theories may be tomorrow's has-beens, and if we accept the proposition that no conceptual framework that is set in concrete can survive, then how in the history of ideas can Piagetian theory survive, and in what form?

It is assumed that man as a biological entity does have a biological integrity as well as a psychological perspective and integrity. One central aim among others in the science of development is the search for universal human functions, and the search within this universality to discover sources that account for deviations or comparatives among varying human groups. It is for this reason that the theory of genetic epistemology as expounded by Piaget has such a profound attraction.

Piaget and his colleagues have constructed a comprehensive, interdisciplinary model for the study of man. They have assimilated knowledge from an array of disciplines—philosophy, psychology, biology, mathematics, sociology—and have striven to blend these into a most comprehensive, integrative, modern theory of the development of intelligence. The theory or the system is in process. It is a developing system. What follows is a presentation of a reasonable and heuristic framework as a way of looking at Piagetian theory, perhaps much the same way as Piaget himself views the history of the development of human knowledge and of the child.

Let us view scientific systems as living systems, systems that follow the principles of growth. If they don't, they will die, they will ossify, they will loose their flexibility and adaptability. To perceive of a conceptual system as living and open is to perceive it as a growing, coherent mass that will derive its viability and its vitality from the encounters it has with the social and physical world. In order to grow, this system will be by nature engaged in dialectics, in contradictions, in compromises, and in reconceptualizations, but with an ever-growing dynamic and momentum. Under these conditions it is apparent that Piagetian theory cannot be viewed as a given, fixed set of principles and facts, but rather as an open system that must assimilate new information and produce new accommodations, just as the child develops from a sensorimotor thinking organism to one capable of propositional logic.

It can be argued, of course, that such a perspective precludes the integrity of the theory and results in a new theory or a new organism with a new identity. Consequently the theory has lost its inherent integrity. To that argument it can be said that to the degree the theory has been forced to change, either in fact or in perspective, to that degree it might have been in error. Science is the engagement in a series of acts that are approximations. By definition the scientific enterprise is an enterprise of constant movement—movement that is supportive or contradictory or additional. In fact, the distinction between a dogma and science rests on the ever-changing nature of science in the face of new ideas and new findings. This was summarized very nicely by Inhelder when, in the concluding remarks at the McGraw conference on ordinal scaling in 1969, she said, "It is very refreshing to be confronted with strong criticism and I hope that the Piagetian family will never become a church with its own ten commandments" (Inhelder and Piaget, 1971: 210).

What are the implications of this point of view? How does a theoretical position keep from becoming a church? How does growth proceed without destroying the original organism or, to put it another way, how does growth proceed without the loss of the original framework? The question is a profound developmental question of how change in scientific theory occurs.

The answer begins with the proposition that all theory is a product of human construction, just as Piaget would hold that reality is a product of the child's construction. We construct theory as part of our construction of reality. To be sure, in such constructions there are basic and fundamental propositions by which reality is defined and it may be that these basic definitions must hold until the evidence is overwhelming that one must change. This may take many, many generations, as it took the time from Newtonian physics to Einstein's theories to create a different perspective in the science of physics. But then it must be kept in mind that, just as not all Newtonian mechanics has been superseded, not all previous knowledge need be rejected.

Piaget has come to two basic ideas that he claims "are central for my point of view which, moreover, I have never given up. The first is that since every organism has a permanent structure which can be modified under the influence of the environment but is never destroyed as a structured whole, all knowledge is always assimilation of a datum external to the subject's structure. . . . The second is that the normative factors of thought correspond biologically to a necessity of equilibrium by self-regulation; thus, logic would in the subject correspond to a process of equilibrium" (Piaget, 1971a: 8).

Subsidiary to these basic assumptions is the developmental perspective that forms a core research question, "is it possible to detect broad periods in development with characteristics that can be applied in a general manner to all the events of these periods?" (Piaget, 1971b: 2). He goes on to say "we are looking for total structures or systems with their own laws, systems which incorporate all their elements and whose laws cover the entire set of elements in the system. It would be these structures which become integrated with development" (Piaget, 1971b: 3).

Immediately on reading these statements, one begins to see the directions that subsequent thinking has taken on the relationship between the organism-environment interaction and on the significance of an equilibration model that operates through certain principles of self-regulation. Related, of course, is the concept of structure. Thus, for Piaget, some propositions are fundamental. This does not define how and what he will proceed to do. It is important, then, to present Piaget's own words that define his choice of moving into the camp of the *scientist* in contrast to the camp of the *philosopher*. This distinction is critical, because accepting the rules of the game of science defines a commitment to a methodology that leads to the discovery of facts and also to the testing of their validity. It is better to present Piaget's own words, which state his position clearly:

> Although speculative reflection is a fertile and even necessary heuristic introduction to all inquiry, it can only lead to the elaboration of hypotheses, as sweeping as you like, to be sure, but as long as one does not seek for verification by a group of facts established experimentally or by a deduction conforming to an exact algorithm (as in logic), the criterion of truth can only remain subjective, in the manner of an intuitive satisfaction, or "self-evidence," etc. (Piaget, 1971a: 11–12)

His statements are even stronger when he comes to the canons of science, where he says

> . . . there is a kind of intellectual dishonesty in making assertions in a domain concerned with facts, without a publicly verifiable method of testing, and in formal domains without a logistic one . . . . the sharpest possible distinction should at all times be made between personal improvisation, the dogma of a school or whatever is centered on the self or on a restricted group, and, on the other hand, the domains in which mutual agreement is possible, independently of metaphysical beliefs or of ideologies. Whence the essential rule of only asking questions in such terms that verification and agreement is possible, a truth only existing as a truth from the moment in which it has been verified (and not simply accepted) by other investigators. (Piaget, 1971a: 12)

But Piaget also argues that the search for truth cannot be obtained through the single efforts of one investigator. He says so clearly:

> Thus it follows that either we must adopt systematically a method of cooperation as in science, where truth is only achieved as a result of verifications carried out by many co-workers in the field of facts and that of deduction; or else the self, believing itself free, is unconsciously affected by the suggestions or the pressures of the social group—this we cannot accept, for sociocentrism, like egocentrism, is diametrically opposed to rational cooperation. (Piaget, 1971a: 16)

Piaget places himself squarely in the camp of the scientist where the testing of hypotheses by verifiable methodologies is paramount. But the findings obtained in this way do not necessarily lead to agreement because, as he says, "I was, however, convinced that there was no such thing as a pure fact, but that, as Duhem, Poincaré, and so many others have shown, it always involves an interpretation (which, nevertheless, is in itself a refutation of positivism or logical empiricism)" (Piaget, 1971a: 32).

Thus an honest examination of facts, even when obtained under agreed-upon conditions, combined with an elaborated and formalized interpretation, can lead research epistemologists to disagree with each other. Such discussions may lead to revisions or more precisely stated hypotheses so as to come closer to agreement. In any case, resolution, if any, leads to progress. This is another indication of a dialectic where a set of facts formulates the thesis, and new facts arise that may contradict the earlier ones, and their reconciliation or confrontation may result in a new synthesis.

What are the sources of facts for Piaget? For him, the way to get "fact" is through scientific investigations, where the essential rule is ". . . only asking questions in such terms that verification and agreement is possible, a truth only existing as a truth from the moment in which it has been verified (and not simply accepted) by other investigators" (Piaget, 1971a: 12).

Piaget eschews philosophy as a means for solving problems because problems must be couched in terms potentially verifiable. For Piaget there is only one road to understanding the growth of knowledge. The issue resolves itself to the problem of what primary and secondary questions one must ask, and how process for obtaining verifiable answers emerges.

To answer the basic question of how knowledge grows, we embark on a scientific theory of genetic epistemology. In effect, Piaget is a constructor and is constructing genetic epistemology, which is his scientific system to study the ontogenesis of knowledge.

In his advocacy of genetic epistemology as the subject matter of concern, Piaget has, as mentioned, made the following commitments: (1) to seek knowledge that is verifiable; and (2) to examine facts through an interdisciplinary endeavor. As Piaget says, "the criterion of the success of a scientific discipline is intellectual coöperation and since my disenchantment with philosophy I have been increasingly of the opinion that any individual piece of work was vitiated by a latent defect, and that to the extent to which one would be able to speak of 'Piaget's system,' this would be a conclusive proof of my failure" (Piaget, 1971a: 29).

Thus Piaget is advocating a cooperative interdisciplinary effort where his own point of view blends with those of others; where he, in effect, may be the intellectual leader in cooperation with other scientific minds. Thus, to study genetic epistemology (by the way, a term coined by J. M. Baldwin in 1915), one must have some familiarity with logic, mathematics, physics, cybernetics, and also the history of science.

How did Piaget proceed to study the development of knowledge? First, he rejected the logical positivism or the logical empiricism and gave way to what he calls an interactional constructivism, which is the concern for the evolution of structures by an active organism that constructs its reality as it is embedded in and engaged with the environment.

However, to study the development of knowledge requires a methodology and Piaget has reported two major methodological efforts. One is the careful observation of young infants (his own), not only in their spontaneous behavior, but when presented with a series of contrived tasks that were developed in order to test for specific abilities, such as the comprehension of the object, means and relationships, and solving various kinds of problems that the infant might or might not engage in in the course of his daily routine. The second strategy is to embark on experiments that have been described in great detail in his numerous writings and that essentially involve the presenting of tasks to children and asking children to solve the problems apparent in these tasks. These range from the classical problem of conservation of mass or number to the more complex problems with adolescents in such areas as the pendulum probabilities, propositional logic, etc.

Piaget's genius is exemplified in his devising the methods for obtaining the facts and the interpretation of these facts from early interviews with children. Discovery of the structural development of thought was to a large measure grounded in data obtained from interviews or observations of different children with different tasks at different chronological ages.

However, it must be made clear that Piaget's interpretation of these facts differed from other observers. The reason in part is that he had a conceptual system within which to interpret the phenemona. That is the perspective he brought to bear on the responses of the children derived from an acceptance of certain doctrines derived from logical deductions, biological knowledge, and knowledge of mathematics. But the procedures he employed to construct his system, which is his integration and interpretation of these facts, followed the traditions of science and evolved into a methodology that is communicable, replicable, and can lead to verification.

One very important difference between Piaget's *method clinique* and the methodologies employed in most experiments with children is the utilization of the inquiry. Although the aim is usually to create experiments that are highly standardized in method and inquiry, in effect operating with the chemistry experiment as a paradigm so that control is presumed for all conditions except those variables to be manipulated, Piaget veered from this course and asked various questions of the subject. This interrogation has its own scientific justification in that: (1) it recognizes the individual difference among individuals' experiences; and (2) it recognizes the fact that individuals construct their experiences differentially.

However, the objective of the question is consistent in getting to understand as best as possible the child's rationale and understanding of the problem before him. Thus Piaget's observation and his *method clinique* were applied to individual children who were presented with an array of tasks constructed by adults for adults' understanding of how children think. The contrived nature of the experiments, in the sense of the problem presented, has its logic in the sense that problems were set up to answer particular kinds of questions. Because Piaget has categorized knowledge, so to speak, into various domains dealing with various classes of problems, these experiments utilized tasks that were samples from that array. Thus he studied speed, time, causality, geometry, number, concept of the world, and so forth.

What can education contribute to the Piagetian system and how can a true and honest interaction emerge? Why education? The educational enterprise provides one environment in which children are presumably engaged in knowledge development where the primary task of the educational establishment is a commitment to teach children subject matter, to provide opportunities for mastery of basic intellectual skills, and to provide opportunities for the utilization of these skills in order to enhance the knowledge state of the individual. To accomplish these objectives, educators have to make decisions as to teaching strategies, selection and utilization of the materials, and the social organization of classrooms and schools, and evolve methods of managing children in large groups. The school becomes, in effect, the place where vast bodies of knowledge can be developed.

The educational enterprise in the United States as a public system has as its clientele millions of children who enter the system at age 5 and continue on for at least eight to 10 years. The populations, as we know, are diverse in terms of racial, ethnic, and socioeconomic origin. The educational philosophies, goals, and objectives are also varied.

Education as an institution in this country is varied depending upon the section of the country, the size of the community, and the composition of that community. Thus educational objectives are diverse and priorities are unclear, or to say the least, highly varied. For some, education is the mastery of the basic skills and the orientation is toward some vocational mastery. For others, education is the broadening and expanding of the horizons of individuals. Educational philosophies and educational strategies have come and gone. Just note in the last 20 years the number of different schools of thought regarding the teaching of reading, which epitomizes the vast array of differential perspectives and philosophies in the environment. Even today we have news of book burning and censorship, where the schools are seen as the vanguards of purity and where young minds are seen as vulnerable to books of sex and violence. The schools, at least at the secondary level, have noted increases in violence, vandalism, and distress. Education in the United States faces serious educational, psychological, social, and financial problems, which provide a backdrop to a view of classroom reality that does not necessarily emerge in our scientific experiments. The number of variables is overwhelming. The complexity is considerable. The lack of specification of variables and their consequences precludes precise statements about causes and effects or correlational consequences.

The point of this chapter is not to bemoan the state of American education, which in and of itself deserves considerable thought and reflection before we pass such stringent judgment on our public educational system. Our society has already placed burdens on educational institutions that one must in reflective moments ask, "Is that the place and are they the people to solve those problems?"

With that aside, consider the relevance of education for Piagetian theory. To do that requires one more review of the history. After all, developmentalists are concerned with the experiential base from whence structures emerge. For whatever reason, in the sociology of education Piagetian theory from 1956 on has become increasingly influential. The influence is a one-way street. The educators have looked to Piagetian theory for help, ranging from organization of classrooms to organization of curricula and teaching strategies, from creating of experiments to arguing about reporting progress to classroom organization, etc. Where the theory is massive and comprehensive as Piaget and his colleagues have developed it, one can dip in and abstract ideas that make sense for any of the issues deemed important in the classroom setting. The Piagetian idea of self-regulation, for example, makes sense for the teacher oriented towards a permissive classroom, and now Piagetian theory is used piecemeal to justify the open, free classroom where children can regulate their own behavior. But this is a decontextualized abstraction. For Piaget it is not self-regulation in isolation, but it is self-regulation as intertwined with the concept of equilibration and the active organism's engagement with objects.

Let it be recalled that Piaget's data base comes from the observations and the interviews. The data do not come from classroom observations or reports of teachers. What we have is an altogether too familiar theme in which the application of Piagetian principles to education is made without an adequate scientific investigation of how one translates these data and turns these findings into strategies of application. The literal application of Piagetian stages, for example, to classrooms without firmly establishing ways of verifying the responses that are indicative of these stages or conditions of them do not provide an adequate test. An integral step—creating those relevant operations in classroom settings that are derived from the theory—is skipped. Attempts, of course, have been made by many investigators to do so within the many programs, especially at the preschool level, that claim to be derived from, based on, or be extrapolations of Piagetian theory. However, the programs evaluate their effectiveness too often by using instruments that are unrelated to the nature of the program. The changes that would be expected to emerge should be those structural changes that manifest themselves in particular ways that children think, approach problems, and reason. On the other hand, to say that we can't evaluate the effectiveness of a program then raises an even more serious question, one of which Piaget himself would be inclined to be suspicious, if his position of verification is consistent. The recent volume by Inhelder, Sinclair, and Bovet (1974) on cognitive development and learning indicates how the training studies on which they have embarked are evaluated relative to rather clear objectives. What are the objectives that educators employ when they adopt a Piagetian orientation to their program? What is the nature of the application of Piagetian theory to education and what, if anything, can be learned by using the educational medium as a data base?

The answer to the question begins with the following three givens: that genetic epistemology is a systematic conceptual scheme that has as its objective understanding how knowledge develops; that its current data base is experimental (numbers of children were tested and interviewed individually using the series of tasks essentially related to the physics and mathematics type problems); and that Piaget himself has been interested and has written provocative essays on his views on education but where no data or methodology are directly tested in the educational process. Thus to employ the theory in the educational process is a major leap, in fact, a belief and a value in part based on interpretation of empirical facts and in part based on acts of faith.

There are two important considerations here that can fulfill what for Piaget is interdisciplinary cooperation contributing to the development of the theory by providing new information.

Two types of educational experiences are possible. The first are training studies that have been done in this country and the second are classroom teacher-child interactions. The training studies do have something to offer Piaget and his colleagues that should be incorporated into the theory. These studies, although essentially experimental in nature, do provide some support for some notions of structural congruence and development and raise questions for others. For example, one training study (Sigel, Roeper, and Hooper, 1966), using multiple strategies, contributed to transformation in cognitive structures, and after training, children in the training condition conserved the data that had to be dealt with. The study can be criticized because it did not isolate the particular cognitive agent used by transitional children of a very high IQ; however, the results cannot be dismissed because the high-IQ control children who had no training were still nonconservers in mass and weight even though in terms of mental age they were equivalent to those who were trained to conserve mass and weight. Also, what does it really mean to be transitional? Transitional between what and what? Is transition merely to be defined as unstable, or is it to be defined in more statistical terms of two out of three correct responses? Arguments of this kind avoid the issue. As developmentalists interested in transformation, we should be concerned with the process of transformation and determine what it means, that is, what the fact that a child is "transitional" means. Furthermore, what does it mean when a child with an IQ of 140 cannot conserve? What does that tell us about IQ as measured on the Stanford-Binet test, and what does that tell us about conservation? These are not philosophical questions. These are questions probing in depth the meaning of terms and concepts that are fundamental to our understanding of ongoing developmental processes. That structures evolve at different rates and earlier than expected is an interesting problem because we may ask the source of such developmental rates. It does confirm the fact that, as Piaget has so often stated, chronological age is not an adequate criterion by which to define a child's cognitive status. It may be a crude guide, but it is not precise.

A second relevant issue is the multiplicity of strategies for training the children's competence in classification, reversibility, and seriation. One could, as Beilin (1969) has, propose a design where each of these strategies plus combined strategies could be used in a more ambitious training program. It may well be that no single strategy in and of itself is sufficient but that the collection of them is. There is some evidence that training makes a difference but, to be sure, the final test is what happens in the long run and whether or not these training experiments are theoretical exercises or have pedagogical value.

A more critical area of interaction between education and Piagetian theory is in observations of children in classroom settings. The fact is that most of our knowledge of cognitive growth comes from restricted and constrained experimental environments. Much as the *méthod clinique* is tuned in to the child and much as it allows for a relatively narrow band of data, it is still limited and lacks the ecological validity vis-à-vis the classroom. A paradigm based on ecologically based observation and adult-child engagements is required. First, we can obtain a more complete picture of a child's ongoing functioning from observing him in the habitat of the classroom. Piaget makes much of the role of the experience but the data base for this is not exhaustive. In fact, it is highly interpretive of what Piaget or his colleagues observed during interviews. Our studies, even in the training studies that approximate classroom activity, still have a certain contrived element. But the assessment in our training studies (most of it is a pre/post evaluation) is not an examination of the incremental changes that occur in the process of acting. While watching a child build a block tower, we don't see or measure, for example, the incremental movements that he engages in during the completion of that tower. We frequently think of the beginning and the end, the disarray of the blocks and the tower, but the process orientation that builds on itself and feeds on itself is not usually part of our evaluation. So we can say at the moment that our data base tells us how a child reasons and solves problems at one time and how he does it a second time and we infer that the differential program treatment accounts for this difference. This may lead to many false positives because we may find that a variety of untouched or unsuspected variables that existed in one setting may account for change. Thus replications of such studies may often have some difficulty. The critical area is the change process in relatively small incremental units in many areas, logico-mathematical, social, linguistic, etc. The more basic need is the opportunity to observe cognitive functioning *in vivo* and over a wide area of behaviors and content areas rather than in experiments that tend to be quite narrow, that is, predefining a problem and eliciting the child's answer to it.

As indicated above, another criticism of the experimental procedures, and even the interview, is that we learn about the child's performance vis-à-vis *our* task—the adult's, not the child's. We do not question where the logical necessity is for the solution of his process other than trying to please us. What is needed is to work through various kinds of observation in the child's school habitat. In a study done some years ago (Sigel, Secrist, and Forman, 1973), 3-year-old children in a preschool program at the State University of New York at Buffalo were presented with an array of blocks described by Inhelder and Piaget in *The Early Growth of Logic in the Child* (1969). Our interest was in observing how children categorize or classify these blocks. We videotaped their play and analyzed the spontaneous creations. To be sure, the task we presented the children with was ours in the sense of providing him with an array of blocks. However, we could not interrogate the child or instruct him, but merely say, "Put these together as you wish." The interrogation obviously would be ineffective with children this young. We videotaped these children at four time-intervals about 8 months apart. Close examination of the behavior of the children revealed interesting changes, both within situations and between situations in relation to the objects. We were able to notice how the children related to the objects, what they did with them, how they constructed towers with them, how they made decisions about which blocks to use and which to reject. George Forman of the University of Massachusetts engaged in a very complex and detailed analysis of these behaviors which he refers to as the grammar of action. The important thing for us now is that by such detailed observation we could observe, literally before our eyes, the transformation of the child's motor action to some kind of internal representation where a child would disregard a block in favor of another because he had just previously used that discarded one and found that it did not serve whatever purpose he had in mind. In a sense we observed what was prototypic of what one might call reflective abstractions, that is, scanning, comparing, hesitating before action, and selecting the appropriate block for the particular space that was to be filled. Data of this type provide a wider spectrum than if we concerned ourselves with just the product of the construction.

A second and more perplexing phenomenon was observed in noting contradictions between test performance and classroom performance in the same area, for example, number and language (Sigel, 1974). The context in which the child is engaged makes a difference, not only context as defined by the physical space, but by the task to be engaged. Thus, observing carefully how children deal with questions by teachers becomes an important ingredient for our understanding of the transformations that are occurring in the experience of these children. Third, a way of looking at the question could be testing the theory in a classroom environment, which would again allow for more information, this time by having the experimenter or teacher engaging in the child's stream of behavior. This type of strategy is used by Dr. Edward Chittenden, who suggests that by engaging in such a stream of behavior one is able to find out where the child is, where he is going, and where he came from. But it must be done unobtrusively; it must be done in such a way as to minimally alter the child's intentions.

By observing children in classroom situations, by engaging them naturally in conversations and discussions, as well as obtaining other recollections, even on a short-term basis, information should be provided that might support, contradict, or in some other way influence our theoretical statement. This additional paradigm, the use of observations in living settings, may provide us with the kinds of outcomes that would be important in testing the validity of a number of Piagetian concepts for education.

REFERENCES

Beilin, H. 1969. Stimulus and cognitive transformation in conservation. In D. Elkind and J. H. Flavell (eds.), Studies in Cognitive Development: Essays in Honor of Jean Piaget. New York: Oxford University Press.

Heidbreder, E. 1933. Seven Psychologies. New York: Appleton.

Inhelder, B., and Piaget, J. 1969. The Early Growth of Logic in the Child. New York: W. W. Norton.

Inhelder, B., and Piaget, J. 1971. Closing remarks. In D. R. Green, M. P. Ford, and G. B. Flamer (eds.), Measurement and Piaget, New York: McGraw-Hill.

Inhelder, B., Sinclair, H., and Bovet, M. 1974. Learning and the Development of Cognition. Cambridge, Mass.: Harvard University Press.

Piaget, J. 1971a. Insights and Illusions of Philosophy. New York: World Publishing Company.

Piaget, J. 1971b. The theory of stages in cognitive development. In D. R. Green, M. P. Ford, and G. B. Flamer (eds.), Measurement and Piaget. New York: McGraw-Hill.

Sigel, I. E. 1974. When do we know what a child knows? Human Development 17: 201–217.

Sigel, I. E., Roeper, A., and Hooper, F. H. 1966. A training procedure for acquisition of Piaget's conservation of quantity: A pilot study and its replication. The British Journal of Educational Psychology 36:301–311.

Sigel, I. E., Secrist, A., and Forman, G. 1973. Psycho-educational intervention beginning at age two: Reflections and outcomes. In J. Stanley (ed.), Compensatory Education for Children Ages 2–8. Recent Studies in Educational Intervention. Baltimore, Md.: Johns Hopkins University Press.

Author Index

225

Subject Index